Patterns for Guernseys, Jerseys and Arans

Fishermen's Sweaters from the British Isles

Gladys Thompson

second revised edition

Dover Publications, Inc., New York

This Dover edition, first published in 1971, is
an unabridged, revised republication of the work
originally published in 1969 under the title *Patterns
for Guernseys and Jerseys*. It is reprinted by special
arrangement with B. T. Batsford Limited, London,
publisher of the original edition.

*International Standard Book
Number: 0-486-22703-0
Library of Congress Catalog Card
Number: 71-136140*

Manufactured in the United States of America
Dover Publications, Inc.
180 Varick Street
New York, N. Y. 10014

Contents

NOTE TO AMERICAN KNITTERS

This excellent book was originally written for the British market and therefore calls for the use of British materials, some of which are not generally available in the United States. The five-ply yarn called for in many of these patterns is one example, and I suggest that you substitute a good American sports yarn.

In Britain the system for denoting sizes of needles is the reverse of the American system; therefore the 13 or 14 needles specified herein are actually very fine needles.

The sweaters in this book are designed to be wind and waterproof, being very tightly knit on #2, #1 or #0 (US) needles at a gauge, or tension, of 8 to 9 stitches to an inch. Some American knitters prefer to work at a gauge of 5 stitches to one inch, and may like to use knitting worsted for this.

All wools have a preferred or optimum gauge (number of stitches to one inch) for a given project which is usually given at the beginning of knitting instructions. Tight knitters need larger needles to achieve optimum gauge; loose knitters can attain it with smaller needles.

The only way to find out what size needles *you* should employ is to experiment. Cast on 30 stitches with the wool and needles you wish to use. Work in stocking-stitch for 3″ to 4″. Take the piece off the needle and steam it gently to block it. Lay it on a table and place two pins exactly 3″ apart horizontally, at about the center. Count the number of stitches between the pins and divide by three. The result is the number of stitches you are getting to an inch and represents your gauge. Do not neglect ½ stitches, ⅓ stitches or ¼ stitches; they are vitally important. If you have more stitches, or fractions of a stitch than specified, try a larger needle. If you have less, try a smaller needle.

If the instructions give you the necessary gauge "when measured over stocking-stitch," you are safe even if you plan to use cable or Aran patterns. However, since cable and Aran patterns need more stitches per completed inch than plain knitting, extra precautions are necessary if the instructions specify gauge "in pattern." The only way to find out how many more stitches might be needed is to cast on the number of stitches given for the front and try the patterns for four or five inches. If the resulting piece is not the right width, keep trying with larger or smaller needles according to whether the piece is too wide or too narrow. Don't rip your nice big swatch; it will do for the start of a fine cap.

It is worth your while to take some pains with your gauge before starting a project, as it may save you possible disappointment and ripping later on.

Good Knitting!

ELIZABETH ZIMMERMAN

Babcock, Wisconsin
May, 1971

Preface

This book is a revised edition of *Guernsey and Jersey Patterns* published in 1955, omitting some of the knitting history and stories, but giving more patterns, and including several new items which have been discovered since the first book was written. These include full directions for knitting a Channel Islands guernsey. Also one from Fife in anchor pattern, and full directions for making two sets of sweaters and cardigans adapted for ladies' wear, from my patterns by the Womens Home Industries. They are knitted in Filey and Seahouses designs. Earlier Filey patterns dating from 1822 have been included, also a Sheringham and two Norfolk guernseys.

The patterns seen on Fishermens' guernseys have always interested me, and knowing that whilst the fishing families continued to knit them, the patterns would be safe, I also knew they were never written down; so I started years ago to learn and note them for reference. The patterns are traditional, and belong to families and places, and often have local names either connected with the sea or the men's occupation.

In 1938 I sent a group of fishermen dolls to an exhibition in London. The four fishermen wore different patterned Yorkshire guernseys, and two fisher-women were included in the group, one wearing a lilac sun-bonnet, and knitting a tiny guernsey; the other in a black dress with a crochet shawl. Queen Elizabeth, The Queen Mother, saw them and asked me their history, and I told her I hoped to write a book about the patterns. She was very interested, and made me promise to carry out this idea.

Acknowledgement

The author would like to acknowledge the great help and kindness received whilst collecting information for this book from Her Majesty Queen Elizabeth the Queen Mother, Lady Cecilia Howard, Miss Rose, the Scottish Women's Rural Institutes, Mr Lucas of the National Museum, Dublin, Mrs Marshall Frazer, and Miss Doris Cleverly.

She also wishes to acknowledge the following owners of guernseys who allowed them to be photographed, and the patterns saved for reference: Mr Matt Cammish for fig. 18; Mrs D Thompson for figs. 30 and 48; Miss Verrill for fig. 68; Lady Cecilia Howard for fig. 96; Mrs Wilson for fig. 124; Mrs Forman for figs. 135 and 136; Vice-Admiral and Mrs Jack Egerton for figs. 137 and 140; Mr Lucas, Dublin for figs. 141 and 143; Miss Betty Hennell for fig. 146; Mrs P A Dillon Gibbons for fig. 149; Mrs Maufe for fig. 151; Miss Gahan for figs. 153, 155, 157, 158 and 159; Miss A D Hamilton for fig. 160; and the Yorkshire Federation of Women's Institutes for fig. 1.

The author would also like to record thanks to Mr Lambert Smith of Whitby for kind permission to use the Sutcliffe photographs, figs. 53, 56 and 69; Mrs Appleton for fig. 69; Mr Jenkinson Overy for fig. 49 and to Mr Michael Harvey for figs. 82, 84, 85, 88 and for his kind permission to reproduce text on pages 81 to 85. She greatly appreciates also the help received from Mr S Royle and Mr Masser who were responsible for many of the excellent photographs, and from Mr H Stott who drew many of the graphs. For other help with knitting patterns the author would like to record her thanks to Miss Mary Colbert, Mrs Cowie and Mrs Laidlaw, and to Mrs O'Rourke for her help in correcting the patterns.

Jerseys and Guernseys

The words 'jersey' and 'guernsey' are often discussed, and to clarify this I quote some paragraphs from a letter written by the late Lieutenant Colonel Marshall Frazer, which appeared in *The Sunday Times* some years ago.

'Dr Rex Binning seeks an explanation of the difference between the two garments which took their names from the two bailiwicks of the Channel Islands. Almost invariably guernseys are in thick dark blue wool, whilst jerseys are thinner, and of various colours. Jerseys became better known owing to the very large number of Jersey men who entered the Newfoundland enterprises about 1600, and gave rise to local shipbuilding, and the supply of woollen garments for the mariners.

'The two garments are really identical in shape, but differ by reason of the jersey knit (*Ouvre* in the patois), which is unlike any English, French or Guernsey type, but it would take an expert in wool-craft to tell the difference.'

The shape of the guernsey is definitely square—reminiscent of the short smock worn by country or farm workers years ago, and built for hard wear, with quality and good workmanship throughout.

When starting to knit a guernsey, many of the fishermen's wives cast on in double wool, and also cast off the cuffs in the same way. This looks rather bulky, but adds to the strength of the garment. Seam stitches are always used, starting where the welt finishes, and gussets are worked under each arm from an increase in the centre of the seam stitches and finish with the pattern half way down the sleeve. The seam stitch continues to the cuff. These gussets add years to the wearing qualities of the guernseys.

The sleeve stitches are picked up round the armhole and knitted on four needles. The neck is also knitted on the round, making a stand up collar about two inches high. In Scotland the neck band is fastened by buttons and strong buttonholes. This makes a neat finish without stretching the neck band each time the garment is pulled over the head.

There are many variations in shoulder-strap patterns and often, as at Runswick, it is the only decoration on a plain guernsey.

The old knitters worked the wearer's initials into the jersey above the welt before the pattern started. This is shown in figure 25. Sometimes the fisherman's name was knitted in full.

In Yorkshire, the dark-blue fishermen's jerseys are always called Guernseys or ganseys. They are made without a seam, on a set of five 18 in. steel needles, but these sets are almost unobtainable now, and long sock, or round needles can be used instead, size 12 to 14, according to the type of wool used. The wool can be bought at Richardson's in Whitby, or Hammonds of Hull, and is special 5-ply worsted for guernseys. It is known in Yorkshire as 'wassit', and is sold by the hank, hesp or cut, and roughly 24 to 26 oz are used for a guernsey.

In Scotland a 6-fold black, or dark blue wool is used, much softer than the wool knitted this side of the Border, and the needles are shorter and sometimes sold in sets of eight.

Most of the stitches and patterns have names, and are called after everyday objects noticed at sea, and used by the fishermen in their daily work. For instance ropes of every kind, Diamonds (the shape of fishing net mesh) also Ladder Stitch, 'Print o' the Hoof', Herring Bone, Anchor, and Triple Sea Wave. A list is given, but there are probably many I have not come across.

The following stitches and patterns will be found on the different guernseys shown in this book.

1 Cable or rope stitch.
2 Steps.
3 Zigzag, so called from the paths up cliffs, or lightning.
4 Double zigzag, known in Scotland as 'marriage lines' or 'ups and downs'.
5 Ladder stitch.
6 Diamonds. The shape of net mesh worked in plain, purl, moss and double moss.
7 Net mask; meaning net stitch. A Flamborough pattern, also called herring mask.
8 Print o' the hoof. Hoof marks in the sand (a double plait).
9 Hit and miss it. Double moss stitch.
10 Sand or shingle. Double and single moss stitch.
11 Poor man's wealth. Several rows purl knitting, so called as it is difficult to count.
12 Betty Martin. Used in Filey, Whitby and Scotland.
13 Honeycomb. Flamborough and Scotland.
14 Tree of Life, fern or cone pattern. Scotland, Fair Isle and Northumberland.
15 Herring bone or feather. Scottish Fleet and Filey.
16 Hearts. Scottish Fleet and Fife.
17 Anchor pattern. Scottish Fleet and Fife.
18 Flag or kilt. Whitby and Scotland.
19 Triple sea wave. Northumberland and Border.
20 Rig and fur (ridge and furrow) used in Runswick and Staithes for shoulder straps.
21 Armada. Old Fair Isle pattern from the Spaniards.

A Channel Islands' Guernsey

Messrs de Cartaret and le Patourel of Guernsey, Channel Islands have kindly allowed me to include their pattern, and gave me the following information: 'The guernsey is in an island traditional style. At one time there were different family, or occupational designs, such as fishermen and farmers. But these different styles are not usually made now, as most knitters make the standard style, as in ours, which was based on an old composite pattern, and left to us by someone years ago.'

This guernsey is simple in design, but has its own characteristics, showing decorative ribbing and side vents, with gussets at neck and under-arm, and set in sleeves with the armholes cut, or with a knitted edge.

Materials

5 ply worsted wool. Size 12 or 13 needles (11 required).

38 in. chest: approximately 150—170 stitches for front and back (300 altogether).

44 in. chest: approximately 198 on size 13 needles.

For children's sizes chest 24, 28, 32, knitted in 4 ply worsted on No. 13 needles. Instruction for stitches, etc., in brackets, otherwise everything else the same as large size (98, 116, 134).

To cast on knotted edge by thumb method. Use double wool on left hand, putting right hand wool around needle between each cast on stitch.

The body

Cast on required stitches for front on five needles. Knit 24 rows (16, 16, 20 rows) garter-stitch: Knit similar piece for back. Join together, and knit 8 (6) rounds in k2 p2 rib, making a seam stitch on each side by knitting plain one row and purl the next. On next round, knitting in stocking stitch increase one stitch at beginning and end on each needle, 20 stitches altogether. Continue in plain knitting till required length allowing approx. 10 in. (6½, 7, 7½ in.) for armhole.

Armhole

Cast on 7 stitches over each seam stitch. Continue knitting all stitches plain except 12 stitches before and after each seam stitch. In 1st round knit each set of these 25 stitches as follows: Knit 25 2nd round—purl 6, knit 6, purl 1, knit 6, purl 6. Continue with this pattern at armhole edges till you have the required depth for armhole. (Alternately the armhole may be done by continuing knitting back and front separately, and working in the garter stitch pattern with 3 or 4 plain stitches at each end.)

To join shoulders

Divide stitches for shoulders, allowing approximately 46 (30, 36, 42) on front shoulders, and 47 on back, the remainder for neck ribbing. Knit to neck edge of shoulders, join front and back together by knitting the two lots of stitches together, next row cast off (on right side of work) finishing with the 47th stitch left on needle at neck edge. Knit across neck, work other shoulder to match finishing with the 47th stitch on needle. With this stitch start neck gusset, continue by knitting one stitch from back and front alternately (1 row plain, 1 row purl) till 19 stitches (15, 15, 17 stitches). Knit across to other shoulder and repeat gusset on the other 47th stitch. K2 p2 rib on remaining stitches and gussets for approximately 2 in. Cast off in rib.

Sleeves

Cast on 20 stitches on each of 4 needles, 80 (44, 52, 60 stitches). Knit cuff in k2 p2 rib, approx. 4 in. (3 in.). Change to stocking stitch and increase 2 stitches on each needle in the first round and one extra stitch at beginning for seam. Knit 6 rounds, then increase one stitch on each side of seam stitch. Continue in this way increasing every 6th round till 121 stitches (77, 87, 99 stitches). Knit without increasing till sleeve is required length, allowing approximately $2\frac{1}{2}$ in. for gusset (i.e. if 20 in. sleeve required, make sleeve $17\frac{1}{2}$ in. before commencing gusset).

Gusset

Increase one stitch on each side of seam stitch in next round. Continue by increasing one stitch on each of these increase stitches, on every 2nd round till 12 stitches (6, 8, 10) each side of seam stitch. Continue knitting gusset plain, but knit 6 rounds on remaining stitches in k2 p2 rib. Next round cast off ribbing, then continue gusset by decreasing 1 stitch each end of gusset on every plain row till 4 stitches left. Cast off. Keep seam stitch running through gusset.

To insert sleeve

If increased armhole has been made, cut along seam stitch of increased stitches, turn in and hem. Sew top of sleeve to hem. Other method, sew in, in ordinary way.

Patrington and Withernsea

1 This Guernsey was exhibited in Canada, the United States, Australia and
New Zealand

Many years ago, Patrington was a small fishing village with a creek harbouring its boats. This is no longer the case, but just below the village, towards the Humber, Haven Side shows the site of the old harbour.

Patrington and Withernsea possess the lovely guernsey pattern which is shown in figures 1–4. It was knitted by the late Mrs Foster of Withernsea. It was included in the British Council Overseas Exhibition. This guernsey has rather a shallow yoke, composed of alternate panels of ladder stitch and double moss, divided by rope stitch, two ropes side by side form the centre back and front, and down the sleeves. The directions are as follows:

Cast on 328 stitches using double wool for the cast on.

The stitches are divided equally on to 4 long steel needles, as 5 needles are used in the making. The welt is knitted in 2 plain, 2 purl for 3½ inches, followed by 9½ inches of plain knitting with 2 seam stitches, of 2 purl each worked up the sides, using 2 of the welt purl ribs to carry this out with an equal amount of stitches left for front and back between the side seams. The seam stitch can be seen at left side above the welt in figure 1.

When the 9½ inches have been worked the under-arm gussets start by increasing 2 stitches in the centre of the side seams, thus making 1 purl, 2 plain, 1 purl. The 2 plain stitches form the gusset. Continue the plain knitting for the body, increasing each gusset by 2 stitches every 7th round until there are 10 stitches in each. These increases are made 1 stitch in from each gusset edge, not on the outside stitch.

The yoke pattern now starts by working 3 rounds of purl, keeping the gussets ii pattern and increasing as before.

1st row *K18, p2, k6 (for cable), (p2, k2) 4 times, p4, k6, p2, k18,* (p2, k6) twice, p2. Repeat once between stars. Work gusset and repeat row 1, finishing round with second gusset.

2nd row Same as row 1.

3rd row *K18, p2, k6, p4, (k2, p2) 4 times, k6, p2, k18,* (p2, k6) twice, p2. Repeat once. Same pattern for back each round.

4th row Same as row 3.

5th and 6th row Repeat rows 1 and 2 once.

7th row P20, cross cable, p4, (k2, p2) 4 times, cross cable, p22, cross cable, p2, cross cable, p 22, cross cable, p4, (k2, p2) 4 times, cross cable, p 20. Knit gusset and repeat row 7 for back. Repeat from row 1 for ladder stitch and cables, but the double moss panels do not repeat correctly, so work these from graph.

When the gussets are 20 stitches wide, the front and back must be divided for the armholes. The 22 stitches of each gusset should be slipped off on to wool or holder, whilst the front and back of guernsey are knitted separately. The size of the armhole can be gauged, as 11 ribs of purl in the ladder pattern are worked from the division of back and front to the shoulders. See figure 1.

The shoulders are cast off together on the right side of work, forming a ridge. See figure 4.

124 stitches are picked up for the neck and worked in k2, p2, for 21 rounds. Cast off plain in double wool.

132 stitches are picked up for each sleeve, not including the gusset stitches; these are knitted in with the sleeves.

Two cables side by side are knitted from the shoulder, the ridge acting as centre for the pattern. See figure 4.

The purl pattern is continued down the sleeve, finishing with the cables after 7 purl ribs round the sleeve have been completed.

10

The gussets are decreased each side every 7th row, and the sleeve pattern finishes with 3 rows of purl where the gussets end. The seam stitch of 2 purl is carried on to the cuff. Continue in plain knitting, decreasing one stitch each side of seam stitch every 6th round till the cuff is reached. 80 stitches knitted in 2 plain, 2 purl, form the cuff welt.

Sleeve length, 22 inches. Sleeve pattern, about one-third the length of the sleeve without the cuff.

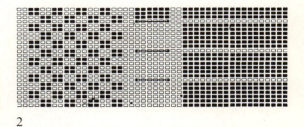

2
3   Double moss, cable and ladder patterns

4   Another view of figure 1 showing shoulder strap as decoration

Flamborough

5   Diamond moss and cable pattern

13

This is an old Viking settlement, and some of the fishermen bear a striking resemblance to their Scandinavian forbears. There are many fishing families in the village, but only about a dozen boats go out now compared to the forty or fifty in former days. Fishing is still a means of livelihood, but the village has become one of the beauty spots of Yorkshire, and visitors are also a source of income.

These people come from Viking stock, and many of the words used still show this. 'Mask' is Norwegian for 'stitch', and 'herring mask' and 'net mask' are the names of two patterns that have been in use for hundreds of years.

Flamborough is noted for fine guernsey knitters, and the older women still knit, but some of the younger ones find the work tedious and heavy, and so another old craft is gradually fading away, and more machine-made jerseys are worn by the fishermen. The patterns used here are elaborate and distinctive, and though there is a similarity amongst them they are easy to recognise. Different families vary the detail in the size and filling of the diamonds and the width of the moss stitch pattern.

FLAMBOROUGH PATTERN I
Diamond

Figure 5
Pattern multiple 41

This is a variation of Flamborough V. The centre section and front including 2 ropes (chart 6) is 51 stitches wide. The two sections, one on each side, are 41 stitches each with a 3 moss panel next the sleeve, and a 2 plain rib each side of the 3 moss stitches (figure 7), making 149, and a total of 298 for the pattern. Cast on with double wool 296 stitches for the welt and increase 2 more for the pattern.

A 6-inch welt is worked in k2, p2, then 1½ inches plain knitting, making a seam stitch each side of 2 purl, and working on from 2 of the purl ribs in the welt. The directions for knitting the pattern follow shortly—the diamonds are in moss stitch with 3 rows of plain knitting between each diamond.

The gusset starts about 14 inches from the bottom of the guernsey, and the directions for making it are the same as those given for Patrington. The shoulders

are worked in 5 ribs of purl 2 rows deep, alternating with 5 ribs of 2 plain, back and front, and are cast off together on the inside.

The sleeve pattern shows a slightly smaller diamond see chart 8. The guernsey was knitted by me and went with the British Council Loan Collection on a world tour.

A variation of the diamond pattern seen at Flamborough and in many Scottish guernseys is also given in Flamborough V and may be used instead of the moss stitch if preferred.

The sleeve graph does not give the rope pattern, but it is used to separate the main pattern.

1st row P2, k6, p2, k3, (p1, k1) twice, p1, k16, (p1, k1) twice, p1, k2, p2, k6, p2.
2nd row P2, k6, p2, k2, (p1, k1) twice, p1, k16, (p1, k1) twice, p1, k3, p2, k6, p2.

3rd row Same as row 1.

4th row P2, k6, p2, k2, (p1, k1) twice, p1, k8, p1, k7, (p1, k1) twice, p1, k3, p2, k6, p2.

5th row P2, k6, p2, k3, (p1, k1) twice, p1, k6, p1, k1, p1, k7 (p1, k1) twice, p1, k2, p2, k6, p2.

6th row P2, cross cable left over right, p2, k2, (p1, k1) twice, p1, k6, (p1, k1) twice, p1, k5, (p1, k1) twice, p1, k3, p2, cross cable left over right, p2.

7th row P2, k6, p2, k3, (p1, k1) twice, p1, k4, (p1, k1) 3 times, p1, k5, (p1, k1) twice, p1, k2, p2, k6, p2.

8th row P2, k6, p2, k2, (p1, k1) twice, p1, k4, (p1, k1) 4 times, p1, k3, (p1, k1) twice, p1, k3, p2, k6, p2.

9th row P2, k6, p2, k3, (p1, k1) twice, p1, k2, (p1, k1) 5 times, p1, k3, (p1, k1) twice, p1, k2, p2, k6, p2.

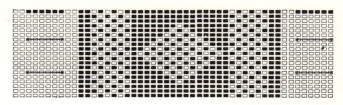

6

7 Detail of pattern showing shoulder strap and gusset under the arm

10th row P2, k6, p2, k2, (p1, k1) twice, p1, k2, (p1, k1) 9 times, p1, k3, p2, k6, p2.

11th row Same as row 9.

12th row Same as row 8.

13th row Same as row 7 but cross cable twice as in row 6.

14th row Same as row 6.

15th row Same as row 5.

16th row Same as row 4.

    This pattern is now repeated from row 1, crossing the cable every 7th row.

Sleeve section

1st row K3, (p1, k1) twice, (p1, k6) twice, (p1, k1) twice, p1, k3.

2nd row K2, (p1, k1) twice, p1, k6, p1, k1, p1, k6, (p1, k1) twice, p1, k2.

3rd row K3, (p1, k1) twice, p1, k4, (p1, k1) twice, p1, k4, (p1, k1) twice, p1, k3.

4th row K2, (p1, k1) twice, p1, k4, (p1, k1) 3 times, p1, k4, (p1, k1) twice, p1, k2.

5th row K3, (p1, k1) twice, p1, k2, (p1, k1) 4 times, p1, k2, (p1, k1) twice, p1, k3.

6th row K2, (p1, k1) twice, p1, k2, (p1, k1) 5 times, p1, k2, (p1, k1) twice, p1, k2.

7th row Same as row 5.

8th row Same as row 4.

9th row Same as row 3.

10th row Same as row 2.

11th row Same as row 1.

12th row K2, (p1, k1) twice, p1, k13, (p1, k1) twice, p1, k2.

13th row K3, (p1, k1) twice, p1, k13, (p1, k1) twice, p1, k3.

Repeat from row 1.

FLAMBOROUGH PATTERN II
Net Mask

Figure 11
Pattern multiple 41

284 stitches for welt—4 cables across the front, diamond centre, otherwise the same as Flamborough I.

1st row *P2, k6, p2, k2, (p1, k1) 3 times, (p1, k6) twice, (p1, k1) 3 times, p1, k2, *p2, k6, p2.

2nd row *P2, k6, p2, k3, (p1, k1) twice, p1, k6, p1, k1, p1, k6, (p1, k1) twice, p1, k3, *p2, k6, p2.

3rd row *P2, k6, p2, k2, (p1, k1) 3 times, p1, k4, p1, k3, p1, k4, (p1, k1) 3 times, p1, k2, *p2, k6, p2.

4th row *P2, k6, p2, k3, (p1, k1) twice, p1, k4, p1 k5, p1, k4, (p1, k1) twice, p1, k3, *p2, k6, p2.

5th row *P2, k6, p2, k2, (p1, k1) 3 times, p1, k2, p1, k7, p1, k2, (p1, k1) 3 times, p1, k2, *p2, k6, p2.

6th row *P2, k6, p2, k3, (p1, k1) twice, p1, k2, p1, k9, p1, k2, (p1, k1) twice, p1, k3, *p2, k6, p2.

7th row Cross cable twice in this row, otherwise same as row 5.

8th row Same as row 4.

9th row Same as row 3.

10th row Same as row 2.

11th row Same as row 1.

Repeat pattern from row 1. The cables are crossed every 7th row.

16

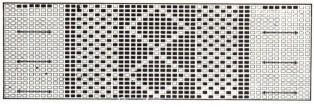

9

4th row (K1, p1) 3 times, k3, p1, k5, p1, k3, (p1, k1)
   3 times.
5th row (P1, k1) 4 times, p1, k7, (p1, k1) 4 times, p1.
6th row Same as row 4.
7th row Same as row 3.
8th row Same as row 2.
9th row Same as row 1.

Repeat from row 1.

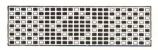

10 The left hand side of the
    chart should show one
    more line of moss stitch

Sleeve pattern
Multiple of 18

1st row (P1, k1) 3 times, (p1, k5) twice, (p1, k1) 3
   times, p1.
2nd row (K1, p1) 3 times, k5, p1, k1, p1, k5, (p1, k1) 3
   times.
3rd row (P1, k1) 3 times, (p1, k1) 3 times, (p1, k1) 3
   times, p1.

11   A very popular Flamborough pattern

FLAMBOROUGH PATTERN III
Net Mask and Honey Comb

Figure 13

Pattern multiple 45

294 stitches are cast on in double wool, the diamond again in centre, front and back. Welt 3 inches deep in k2, p2.

Gusset direction same as Patrington and shoulders finished as in Flamborough I.

Length of guernsey 22 inches.

Pattern 17 inches.

Sleeve 20 inches.

1st row *P2, k6, p2, k2, (p1, k1) 4 times, (p1, k6) twice, (p1, k1) 4 times, p1, k2, *p2, k6, p2.

2nd row *P2, k6, p2, k16, p1, k1, p1, k16, *p2, k6, p2.

3rd row *P2, k6, p2, k2, (p1, k1) 4 times, p1, k4, p1, k3, p1, k4, (p1, k1) 4 times, p1, k2, *p2, k6, p2.

4th row *P2, k6, p2, k14, p1, k5, p1, k14, *p2, k6, p2.

5th row *P2, k6, p2, k2, (p1, k1) 4 times, p1, k2, p1, k7, p1, k2, (p1, k1) 4 times, p1, k2, *p2, k6, p2.

6th row *P2, k6, p2, k12, p1, k9, p1, k12, *p2, k6, p2.

7th row P2, cross cable in next 6 stitches, p2, k2, (p1, k1) 4 times, p1, k2, p1, k7, p1, k2, (p1, k1) 4 times, p1, k2, *p2, cross cable, p2.

8th row Same as row 4.

9th row Same as row 3.

10th row Same as row 2.

11th row Same as row 1.

12th row *P2, k6, p2, k17, p1, k17, *p2, k6, p2.

13th row *P2, k6, p2, k2, (p1, k1) 4 times, p1, k5, p1, k1, p1, k5, (p1, k1) 4 times, p1, k2, *p2, k6, p2.

14th row *P2, cross cable, p2, k15, p1, k3, p1, k15, p2, *cross cable, p2.

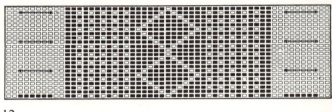

12

13   This pattern is also seen in Scotland

15th row *P2, k6, p2, k2, (p1, k1) 4 times, p1, k3, p1, k5, p1, k3, (p1, k1) 4 times, p1, k2, *p2, k6, p2.
16th row *P2, k6, p2, k13, p1, k7, p1, k13, *p2, k6, p2.
17th row *P2, k6, p2, k2, (p1, k1) 5 times, p1, k9, (p1, k1) 5 times, p1, k2, *p2, k6, p2.
18th row Same as row 16.
19th row Same as row 15.
20th row Same as row 14.
21st row Same as row 13, but cross cable.
22nd row Same as row 12.

Repeat pattern from row 1, crossing cables every 7th row. Sleeves are worked in honey comb pattern from armhole to just above the elbow.

FLAMBOROUGH PATTERN IV

Figure 15
Pattern multiple 37

Cast on 284 stitches in double wool for the welt, which is 3 inches in depth and knitted in 2 plain, 2 purl. A seam stitch of 2 moss is carried up each side from top of welt, and 2 inches of plain knitting is then worked before the pattern starts. One of the diamond panels forms the centre, back and front.

This pattern is very like Flamborough I, Diamond but the diamonds are smaller and further apart, and the moss stitch narrower.

The gusset is the same as in the Patrington guernsey —directions will be found there for working it. The shoulders are the same as Flamborough I Diamond (Mrs Major). This pattern can be knitted from the graph. The sleeve directions are given, but it is an odd pattern and not symmetrical. After the gusset is finished, the decreasings are carried on in the sleeves, each side of the seam stitch, but never increasing or decreasing on the stitch next the seam, always leaving one clear stitch each side. The decreasing finishes when the cuff is reached. This is worked in k2, p2, to match the welt.

Pattern for half-sleeve

1st row P2, k6, p2, k2, (p1, k1) 3 times, p1, k3, (p2, k6) twice, p2, k2, (p1, k1) 3 times, p1, k3.
2nd row P2, k6, p2, k3, (p1, k1) 3 times, p1, k2, p2, k6, p2, k6, p2, k3, (p1, k1) 3 times, p1, k2.
3rd row (P2, k2) 3 times, (p1, k1) 3 times, p1, k3, (p2, k2) 5 times, (p1, k1) 3 times, p1, k3.
4th row (P2, k2) twice, p2, k3, (p1, k1) 3 times, p1, k2, (p2, k2) 4 times, p2, k3, (p1, k1) 3 times, p1, k2.

These 4 rows repeated make the pattern for the sleeve.

Length from neck without collar 22 inches.
Pattern 17 inches.
Sleeve, full length, 20 inches.

14

15

16

17

Diamond seen at Flamborough, Filey and in Scotland

Figure 17

1st, 2nd and 3rd rows K15.
4th, 5th rows K7, p1, k7.
6th, 7th rows K6, p1, k1, p1, k6.
8th, 9th rows K5, (p1, k1) twice, p1, k5.
10th, 11th rows K4, (p1, k1) 3 times, p1, k4.
12th, 13th rows K3, (p1, k1) 4 times, p1, k3.
14th, 15th rows K2, (p1, k1) 5 times, p1, k2.
16th, 17th rows K1, (p1, k1) 7 times.
18th, 19th rows Same as 14, 15.
20th, 21st rows Same as 12, 13.
22nd, 23rd rows Same as 10, 11.
24th, 25th rows Same as 8, 9.
26th, 27th rows Same as 6 and 7.
28th, 29th rows Same as 4 and 5.

Repeat pattern from row 1.
This stitch is also seen in Fisher Row chart 94.

20

Filey

18   This guernsey is over forty years old and was worn by Matt Cammish in the
Navy during the Second World War

When I first remember Filey, every doorway in the old town held a knitter, in a black or coloured sunbonnet, with her needles flicking in and out so quickly, that it was impossible to follow their movement. One 'pin' would be tucked into a 'shear' under her arm. These knitting sheaths were made of print, small cases a few inches long, and filled tightly with quills—they held one needle, leaving a hand free for quicker movement with the wool. Sometimes a wisp of straw rolled tightly was used instead. Wooden knitting sheaths and sticks were also seen, and the sheaths were occasionally beautifully carved. They were used stuck into, or through, the waistband. They are also mentioned under Whitby and Flamborough. In Staithes and Flamborough, knitting tippies, like those seen in Shetland were worn, these were small leather pouches. The one seen at Staithes was pierced with several holes, into one of which the pin was stuck, and held round the waist by a leather band. The Flamborough tippie was a flap of leather pierced by two holes, through which a strong 'bit of band' was threaded and twisted round the long knitting needle, this tippie was fastened round the waist in the same way. The old cobbled sloping sea wall was still in existence then. It had been built with large stones of different shapes cemented together, and some were worn away by the action of the tide, and the resulting holes were transformed· into tiny pools filled with sea water and shells and fringed with sea weed.

Down by the cobble landing you may come across some of the fishermen who remember the old days, and if you ask them about Lizzie Ann, a smile comes over their faces, for she was related to many of the families living in the old town.

She was a remarkable women, and though she only had one hand (the other arm ended at the knuckles) she was one of the hardest workers in Filey. A great Chapel supporter, she also helped at the Vicarage and on other days went out cleaning and white washing. During the summer her house was overflowing with visitors and the same people came to her year after year. She was also a great knitter, and through her I came to know many of the Filey patterns and to learn the names of the different stitches. I often slipped up to her cottage in the evenings and listened to her lovely East Yorkshire dialect and learnt to knit the different patterns she was always ready to show me. She talked very fast, and it was difficult to follow all she said. She called her knitting needles 'Pins'.

The patterns belong to families and places and often have local names, either connected with the sea, or the men's occupation. One of the Filey patterns is known as 'Betty Martin'—evidently a knitting celebrity, though she still remains only a name and a pattern to me.

Guernsey hunting becomes rather an obsession, but the search for them is fun—memorising them off the fisherman's back or front, (back, if he is baiting lines, painting boats or other engrossing jobs which entail a bending position!) Front, if he'll talk!

Fortunately, most of the patterns are repetitions, and if a section is memorised, the rest can be worked out on an old envelope round the corner—often the man wanders away before you have taken it all in, then he has to be chased down the sea wall, or harbour, to verify and make certain.

One day I found myself in Queen Street in the old town, and I called at a whitewashed stone cottage with walls at least a foot thick. An old lady opened the door, and when she heard I wanted guernsey patterns she asked me into the kitchen. A tortoiseshell cat sat by the fire, and an old man lay asleep on his side on a horsehair sofa. She asked me to sit down and went to fetch some guernseys from up the yard. She showed me one or two, and then pointing to the sofa said, 'Tak a leeak at yon gansey he's wearing; yer can tun him over and see t'pattern!" Thank goodness our talking woke him, and I had a look without having to 'tun him over'. They were a charming old couple, and were the parents of George Overy shown in figure 49.

Matt Cammish also lives in Queen Street, and figure 18 shows a guernsey belonging to him that has been in constant wear for over forty years, and worn by his father before him. Matt, junior, wore it when he was in the Navy during the war.

A lady living outside Scarborough told me that this guernsey belonged to a Filey man who brought her fish once a week. I asked her to try to borrow it for me, and about a week later a parcel arrived, smelling strongly of fish! The colour of the wool was the lovely grey blue, only found in the very old guernseys; it was like the sea on a stormy day.

One sleeve had been re-knitted from the shoulder and the join shows plainly in the picture, figure 18, the other knitted in a different blue from the elbow to the wrist, and the collar and welt had been renewed several times. The wool was almost shiny with wear. The pattern was knitted in double moss diamonds with cables and panels of Betty Martin; this particular type of moss stitch is sometimes found at Flamborough and in the Scottish guernseys. Directions for knitting this pattern are given in Flamborough V.

The group of the four Crimlisk brothers (figure 41) show some of the simple early patterns: graphs on page 45. The left-hand figure wears pattern 43, the man above pattern 45, and the other man in the sealskin cap pattern 47.

FILEY PATTERN I
Matt Cammish's Guernsey

Figure 18

Knitted in multiple of 47 stitches. The pattern shows 49, as the outside purl stitches are included twice to balance pattern.

1st row (P2, k2) repeat twice, p2, k6. These 6 stitches are worked as a cable and the knitting crossed from left to right every 7th row, (p2, k2) repeat twice, p2, k6, p1, k6, p2.

2nd row Same as row 1.

3rd row P2, k10, p2, k6, p2, k10, p2, k5, p1, k1, p1, k5, p2.

4th row Same as row 3.

5th row (P2, k2) repeat twice, p2, k6, (p2, k2) repeat twice, p2, k4, p1, k1, p1, k1, p1, k4, p2.

6th row Same as row 5.

7th row P2, k10, p2, cross cable, p2, k10, p2, k3, (p1, k1) twice, p1, k3, p2.

8th row Same as row 7.

9th row (P2, k2) repeat twice, p2, k6, (p2, k2) repeat twice, p2, k2, (p1, k1) repeat 3 times, k2, p2.

10th row Same as row 9.

11th row P2, k10, p2, k6, p2, k10, p2, k1, (p1, k1) repeat 4 times, p1, k1, p2.

12th row Same as row 11.

13th row (P2, k2) repeat twice, p2, k6, (p2, k2) repeat twice, p2, k2, (p1, k1) repeat 3 times, p1, k2, p2.

14th row Same as row 13. Cross cable.

15th row P2, k10, p2, k6, p2, k10, p2, k3, (p1, k1) repeat twice, p1, k3, p2.

16th row Same as row 15.

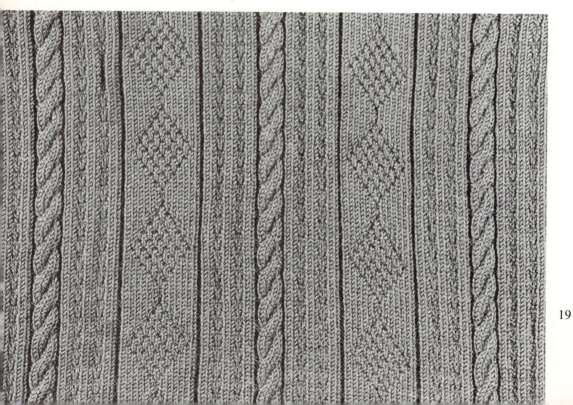

19

17th row (P2, k2) repeat twice, p2, k6, (p2, k2) repeat twice, p2, k4, (p1, k1) repeat twice, p1, k4, p2.

18th row Repeat 17.

19th row P2, k10, p2, k6, p2, k5, p1, k1, p1, k5, p2.

20th row Repeat 19.

21st row (P2, k2) repeat twice, p2, k6, (p2, k2) repeat twice, p2, k6, p1, k6, p2.

22nd row Repeat 21. Cross cable.

23rd row P2, k10, p2, k6, p2, k10, p2, k6, p1, k6, p2.

24th row Repeat 23.

These 24 rows complete 1 section. 4 rows must be knitted between each diamond, with a purl stitch in the centre of each rib connecting the diamonds.

FILEY PATTERN II

Mr G. Overy

Figure 21
Multiple 41

This consists of two panels: one of zigzag pattern, 11 stitches wide; the other worked in double moss stitch with border of k2 each side. Cable divides the panels and is crossed every 7th row. 320 stitches cast on double for the welt, depth of welt 3 inches with 1 row of purl at the top.

Shoulders 6 double rows purl and plain.

Sleeves patterned half-way down, not including cuff.

Gussets 8 plain stitches with 1 purl stitch each side, starting from bottom of pattern which begins after 1½ inches of plain knitting have been worked above the welt. The gusset rises to 30 stitches wide under arm, and finishes in the sleeve with the pattern. No seam stitch.

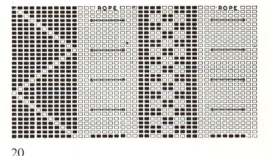

20

21   The pattern used by Mrs Overy

1st row P2, k6, (p2, k2) 3 times, p2, k6, p3, k10.

2nd row P2, k6, (p2, k4) twice, p2, k6, p2, k1, p1, k9.

3rd row P2, k6, (p2, k4) twice, p2, k6, p2, k2, p1, k8.

4th row P2, k6, (p2, k2) 3 times, p2, k6, p2, k3, p1, k7.

5th row P2, k6, (p2, k2) 3 times, p2, k6, p2, k4, p1 k6.

6th row P2, k6, (p2, k4) twice, p2, k6, p2, k5, p1, k5.

7th row P2, to cross cable, work as follows: slip next 3 stitches onto spare needle and drop to back. K next 3. Then knit stitches on spare needle, then (p2, k4) twice, p2, cross cable as before, p2, k6, p1, k4.

8th row P2, k6, (p2, k2) 3 times, p2, k6, p2, k7, p1 k3.

9th row P2, k6, (p2, k2) 3 times, p2, k6, p2, k8, p1, k2.

10th row P2, k6, (p2, k4) twice, p2, k6, p2, k9, p1, k1.

11th row P2, k6, (p2, k4) twice, p2, k6, p2, k10, p1. Directions are now given for zigzag pattern only, up to the 20th row. Cables are crossed every 7th row, and double moss can be followed from the chart: Filey II.

12th row Same as 10.

13th row Same as 9.

14th row Same as 8.

15th row Same as 7.

16th row Same as 6.

17th row Same as 5.

18th row Same as 4.

19th row Same as 3.

20th row Same as 2.

Repeat from row 1.

FILEY PATTERN III
Zigzag and Ladder Stitch

Multiple of 61

This pattern found at Scarborough, was knitted at Filey by Mrs Overy of Queen Street. Patterns 2, 4 and 12 were also knitted by her, and 3 is a mixture of patterns 1 and 2. The guernsey worn by Mr G. J. Overy at Scarborough is also a mixture of 1, 7 and ladder stitch.

22

FILEY PATTERN IV
Steps and Moss

Figure 24
Multiple of 33

Two panels are used in this pattern. They are divided by cables 4 stitches wide. Shoulders worked in garter stitch. The first panel in step stitch 7 wide consists of 4 rows plain and 2 rows purl repeated. The second panel is worked in moss stitch 10 wide and bordered each side by k2.

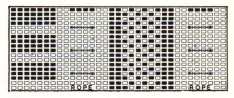

23

24　Smaller cables

FILEY PATTERN VII

Multiple of 19

One panel of a favourite Filey moss stitch which I call single double. It is worked as follows: K2, p1, k1, p1, k1, p1, k2, for 2 rows, then k3, p1, k1, p1, k3, for 2 rows; repeat these 4 rows all through. This panel is bordered by cables each side.

Irish moss stitch

Cast on any even number of stitches.
2 rows k1, p1, k1, p1.
2 rows p1, k1, p1, k1.

Directions for side diamond pattern

Cast on about 100 stitches according to thickness of wool and size of needles. After the welt the pattern starts at the side seam with 3 stitches of Irish Moss, a cable pattern of 2 purl 6 plain 2 purl, next the diamond pattern worked in Irish Moss stitch, followed by the single crossover pattern working up to the centre panel. The diamond and crossover are not given under one heading, as they do not repeat evenly.

Front

Cast on 13 stitches

1st row P5, k1, p1, k1, p5.
*2nd row K5, p1, k1, p1, k5.
3rd row P4, s1b, k1, pss, k1, s1f, p1, kss, p4.
4th row K4, (p1, k1) twice, p1, k4.
5th row P3, s1b, k1, pss, k1, p1, k1, s1f, p1, kss, p3.

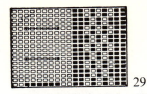

29

6th row K3, p1, (k1, p1) 3 times, k3.
7th row P2, s1b, k1, pss, (k1, p1) twice, k1, s1f, p1, k22, p2.
8th row K2, (p1, k1) 4 times, p1, k2.
9th row P1, s1b, k1, pss, (k1, p1) 3 times, k1, s1f, p1, kss, p1.
10th row (K1, p1) 6 times, k1.
11th row S1b, k1, pss, (k1, p1) 4 times, k1, s1f, p1, kss.
12th row P1, (k1, p1) 6 times.
13th row S1f, p1, kss, (p1, k1) 4 times, p1, s1b, k1, pss.
14th row (K1, p1) 6 times, k1.
15th row P1, s1f, p1, kss, (p1, k1) 3 times, p1, s1b, k1, pss, p1.
16th row K2, (p1, k1) 4 times, p1, k2.
17th row P2, s1f, p1, kss, (p1, k1) twice, p1, s1b, k1, pss, p2.
18th row K3, (p1, k1) 3 times, p1, k3.
19th row P3, s1f, p1, kss, p1, k1, p1, s1b, k1, pss, p3.
20th row K4, (p1, k1) twice, p1, k4.
21st row P4, s1f, p1, kss, p1, s1b, k1, pss, p4.
22nd row K5, p1, k1, p1, k5.
23rd row P5, s2f, k1, knit first stitch on spare needle, purl second stitch, p5.
24th row K6, p2, k5.
25th row P5, k1, s1f, p1, kss, p5.

Repeat from row 2.*

FILEY PATTERN VIII

Figure 30

This jersey, knitted by me for my daughter-in-law, has no gussets and the neck band is lower than in a man's guernsey.

The zigzag pattern can be followed from the chart for Filey II, but the rib for this pattern is 13 stitches wide instead of 11, 1 plain stitch being left up each side of the zigzag.

The sleeve pattern block of Flamborough III gives the same moss and cable pattern, and the rib of the diamond is 13 stitches wide as for the zigzag. This pattern can be worked from these two charts. Initials are knitted in above the welt C.J.T., but the letters are clearer in Filey V, S.M.T. See figure 25.

30   Zigzag, moss and cables

FILEY PATTERN IX

Figure 32

1st row P2, k6, cable, p2, (k5, p2) twice, k6, cable, p2, k2, m5, k2.

2nd row *P2, k6, p2, k4, p4, k4, p2, k6, p2, k3, m3, k3.

3rd row P2, k6, p2, k3, p1, k1, p2, k1, p1, k3, p2, k6, p2, k2, m5, k2.

4th row P2, k6, p2, k2, p1, k2, p2, k2, p1, k2, p2, k6, p2, k3, m3, k3.

5th row P2, k6, p2, k1, p1, k3, p2, k3, p1, k1, p2, k6, p2, k2, m5, k2.

6th row P2, k6, p3, k4, p2, k4, p3, k5, p2, k3, m3, k3.

7th row P2, cross cable, p2, (k5, p2) twice, cross cable, p2, k2, m5, k2.

Repeat from row 2* Cross cable every 6th row.

31

32   Moss, cable and herringbone pattern

32

FILEY PATTERN X

Figure 34

1st row *P2, k6, p2, k3, m7, k3, p2, k6, p1, k6, p2, k3, m7, k3, p2, k6, p2.

2nd row P2, k6, p2, k2, m9, k2, p2, k5, p1, k1, p1, k5, p2, k2, m9, k2, p2, k6, p2.

3rd row P2, k6, p2, k3, m7, k3, p2, k4, p1, k3, p1, k4, p2, k3, m7, k3, p2, k6, p2.

4th row P2, k6, p2, k2, m9, k2, p2, k3, p1, k5, p1, k3, p2, k2, m9, k2, p2, k6, p2.

5th row P2, k6, p2, k3, m7, k3, p2, k2, p1, k7, p1, k2, p2, k3, m7, k3, p2, k6, p2.

6th row P2, k6, p2, k2, m9, k2, p2, k1, (p1, k4) twice, p1, k1, p2, k2, m9, k2, p2, k6, p2.

Repeat from row 1*. Cables are crossed in this row and every following 6th row.

33

34   Moss, cable and herringbone. One of the best Filey patterns

FILEY PATTERN XI

Figure 36

Multiple of 43

A large panel of single moss stitch 27 wide is flanked each side by a variation of cable stitch known locally as 'Print o' the Hoof' (a horse's hoof mark in the sand). The moss pattern can also have 1 or 2 plain stitches at each side of the moss as a border.

This cable is worked as follows and has 12 stitches instead of the usual 6 and knitted plain for the first 6 rounds, then slip first 3 stitches onto a spare needle, place at back, knit next 3 knit stitches on spare needle, slip next 3 on spare needle to the front, knit 3 stitches on spare needle. After this, knit 6 plain rows and then repeat cable crossing as above every 8th row. Continue thus till pattern is finished. Should be worked on fine needles.

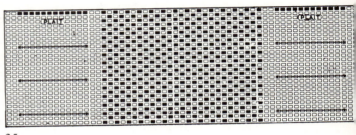

35

36   This plait is also found in Scottish and Aran guernseys

34

FILEY PATTERN XII

Figure 38

Multiple of 62

Two wide panels of 18 stitches each are worked in single moss and outlined by 1 plain stitch used as an edge each side. The moss panels are divided by 2 cables, with a central rib of plain knitting, 4 stitches wide. 4 ribs of 2 purl divide the cables and plain rib. This pattern should be worked on very fine needles.

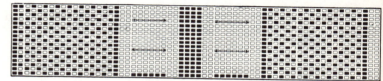

37

38   This pattern should be knitted on very fine needles

39   Detail of under-arm gusset

FILEY PATTERN XIII
Steps and Diamonds

Multiple of 38

Two panels divided by cables. The first 7 stitches wide, of 3 rows of plain, and 1 purl row repeated. The second panel 11 wide with moss stitch diamonds worked on a plain ground.

40

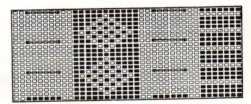

FILEY PATTERN XIV
'PRINT O' THE HOOF' SWEATER

Crew neck

Materials
31 oz Listers Double Six.
1 pair 'A' needles (see tension note).
1 pair 'B' needles (see tension note).
1 set of 'B' needles with points at both ends.
Size
To fit 40 in. chest.

Measurements
Length at centre back = 26 in.
Width across pattern at underarm = 21 in.
Side seam = 16 in.
Sleeve seam = 20 in.

Description

A long crew neck sweater with low set in sleeves. Gussets are worked at underarm. Main part of garment is worked in panels of Filey stitches. Welts, cuffs worked in k2, p2, rib. Only a third of the sleeves at the top is worked in pattern stitch. The lower part is worked in stocking stitch to the cuff. Sleeves are picked up at the top and worked downwards.

Tension

5 stitches and 6 rows to 1 in., measured over stocking stitch, using 'A' needles.

To test tension

Use a portion of the wool and No. 7 needles. Cast on 15 stitches and work 12 rows of stocking stitch. Cast off, but do not press.

Now measure the tension

If you have more than 5 stitches and 6 rows to 1 in., work another sample using No. 6 needles. If, however, the first sample had less than 5 stitches and 6 rows to the inch, test again using No. 8 needles.

The needles used for the correct tension sample are termed 'A' needles in the pattern. You will need two sizes finer for 'B' needles.

It is essential that the tension is absolutely correct

Abbreviations

k=knit; p=purl; st=stitch; sts=stitches; k2 tog =knit 2 together; k2 tog t.b.s.=knit 2 together through back of stitches; inc=increase; dec= decrease.

**Using 'B' needles, cast on 108 stitches (Rope edge).

Work in k2, p2, rib thus:

1st row K3, *p2, k2. Repeat from * ending the last repeat k3.

2nd row K1, *p2, k2. Repeat from * ending the last repeat k1. Repeat these 2 rows until work measures 4 in. from the cast-on edge, ending on a 2nd row and increasing 1 stitch at each end

of the last row. (110 stitches). Change to 'A' needles and work in stocking stitch until work measures 8 in. from the cast-on edge, ending on a purl row. Now work in pattern stitch thus: (multiple of 43 stitches plus 24).

1st row K5, p2, (k4, p2) twice, k8, p3, (k8, p2) twice, (k4, p2) twice, k8, p2, k8, p3, k8, p2, (k4, p2) twice, k5.

2nd row K1, p4, k2, (p4, k2) twice, p8, k2, p1, k1, p7, k2, p8, k2, (p4, k2) twice, p8, k2, p7, k1, p1, k2, p8, k2, (p4, k2) twice, p4, k1.

3rd row K1, slip the next 2 sts onto a cable needle and drop to *front* of work, k2 from main needle, then k2 from cable needle, p2, (k2, p2) 3 times, slip the next 2 sts on to cable needle and drop to *back* of work, k2 from main needle, then k2 from cable needle; slip the next 2 sts on to cable needle and drop to *front* of work, k2 from main needle, k2 from cable needle, p2, k2, p1, k6, p2, cable 4 B, cable 4 F (as before), p2, (k2, p2) 3 times, cable 4 B, cable 4 F, p2, k6, p1, k2, p2, cable 4 B, cable 4 F, p2, (k2, p2) 3 times, cable 4 B, k1.

4th row K1, p4, k2, (p2, k2) 3 times, p8, k2, p3, k1, p5, k2, p8, k2, (p2, k2) 3 times, p8, k2, p5, k1, p3, k2, p8, k2, (p2, k2) 3 times, p4, k1.

5th row K5, p2, (k4, p2) twice, k8, p2, k4, p1, k4, p2, k8, p2, (k4, p2) twice, k8, p2, k4, p1, k4, p2, k8, p2, (k4, p2) twice, k5.

6th row K1, p4, k2, (p4, k2) twice, p8, k2, p5, k1, p3, k2, p8, k2, (p4, k2) twice, p8, k2, p3, k1, p5, k2, p8, k2, (p4, k2) twice, p4, k1.

7th row K1, cable 4 F, p2, (k2, p2) 3 times, cable 4 B, cable 4 F, p2, k6, p1, k2, p2, cable 4 B, cable 4 F, p2, (k2, p2) 3 times, cable 4 B, cable 4 F, p2, k2, p1, k6, p2, cable 4 B, cable 4 F, p2, (k2, p2) 3 times, cable 4 B, k1.

8th row K1, p4, k2, (p2, k2) 3 times, p8, k2, p7, k1, p1, k2, p8, k2, (p2, k2) 3 times, p8, k2, p1, k1, p7, k2, p8, k2, (p2, k2) 3 times, p4, k1.

9th row K5, p2, (k4, p2) twice, k8, p2, k8, p3, k8 p2, (k4, p2) twice, k8, p3, k8, p2, k8, p2, (k4, p2) twice, k5.

10th row K1, p4, k2, (p4, k2) twice, p8, k2, p7, k1, p1, k2, p8, k2, (p4, k2) twice, p8, k2, p1, k1, p7, k2, p8, k2, (p4, k2) twice, p4, k1.

11th row K1, cable 4 F, p2, (k2, p2) 3 times, cable 4 B, cable 4 F, p2, k6, p1, k2, p2, cable 4 B, cable 4 F, p2, (k2, p2) 3 times, cable 4 B, cable 4 F, p2, k2, p1, k6, p2, cable 4 B, cable 4 F, p2, (k2, p2) 3 times, cable 4 B, k1.

12th row K1, p4, k2, (p2, k2) 3 times, p8, k2, p5, k1, p3, k2, p8, k2, (p2, k2) 3 times, p8, k2, p3, k1, p5, k2, p8, k2, (p2, k2) 3 times, p4, k1.

13th row K5, p2, (k4, p2) twice, k8, p2, k4, p1, k4, p2, k8, p2, (k4, p2) twice, k8, p2, k4, p1, k4, p2, k8, p2, (k4, p2) twice, k5.

14th row K1, p4, k2, (p4, k2) twice, p8, k2, p3, k1, p5, k2, p8, k2, (p4, k2) twice, p8, k2, p5, k1, p3, k2, p8, k2, (p4, k2) twice, p4, k1.

15th row K1, cable 4 F, p2, (k2, p2) 3 times, cable 4 B, cable 4 F, p2, k2, p1, k6, p2, cable 4 B, cable 4 F, p2, (k2, p2) 3 times, cable 4 B, cable 4 F, p2, k6, p1, k2, p2, cable 4 B, cable 4 F, p2, (k2, p2) 3 times, cable 4 B, k1.

16th row K1, p4, k2, (p2, k2) 3 times, p8, k2, p1, k1, p7, k2, p8, k2, (p2, k2) 3 times, p8, k2, p7, k1, p1, k2, p8, k2, (p2, k2) 3 times, p4, k1.

These 16 rows form the pattern and are repeated throughout.

Continue in pattern, increasing 1 stitch at each end of the next row and every following 4th row, until there are 124 stitches on the needle, working the extra stitches in stocking stitch.

Continue without shaping, keeping the 7 stitches for gusset at each end in stocking stitch, until 3 complete patterns have been worked altogether.

Slip the 7 stitches at each end of needle onto safety pins and continue in pattern on the centre 110 stitches until 6 complete patterns have been worked from the beginning.**

Yoke

1st row (Right side of work) k1, purl to last stitch, k1.

2nd row Knit.

3rd row Knit.

4th row K1, purl to last stitch, k1.

Repeat these 4 rows 3 times more.

Next row Cast off 35 stitches, purl to last stitch, k1.

Next row Cast off 35 stitches, knit to end.

Neck facing

Next row Cast on 6 stitches, knit to end.

Next row Cast on 6 stitches, knit to end. (52 stitches)

Continue in garter stitch (i.e. every row knit) on these 52 stitches for 1 inch.

Cast off VERY LOOSELY.

Front

Work exactly as for back.

Join shoulder seams by back-stitching on the wrong side approximately $\frac{1}{8}$ in. from edges to ensure neat seams.

Turn the garter stitch facing on to the wrong side of work and neatly slip stitch down to form a 1 in. facing. Then weave together the 6 stitches of back extension and the 6 stitches of front extension so that it fits along shoulder seam.

Sleeves

These are worked from the shoulders with the 7 gusset stitches added on at each end thus:

Using 'B' needles and with right side of work facing, knit the 7 stitches of gusset at beginning of sleeve, then pick up neatly and knit 42 stitches to shoulder seam, then 42 stitches along other side of sleeve to the 7 stitches of gusset at other end, then knit these 7 stitches (98 stitches).

Change to 'A' needles and work in pattern thus:

The half cable at each end and the double moss panel at each end are omitted on the sleeves, also the cables must be reversed on the sleeves so work cable 4 F first then cable 4 B, each time instead of vice versa:

Next row (Wrong side of work) k1, p10, k2, p8, k2, p1, k1, p7, k2, p8, k2, (p2, k2) 3 times, p8, k2, p7, k1, p1, k2, p8, k2, p10, k1.

Next row K11, p2, cable 4 F, cable 4 B, p2, k2, p1, k6, p2, cable 4 F, cable 4 B, p2, (k2, p2) 3 times, cable 4 F, cable 4 B, p2, k6, p1, k2, p2, cable 4 F, cable 4 B, p2, k11.

Next row K1, p10, k2, p8, k2, p3, k1, p5, k2, p8, k2, (p2, k2) 3 times, p8, k2, p5, k1, p3, k2, p8, k2, p10, k1.

Continue in pattern, keeping the 11 stitches at each end in stocking stitch, and decreasing 1 stitch at each end of the next row and every following 4th row until 4 stitches remain in stocking stitch at each end. The 7 gusset stitches at each end have now been decreased. (84 stitches).

Continue in pattern without shaping until 3 complete patterns have been worked.

Now work in stocking stitch only, decreasing 1 stitch at each end of every 4th row until 64 stitches remain.

Continue without shaping until sleeve measures 15½ in. from the picked up stitches at armhole, ending on a knit row.

Next row K1, *p2 tog., p2. Repeat from * ending the last repeat p1. (48 stitches).

Change to 'B' needles and work in k2, p2, rib as for back welt for 4½ in.

Cast off LOOSELY in rib.

Work the second sleeve in the same manner.

1 DO NOT PRESS.
2 Join underarm, gusset and sleeve edges together by back-stitching on the wrong side approximately ⅛ in. from edges to ensure neat seams, but weave together on the right side of work, the ribbing at welts and cuffs.

'PRINT O' THE HOOF' CARDIGAN

Materials
32 oz Listers Double Six.
1 pair 'A' needles (see tension note).
1 pair 'B' needles (see tension note).
1 pair 'C' needles (see tension note).

Size
To fit 40 in. chest.

Measurements
Length at centre back = 27 in.
Width across back at underarm = 20 in.
Side seam = 16½ in.
Sleeve seam = 17 in.

Description
A classic shaped cardigan with long set in sleeves and a 'V' neck. Main part worked in Filey stitches of zigzag, moss stitch and horseshoe cables. Welts, cuffs and front borders worked in k1, p1, rib. An inset pocket on each front. Fastened with 5 buttons.

Tension
5 stitches to 1 in., measured over stocking stitch, using 'A' needles.

To test the tension
Use a portion of the wool and No. 6 needles. Cast on 15 stitches and work 12 rows of stocking stitch. Cast off, but do not press.

Now measure the tension
If you have more than 5 stitches to 1 in., work another sample using No. 5 needles. If, however, the first sample had less than 5 stitches to the in., test again using No. 7 needles.

The needles used for your correct tension sample are termed 'A' needles in the pattern. You will need two sizes finer for 'B' needles, and two sizes finer still for 'C' needles.

It is essential that your tension is absolutely correct.

Abbreviations
k = knit; p = purl; st = stitch; sts = stitches; k2 tog = knit 2 together; k2 tog t.b.s. = knit 2 together through back of stitches; inc = increase; dec = decrease.

Back

Using 'B' needles, cast on 109 stitches (Rope edge).

Work in k1, p1, rib thus:

1st row K2, *p1, k1. Repeat from * ending the last repeat k2.

2nd row K1, *p1, k1. Repeat from * to end.

Repeat these 2 rows until work measures 1 in. from the cast-on edge, ending on a 2nd row and increasing 1 stitch at the end of the last row. (110 stitches).

Change to 'A' needles and work in pattern stitch thus:

1st row P2, k4, p2, k8, p3, (k8, p2) twice, (k4, p2) twice, k8, (p2, k4) twice, p2, k8, p2, k8, p3, k8, p2, k4, p2.

2nd row K2, p4, k2, p8, k2, p1, k1, p7, k2, p8, k2, (p4, k2) twice, p8, (k2, p4) twice, k2, p8, k2, p7, k1, p1, k2, p8, k2, p4, k2.

3rd row (K2, p2) twice, slip the next 2 stitches on to a cable needle and drop to *back* of work, k2 from main needle, then k2 from cable needle, slip the next 2 stitches on to a cable needle and drop to *front* of work, k2 from main needle, k2 from cable needle, p2, k2, p1, k6, p2, cable 4 B, cable 4 F, (p2, k2) 3 times, p2, cable 4 B, cable 4 F, (p2, k2) 3 times, p2, cable 4 B, cable 4 F, p2, k6, p1, k2, p2, cable 4 B, cable 4 F, (p2, k2) twice.

4th row (P2, k2) twice, p8, k2, p3, k1, p5, k2, p8, k2, (p2, k2) 3 times, p8, (k2, p2) 3 times, k2, p8, k2, p5, k1, p3, k2, p8, (k2, p2) twice.

5th row P2, k4, p2, k8, p2, k4, p1, k4, p2, k8, p2, (k4, p2) twice, k8, (p2, k4) twice, p2, k8, p2, k4, p1, k4, p2, k8, p2, k4, p2.

6th row K2, p4, k2, p8, k2, p5, k1, p3, k2, p8, k2, (p4, k2) twice, p8, (k2, p4) twice, k2, p2, k2, p3, k1, p5, k2, p8, k2, p4, k2.

7th row (K2, p2) twice, cable 4 B, cable 4 F, p2, k6, p1, k2, p2, cable 4 B, cable 4 F, p2, (k2, p2) 3 times, cable 4 B, cable 4 F, (p2, k2) 3 times, p2, cable 4 B, cable 4 F, p2, k2, p1, k6, p2, cable 4 B, cable 4 F, (p2, k2) twice.

8th row (P2, k2) twice, p8, k2, p7, k1, p1, k2, p8, k2, (p2, k2) 3 times, p8, (k2, p2) 3 times, k2, p8, k2, p1, k1, p7, k2, p8, (k2, p2) twice.

9th row P2, k4, p2, k8, p2, k8, p3, k8, p2, (k4, p2) twice, k8, (p2, k4) twice, p2, k8, p3, k8, p2, k8, p2, k4, p2.

10th row K2, p4, k2, p8, k2, p7, k1, p1, k2, p8, k2, (p4, k2) twice, p8, (k2, p4) twice, k2, p8, k2, p1, k1, p7, k2, p8, k2, p4, k2.

11th row (K2, p2) twice, cable 4 B, cable 4 F, p2, k6, p1, k2, p2, cable 4 B, cable 4 F, p2, (k2, p2) 3 times, cable 4 B, cable 4 F, (p2, k2) 3 times, p2, cable 4 B, cable 4 F, p2, k2, p1, k6, p2, cable 4 B, cable 4 F, (p2, k2) twice.

12th row (P2, k2) twice, p8, k2, p5, k1, p3, k2, p8, k2, (p2, k2) 3 times, p8, (k2, p2) 3 times, k2, p8, k2, p3, k1, p5, k2, p8, (k2, p2) twice.

13th row P2, k4, p2, k8, p2, k4, p1, k4, p2, k8, p2, (k4, p2) twice, k8, (p2, k4) twice, p2, k8, p2, k4, p1, k4, p2, k8, p2, k4, p2.

14th row K2, p4, k2, p8, k2, p3, k1, p5, k2, p8, k2, (p4, k2) twice, p8, (k2, p4) twice, k2, p8, k2, p5, k1, p3, k2, p8, k2, p4, k2.

15th row (K2, p2) twice, cable 4 B, cable 4 F, p2, k2, p1, k6, p2, cable 4 B, cable 4 F, p2, (k2, p2) 3 times, cable 4 B, cable 4 F, (p2, k2) 3 times, p2, cable 4 B, cable 4 F, p2, k6, p1, k2, p2, cable 4 B, cable 4 F, (p2, k2) twice.

16th row (P2, k2) 3 times, p8, k2, p1, k1, p7, k2, p8, k2, (p2, k2) 3 times, p8, (k2, p2) 3 times, k2, p8, k2, p7, k1, p1, k2, p8, (k2, p2) 3 times.

These 16 rows form the pattern.

Continue in pattern, increasing 1 stitch at each end of the next row and every following 10th row until there are 122 stitches on the needle, working the extra stitches into double moss stitch. (There should be 10 stitches at each end in double moss stitch outside the k2 panel).

Continue without shaping until work measures 16½ in. from the cast-on edge, ending on a wrong side row.

Shape armholes

Keep continuity of pattern stitch.

Cast off 2 stitches at the beginning of the next 2 rows.

Decrease 1 stitch at each end of every right side row until 88 stitches remain.

Now working an edge stitch of k1, work half a cable at each end on the cable rows (i.e. cable 4 F at the beginning and cable 4 B at the end of rows).

Continue without shaping until work measures 26 in. from the cast-on edge, ending on a wrong side row.

Shoulders

Cast off 5 stitches at the beginning of the next 4 rows.

Cast off 6 stitches at the beginning of the next 6 rows.

Cast off remaining 32 stitches.

Left front

Pocket inset

Using 'A' needles, cast on 23 stitches (Rope edge).

Work in stocking stitch for 4½ in., ending on a purl row.

Next row P2, k8, p2, k6, p1, k2, p2.
Next row K2, p3, k1, p5, k2, p8, k2.
Next row P2, k8, p2, k4, p1, k4, p2.
Next row K2, p5, k1, p3, k2, p8, k2, p4, k2.
Next row P2, cable 4 B, cable 4 F, p2, k2, p1, k6, p2.
Next row K2, p7, k1, p1, k2, p8, k2.
Next row P2, k8, p3, k8, p2.

Leave these stitches for the time being.

Using 'B' needles, cast on 51 stitches (Rope edge).

Work in k1, p1, rib as for back welt for 1 in., ending on a 2nd row and increasing 1 stitch at the end of the last row.

Change to 'A' needles and work in pattern thus:

1st row P2, k4, p2, k8, p3, (k8, p2) twice, (k4, p2) twice, k1.
2nd row K3, p4, k2, p4, k2, p8, k2, p7, k1, p1, k2, p8, k2, p4, k2.
3rd row (K2, p2) twice, cable 4 B, cable 4 F, p2, k2, p1, k6, p2, cable 4 B, cable 4 F, (p2, k2) 3 times, p2, k1.
4th row K3, p2, (k2, p2) twice, k2, p8, k2, p5, k1, p3, k2, p8, (k2, p2) twice.

Continue in pattern working each panel as on back and keeping a k1 at front edge until the 16 rows of pattern are completed.

Now increase 1 stitch at the beginning of the next row and the following 10th row (i.e. ending on an 11th row of pattern, working the extra stitches into double moss stitch—54 stitches).

Shape for pocket top

Next row Pattern 23, (p1, k1) 11 times, p1, pattern to end.

Next row Pattern to the rib, (k1, p1) 11 times, k1, pattern 23.

Repeat the last 2 rows once, then the 1st row once more, thus ending on a wrong side row.

Next row Pattern to the rib, then cast off the 23 stitches firmly in rib, pattern to end.

Next row (Wrong side of work) (As a second pattern row) Pattern 23, then with wrong side of pocket inset facing and placed in front of work, pattern across these 23 stitches, then pattern to end.

Continue in pattern, increasing 1 stitch at side seam every 10th row as before, until there are 58 stitches on the needle.

Continue without shaping until work measures 16½ in. from the cast-on edge, ending on a wrong side row and making sure the same number of cables have been worked as on back so that the work teams up.

Slope armhole and neck

1st row Cast off 2 stitches, pattern to end.
2nd row Pattern to end.
3rd row K2 tog, pattern to last 2 sts, k2 tog t.b.s.
4th row As 2nd row.
5th row K2 tog, pattern to end.
6th row As 2nd row.

Repeat rows 3 to 6 inclusive 6 times more, then the 3rd and 4th rows once. (33 stitches).

Keeping armhole edge straight, continue to decrease at neck edge every 4th row 5 times more, AT THE SAME TIME, when work measures 26 in., shape shoulder be casting off 5 stitches twice, and 6 stitches 3 times, on rows beginning at armhole edge.

Right front

Pocket inset

Work as for left front pocket inset, reading the rows backwards to reverse the pattern.

Using 'B' needles, cast on 51 stitches (Rope edge).

Work in k1, p1, rib as for back welt for 1 inch, ending on a 2nd row and increasing 1 stitch at the end of the last row. (52 stitches).

Change to 'A' needles and work in pattern as for left front, but reading the rows backwards to reverse the pattern.

Continue in pattern until the 16 rows of pattern stitch have been completed, then increase 1 stitch at the end of the next row and following 10th row, thus ending on a right side row at side seam.

Slope for pocket

1st row Pattern to last 46 stitches, (p1, k1) 11 times, p1, pattern to end.
2nd row Pattern 23, (k1, p1) 11 times, k1, pattern to end.

Repeat the last 2 rows once, then the 1st row once more.

6th row Pattern 23, cast off 23 stitches firmly in rib, pattern to end.
7th row Pattern to the cast-off stitches, then with wrong side of pocket inset facing and placed in front of work, pattern across these 23 stitches, then pattern to end.

Continue in pattern, increasing 1 stitch at side seam every 10th row until there are 58 stitches on the needle.

Continue without shaping until work measures $16\frac{1}{2}$ in. from the cast-on edge, ending on a right side row.

Slope armhole

1st row Cast off 2 stitches, pattern to end.
2nd row K2 tog, pattern to last 2 stitches, k2 tog t.b.s.
3rd row Pattern to end.
4th row Pattern to last 2 stitches, k2 tog, t.b.s.
5th row As 3rd row.

Repeat rows 3 to 6 inclusive 6 times more, then the 3rd and 4th rows once.

Keeping armhole edge straight, continue to decrease at neck edge every 4th row 5 times more, AT THE SAME TIME, when work measures 26 in. from the cast-on edge, shape shoulder by casting off 5 stitches twice, and 6 stitches 3 times, on rows beginning at armhole edge.

Sleeves

Using 'B' needles, cast on 55 stitches (Rope edge).

Work in k1, p1, rib as for back welt for $2\frac{1}{2}$ in. ending on a 1st row.

Next row Rib 3, * inc 1 in next stitch, rib 3. Repeat from * to end. (68 stitches).

Change to 'A' needles and work in pattern stitch thus:

1st row K1, p2, k4, p2, k8, p3, k8, p2, k8, p2, k8, p3, k8, p2, k4, p2, k1.

2nd row K3, p4, k2, p8, k2, p1, k1, p7, k2, p8, k2, p7, k1, p1, k2, p8, k2, p4, k3.

3rd row K1, (k2, p2) twice, cable 4 B, cable 4 F, p2, k2, p1, k6, p2, cable 4 B, cable 4 F, p2, k6, p1, k2, p2, cable 4 B, cable 4 F, (p2, k2) twice, k1.

4th row K1, (p2, k2) twice, p8, k2, p3, k1, p5, k2, p8, k2, p5, k1, p3, k2, p8, (k2, p2) twice, k1.

Continue in pattern, increasing 1 stitch at each end of the 9th row and every following 8th row until there are 80 stitches on the needle, working the extra stitches into double moss stitch at each end, so that the pattern finishes with 1 more than on back, i.e. with 10 moss stitches at each end, plus a knit stitch.

Continue without shaping until work measures 17 in. from the cast-on edge, ending on a wrong side row and the same pattern row as on back and fronts.

Slope top

Cast off 3 stitches at the beginning of the next 2 rows.

Decrease 1 stitch at each end of the next row and every alternate row until 44 stitches remain.

Cast off 2 stitches at the beginning of the next 8 rows.

Cast off 3 stitches at the beginning of the next 2 rows.

Cast off 4 stitches at the beginning of the next 2 rows.

Cast off remaining 14 stitches.

Work a second sleeve in the same way.

Front border

Join shoulder seams by back-stitching on the wrong side approximately $\frac{1}{8}$ in. from edges to ensure neat seams.

Using 'C' needles, cast on 9 stitches (Rope edge).

Work in k1, p1, rib until the border is long enough to reach from the cast-on edge of right front to neck shaping, then all round neck edge to the beginning of shaping on left front. To ensure correct measurement, neatly tack the border to right front edge and round neck. Do not skimp the length round neck. Now make 5 buttonholes. Use the right front border as a guide, and 5 pins to represent buttons. Place the first pin in the centre of welt (i.e. $\frac{1}{2}$ in. up from the cast-on edge) and the 5th pin on a level with the beginning of neck shaping, which should be $10\frac{1}{2}$ in. down from the top of shoulder, then space the remaining 3 evenly between. Work buttonholes on left front border on rows to correspond with pins thus:

1st row Rib 3, cast off 3, rib 3.

2nd row Rib 3, cast on 3, rib 3.

DO NOT PRESS, BUT DARN IN ALL ENDS.

41   The Crimlisk Brothers: James 1835; John 1832; Francis 1830; Thomas 1841

44

42

43

44

45

46

47

Scarborough

48   A boy's guernsey used as a sample

There is a wonderful charm about this Yorkshire town with the old castle keeping guard, and the grey walls protecting the headland above the harbour. The narrow streets and Ginnels (passages) running up and across the hill have remained the same for generations, and their quaint names—'Old Greece Steps', 'Mast Yard' and St Se*pul*chre Street (with strong emphasis on the second syllable)—take one back to the days when mules and donkeys carried their loads up the wide shallow steps of these narrow streets. The steps still remain, and wandering along you find yards full of shipping junk, ropes, old crab pots, broken-up boats and here and there a figure-head gazing up to the sky with staring eyes.

Down by the harbour and in the fish market, or leaning against the railings, many fishermen can be seen, sometimes showing the whole guernsey, or only a V of pattern with a buttoned-up coat; or a figure in sea-boots and a brown sail-cloth smock, just showing the knitted collar and welt. This is the most exasperating of all, as you are certain that a masterpiece of guernsey knitting is hidden under the brown canvas, and unless the man can be stopped and persuaded to show the pattern, he will disappear like a flash up one of the narrow passages. In the autumn, boats from the Scottish fleet on their way south may be found resting over the weekend, as they don't fish or travel far on Sundays. They come down from Fife, Aberdeen, Banff and the villages along the Forth side, some also from the west coast through the Caledonian Canal. These Northerners in their dark-blue suits and best guernseys are easily recognised, as they seem taller and broader than the average Yorkshire fisherman, but any existing doubts about their nationality is dispelled after you have spoken to them, and their charm of manner and ready smile make them welcome visitors.

49   George Jenkinson Overy in his coble

47

In search of further material I went to see George Jenkinson Overy who was very helpful, but asked me to call back next day as he was just off for bait. When I returned, Mr Overy showed me several guernseys knitted by his mother, and in the sitting room was the picture shown in figure 49 of him returning to harbour in his coble. I asked him if he'd lend it to me as an illustration for my book. He hesitated and said, "It's my most treasured possession, but Ah think Ah can trust yer." (See Filey III for directions.)

Another day I was wandering round the harbour at low tide when I saw down below a fisherman in his boat baiting lines. I could see he had on a good guernsey, so I called to him: "Could you please come up and let me look at your guernsey?" He called back, "If yer want to leeak at mi gansey, yer can coom down yersen." And he knew quite well that I couldn't manage the iron ladders down the harbour side!

SCARBOROUGH PATTERN I

Figure 48

The patterns belonging to Scarborough are not elaborate, the only traditional guernsey has a deep double moss-stitch yoke; this should measure one third of the finished garment. The yoke has an edging of step stitch, starting with the yoke—up the sides of the armholes, merging into the shoulder-strap pattern, and finishing at the back with the yoke (See figure 51). The guernsey in the picture fits a child of six, but gives the idea of the pattern.

320 stitches are cast on, and a narrow welt of 2 rounds plain and 2 rounds purl repeated 6 times. It is easily seen in the picture, and is 3½ inches deep. The same welt is shown in a Staithes pattern (figure 68). In the next round knit 158 stitches plain, 2 purl, 158 stitches plain, 2 purl. These purl stitches are for the seam stitch. Continue this for 6 inches.

The yoke pattern now starts with 2 rounds purl and 2 rounds plain, repeated once, still keeping the seam stitches up the sides.

The true Scarborough gusset is a double one, but to prevent complication the Patrington gusset can be used.

1st row *Yoke: K2, p12, k2, p2, till within 16 stitches of the seam stitch, p12, k2, (p2),* increase in this bracketed p2, twice, for the gusset. Repeat once between stars.

2nd row Same as row 1 without the increase, and working gusset stitches.

3rd row *K14, p2, k2, till within 14 stitches of seam stitch, k14, p1, k2, p1.* Repeat between stars.

4th row Same as row 3.

These 4 rows complete the pattern, increasing in the gusset ribs every 7th round. Continue thus to the armholes. The gusset ribs and the 2 purl stitches are slipped onto a holder, and the front and back knitted separately in pattern up to the shoulders, till the guernsey measures 25 inches in length.

The step pattern continues up the sides of the armholes and over the shoulders. The armholes should measure about 7½ inches to the shoulder top, then cast off together on the right side.

The shoulder pattern is 2 rows of plain and 2 rows of purl repeated 4 times, for front and back. Pick up 124 stitches for the neck and k2, p2, for

21 rounds. Cast off in plain knitting with double wool.

Pick up 160 stitches round the armholes, including gussets. The sleeves are worked in plain knitting, the gusset rib is decreased every 7th row until the rib is finished and the 2 purl seam stitch continues to the cuff, with sleeve decreasings every 5th row. Cuff knitted in 2 plain, 2 purl, for 3 inches. Sleeve length 20 inches.

The Penzance guernsey is often seen in Scarborough, and was evidently copied from the Penzance fishermen who frequented Scarborough and Whitby in the old days in the fishing season.

The Penzance pattern is very plain, but the Scarborough step pattern is usually added, and the guernsey looks well in wear. It is knitted in ribbing of k2, p2. The welt is worked in this rib for 3½ inches, 4 inches of plain knitting above the welt, with the usual seam stitch and gusset. The ribbing now continues to the neck, and the neck band is worked in the same rib. Shoulders are worked the same as figure 25. Sleeves can be plain, or ribbed to the elbow.

Other patterns are often seen in Scarborough, but as a rule they are worn by visiting fishermen, or by men whose wives or mothers knit the patterns belonging to their native place.

The next pattern with the large cable was very effective, and I asked the wearer if I could call on his wife. She lived near the harbour, and was most friendly, and told me about this pattern. I have never come across it before, the centre of the cable stands out in a wonderful way, and looks most intriguing.

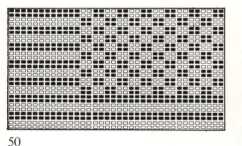

50

51

SCARBOROUGH PATTERN II
Large Cable

Figure 52

Multiple of 29

1st row *P2, k12, p2, k6, p1, k6.* Repeat between stars in each row.

2nd row Repeat row 1 once.

3rd row *P2, k12, p2, k5, p1, k1, p1, k5.*

4th row Repeat row 3 once.

5th row *P2, k12, p2, k4, (p1, k1) twice, p1, k4.*

6th row Repeat row 5 once.

7th row *P2, slip 6 stitches on to spare needle, and drop to back, knit 6, then knit the 6 stitches on spare needle, p2, k3, (p1, k1) 3 times, p1, k3.*

8th row *P2, k12, p2, k3, (p1, k1) 3 times, p1, k3.*

9th row *P2, k12, p2, k2, (p1, k1) 4 times, p1, k2.*

10th row Repeat row 9 once.

11th row *P2, k12, p2, k1, (p1, k1) 5 times, p1, k1.*

12th row Repeat row 11 once.

13th row *P2, k12, p2, k2, (p1, k1) 4 times, p1, k2.*

14th row Repeat row 13 once.

15th row *P2, cross cable, p2, k3, (p1, k1) 3 times, p1, k3.*

16th row *P2, k12, p2, k3, (p1, k1) 3 times, p1, k3.*

17th row *P2, k12, p2, k4, (p1, k1) twice, p1, k4.*

18th row Repeat row 17 once.

19th row *P2, k12, p2, k5, p1, k1, p1, k5.*

20th row Repeat row 19 once.

These 20 rows complete the pattern. Repeat from row 1, crossing cables every 8th row, as they do not repeat correctly with the rest of the pattern.

52

Robin Hood's Bay

This village only produced one pattern, though the Flamborough diamond, cable and moss is sometimes used. But the beauty of the place more than makes up for the lack of knitting interest. It lies between the moors and the sea, with Ravenscar towering up at one end of the bay and the village nestling down to the shore at the northerly end. Arriving by road, the approach is perfect along the meandering lane dipping down from the moors, and climbing the small hills, the lovely sweep of the valley and sea soon meets the eye. The bay, with seaweed-covered rocks and sandy shore, with the cliffs at each end, makes one pause and drink in the whole scene, with its small farms and outlying cottages; and then the village, with its very steep narrow street ending abruptly on the seashore.

Many legends and stories are connected with this bay, and one that was prevalent for many years was the belief that Robin Hood shot an arrow from Whitby Abbey to the bay which bears his name, a distance of about four miles! There were many encounters between fishermen and the Preventive Officers patrolling the coast on the lookout for smuggling, and Robin Hood's Bay was an ideal spot for landing illicit cargoes.

Figure 53 shows some fishermen and their dog—one wearing hip-length leather boots, which are hardly ever seen nowadays; they all wear white rubber boots reaching just above the knee. The man in the boat has on a sealskin cap—much favoured, and often worn with sealskin waistcoats in days gone by.

ROBIN HOOD'S BAY

The knitting directions for the guernsey are easy to follow.

Welt made in k2, p2, for 3 inches. Then 5 inches of plain knitting before starting the deep patterned yoke. It is knitted in moss stitch and small cables.

Pattern multiple 15

1st row *P2, k2, p1, k1, p1, k2, p2, k4. Repeat from*.
2nd row *P2, (k1, p1) 3 times, k1, p2, k4. Repeat from*.

54

These two rows complete the pattern, the cable of k4 is crossed every 5th row.

A moss panel forms the centre of the guernsey, front and back. The shoulders are knitted in 2 rows plain, 2 rows purl, repeated 4 times. It has the usual underarm gusset and plain sleeves.

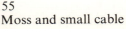

55
Moss and small cable

Runswick Bay

The small village of Runswick is a favourite place for artists, and many pictures of this lovely village have been in the Academy. It is at its best on an early summer evening, and when slowly walking down the many steps you have an opportunity of taking in the full beauty of the scene, and also the delicious scent of pinks and stocks, varied by honeysuckle and roses.

Down below, children's voices could be heard on the sands, and small figures seen hurrying into the sea, and nearer at hand a group of fishermen leaning over the bows of a coble drawn up on the beach. I knocked on Mrs Beswick's door, and when she heard I was interested in Runswick guernseys she asked me in, and went to fetch one she was 'on with'. The true Runswick pattern is knitted in stocking stitch with ribbed shoulder straps and more ribbing each side of the armholes. Mrs Beswick knits a gusset each side of the neck where the shoulder strap finishes. This can be seen in figure 56. My favourite picture of that generation of fisher folk.

Mrs Beswick calls this rib pattern 'Rig and Fur', meaning 'ridge and furrow', and so descriptive of the fields in March when ridged up for potato setting.

Her cottage was charming with lustre-ware bowls and china groups and plates, and several photographs of fishermen. Hanging high on the wall was a fishing coble in Sunderland china.

56

Shoulder strap and gusset worn in Runswick and Staithes

Visitors are put up in nearly all the houses in summer, and it is amazing to see the number of people staying in this tiny place.

I asked about the old Runswick days and where they got their bait, as I had a picture of Runswick bait-gatherers taken over eighty years ago and was told a mussel boat used to come round from Staithes and tipped the bait out onto the beach.

Climbing back up the steps I wished I had seen it all when the picture of the bait gatherers was taken. I also thought of the Sunday evenings many years ago, when the fishermen could be seen winding their way up the steps to the church on the top of the cliff, carrying lanterns and leaving them alight near the porch till the service was over. Their other nights may not have been quite so well spent, as there are wonderful tales of illicit boat-loads creeping in along this coast and often landing, without being caught by the King's Men!

Whitby

The red-roofed town of Whitby lies between the moors and the sea, with the River Esk running through the harbour and dividing the town in half. The place teems with legend and history, and the story of the Abbey standing on the cliff-edge above the town would fill a volume. The many steps leading up there are well worth climbing, for the lovely view is worth the toil.

Down by the river are the yards where Captain Cook served his apprenticeship, and where in later years his boats were built, and thoughts go back to the times when the harbour was used by sailing ships coming up from Cornwall. The photographs I have been lucky enough to obtain of this coast were taken by the late Mr Sutcliffe, and they show the peace and beauty of this part of Yorkshire about eighty years ago.

Whitby guernsey patterns are not very numerous, and are also occasionally seen in Staithes, and the Whitby patterns may have been influenced by the many Scottish fishermen who thronged the town in late August and September for the herring season.

A Musselburgh knitter told me she had shown the Whitby women a lot of her patterns years ago. The flag pattern so often seen here is much used in Scotland.

In one of my wandering moods along the harbour I saw a man in a guernsey coming up the steps from his boat; he was some way off, but I thought his guernsey worth following. I hurried through the holiday-makers, who were watching the fish being packed, and after many bumps in the crowd I caught him up, only to find he was wearing a flag pattern guernsey inside out! Once a pattern disappears up the steps or narrow passages of Whitby it is lost for ever.

Harry Freeman, the well-known cox of the Whitby lifeboat, was honoured for his bravery and seamanship, and his fine character shows in his face (figure 57). His guernsey pattern is given under Staithes, where I first came across it.

The Whitby museum is well worth a visit, its arrangement and lighting are excellent, showing off the pictures painted in the Whitby area by the Wetherell family. I also found a collection of old knitting sheaths, all used in the district. They were usually given as betrothal presents, and the combined initials and date are often found carved on the sheaths; sometimes crosses are added for

57 Harry Freeman, only survivor of Whitby lifeboat disaster 1881

kisses, and a keyhole, denoting the door of their future home. The sheath often has a hook at the end of the chain called a 'clueholder' (clue being the old name for a ball of wool); this hook was also used to support a long or heavy piece of knitting. They are wonderfully made, the chain and sheath carved out of one piece of wood, and the decoration on some of the finer specimens is beautifully carried out, especially when it is realised that the tool used was a pocket-knife.

'Sometimes, as a foundation for the ball of yarn, the windpipe of a goose was made into the form of a ring, the hollow ends being slipped one into the other. Before doing this a few peas were inserted, and the whole, when dry, forming a kind of rattle. On this the yarn was wound, so that if the ball was dropped, its direction and whereabouts were made known by the rattle of the peas. As much knitting was done in the evening by firelight, or perhaps by the additional gleam of the home-made rush light or dip candle, then in vogue, this clever device must have saved the knitters much time and trouble.' Owen Evan-Thomas *Domestic Utensils of Wood.*

Glass rushlight lamps also were used by the knitters, they were shaped like a candlestick and bought for 5*s*. The wick used in these lamps was the centre, or pithy part of the bulrush.

WHITBY PATTERN I
Betty Martin

1st and 2nd rows (K2, p2), 5 times. Repeat as required.
3rd and 4th rows Knit.

These 4 rows complete the pattern, which is often used for sleeves and worked as a panel for yokes, or used as an allover pattern.

58
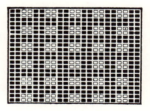

WHITBY PATTERN II

Multiple of 18
1st row P4, k6, p4, k4, p4, k6, p4, k4, p4. Repeat.

This row completes the pattern, but every 7th row the 6 knitted stitches must be crossed to form a cable.

59
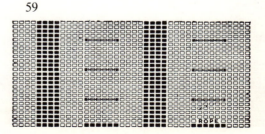

57

WHITBY PATTERN III

Multiple of 30

1st row P2, k3, p2, k6, p2, k3, (p1, k1) 4 times, p1, k3. Repeat.

2nd row P2, k3, p2, k6, p2, k4, (p1, k1) 3 times, p1, k4. Repeat.

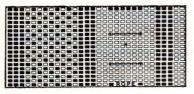

60

61

WHITBY PATTERN IV

Figure 61

Multiple of 20

1st and 2nd rows P2, k6, p2, k10. Repeat.

3rd and 4th rows P2, k6, (p2, k2) 3 times.

These 4 rows make up the pattern. Cross the 6 knitted stitches every 7th row to form cable.

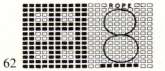

62

63

WHITBY PATTERN V

Figure 63

Multiple of 25

1st row P2, k6, p2, (k3, p3) twice, k3, p2, k6, p2.
2nd row P2, k6, p2, k15, p2, k6, p2.

These 2 rows make up the pattern. Cross cable every 7th row.

64

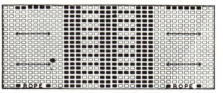

WHITBY PATTERN VI

Variation of Partington pattern

1st row P2, k6, p14, k6, p2, (k2, p2) twice, k2. Repeat.
2nd row P2, k6, p2, k10, p2, k6, p2, (k2, p2) twice, k2. Repeat.
3rd row P2, k6, p2, k10, p2, k6, p2, k4, p2, k4. Repeat.
4th row Same as row 3.

These 4 rows make up the pattern, with the 6 cable stitches crossed every 7th row.

65

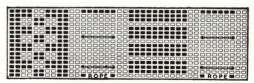

Staithes

   This village, many years ago, was a very flourishing fishing centre, with about four hundred fishermen seeking their living from the sea; and there was also good money earned by trading, and there are many stories told of the smuggling that was carried on along this coast.

   Staithes was completely isolated until the railway came and the people were able to mix with the outer world. Even now there is an atmosphere of secrecy in the narrow streets and passages running downhill to the river and sea, and uphill to the many cottages built one above the other on the cliff, with no road connecting them—only the flagged and cobbled pathways.

As you go down the narrow winding street a group of people may be seen talking together; when you get near where they were, they have melted away, and you feel unseen eyes are watching through windows and cracks of doors.

In Staithes, or 'Steers' as it is pronounced locally, the unmarried women wear coloured print sun-bonnets, but when married, their bonnets are black. In one of the little shops you see these bonnets hanging up for sale, along with the freshly boiled lobsters, crabs and postcards.

As the street winds down to the sea-wall there are glimpses of narrow paved or cobbled yards, grey and white cottages, steps up and down, shafts of sunlight and deep shadows, brightened by splashes of colour from geraniums and nasturtiums in summertime. Down one of these passages I knocked on a cottage door, with a message from an aunt in our village to her niece at Staithes. A smile and a welcome were mine when she knew where I came from, and Miss Verrill took me straight away to see some of the knitters, and she lent me a guernsey that had been worn by her grandfather for many years. The knitted copy is shown in figure 68.

69

70 Detail of pattern

WHITBY PATTERN VII

1st row P1, * (k7, p1)* repeat as required.
2nd row P2, * (k6, p2)* repeat.
3rd row P3, * (k5, p3)* repeat.
4th row P4, * (k4, p4)* repeat.
5th row P5, * (k3, p5)* repeat.
6th row P6, * (k2, p6)* repeat.
7th row P7, k1, repeat.

These 7 rows complete the pattern. Repeat as many times as needed.

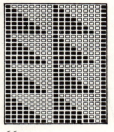

66

WHITBY PATTERN VIII

Multiple of 21

1st row P2, k6, p2, k11, repeat.
2nd row P2, cross cable, p2, k5, p1, k5, repeat.
3rd row P2, k6, p2, k4, p3, k4, repeat.
4th row P2, k6, p2, k3, p5, k3, repeat.
5th row P2, k6, p2, k2, p7, k2, repeat.
6th row P2, k6, p2, k1, p9, k1, repeat.
7th row P2, k6, p2, k2, p7, k2, repeat.
8th row P2, k6, p2, k3, p5, k3, repeat.
9th row P2, cross cable, p2, k4, p3, k4, repeat.
10th row P2, k6, p2, k5, p1, k5, repeat.

These 10 rows repeated as wanted to make up pattern. Multiple of 21. Cables crossed every 7th row.

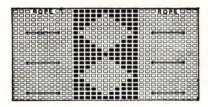

67

STAITHES PATTERN I

Figure 68

This pattern was given me by Miss Verrill of Staithes, and belonged to her grandfather. It was very faded and a lovely grey-blue, and much worn in places. Figure 68 shows this pattern, which I knitted from the original; it was included in an exhibit of Rural Handicrafts sent by the British Council to Canada and America.

A variation of this pattern is shown on a Whitby lifeboat man, taken many years ago; his guernsey shows a deeper panel of plain and purl stitch, and is divided by 3 single purl and plain lines (figure 57). My pattern has narrower panels and the dividing lines are 2 rows of plain and purl, repeated once. I have come across this pattern on Scottish fishermen, and it may have been shown to our knitters by the lassies who used to come down with the herring fleet, to clean and pack the fish. This is the only horizontal pattern noted in Yorkshire—the others are all vertical.

This guernsey is a large size. Length from neck to hem 25 inches. Sleeve from shoulder to cuff edge 20 inches. Pattern on yoke, depth $12\frac{1}{2}$ inches. Plain knitting and welt, $12\frac{1}{2}$ inches. 320 stitches are cast on for the welt and it is worked in 2 rounds plain, 2 rounds purl, repeated 6 times—follows, with moss stitch seam stitches of p1, k1, p1, up each side. The gusset is started in the first round of the yoke pattern, by increasing 1 stitch in the centre of seam stitches (both sides of guernsey) making 2 plain stitches in centre with 1 moss each side. These 2 plain stitches are the beginning of the gusset. It is worked in plain knitting throughout. Increase 1 stitch each side of gussets every 4th round, until there are 20 stitches. The yoke is worked in pattern from commencement of gussets, see chart and detail of pattern (chart 70).

The knitting is divided at the armholes 180 stitches for the front, and the same for the back.

The gusset and moss stitches (22 each side) slipped onto wool or a holder. The front is continued in pattern on 2 needles, but at each armhole edge the first 3 and last 3 stitches are worked in garter stitch. When the neck is reached (25 inches) 60 stitches are put on a holder for the neck and 57 stitches each side are worked in garter stitch for 12 rows, for the shoulders, finishing on a plain row. The back is worked in the same manner; then back and front shoulders are cast off together on the right side, forming a ridge; 60 stitches are left in the centre for neck, back and front, and when shoulders are picked up, 144 stitches are knitted in the neck band. 17 rounds of k2, p2, then 1 plain round, 2 purl rounds, 1 plain round—cast off plain. 158 stitches are picked up for the sleeve, not counting the gusset; sleeve knitting starts with 2 plain rounds and 2 purl rounds, repeated once (but working the gusset and seam stitches in their own pattern) and decreasing one stitch each side every 4th row. Work $1\frac{3}{4}$ inches of plain knitting, then a band of the yoke pattern, see chart 70. Sleeve decreasings start after pattern is finished—decrease 1 stitch each side of seam stitch (2 moss stitches) every 7 rounds, 5 times; every 5 rounds, 13 times; every 3 rounds, 11 times, till 92 stitches are left, work 3 inches in k2, p2, for cuff.

Detail of yoke pattern

2 rounds purl, 2 rounds plain, repeat once.

1st row *Pattern, p2, k2, repeated.
2nd row Knit.
3rd row K2, p2, repeated.
4th row Knit.

Repeat these 4 rows 5 times for each panel. The next 10 rows are (k2 rows, p2 rows) repeat once, then knit 2 rows. Repeat from * until 5 panels are completed. The pattern in sleeves is worked in the same manner without the ribbing.

STAITHES PATTERN II

Figure 72
Multiple of 12
This is composed of p2, k2, p2, k6 for cable, and repeat.

72   71

STAITHES PATTERN III

Multiple of 28

This pattern is the same as No. 68, with a centre panel of double moss stitch outlined each side by k2. This panel continues round the jersey between the cables.

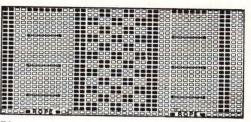

73

STAITHES PATTERN IV

Multiple of 46

Is very attractive when knitted on fine needles, and consists of *p2, k3, p2, k6, for cable, p2, k4, 15 stitches in single moss stitch, k3, p2, k6, for cable, and repeat from *. Continue in this pattern, crossing the cable every 7th row. In most of the Staithes guernseys the shoulder strap is a strong feature continuing from the neck nearly to the elbow. This is also the case at Runswick, as their guernseys are made in plain knitting with the pattern on the shoulders.

74

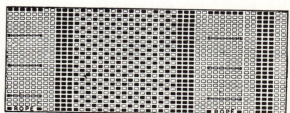

Northumberland

I came across a wonderful guernsey from this county in 1938 at the National Federation of Women's Institutes London Exhibition and made up my mind then and there to meet the knitter and have a heart-to-heart talk with her. But fourteen years passed before the opportunity occurred.

After making enquiries from a group of fishermen, I found Chapel Row and the house where Mrs Laidlaw lived; there were about five dark-grey cottages, slate-roofed, typical Scottish houses in appearance. Only one room in each, a combined kitchen and bedroom. Mrs Laidlaw opened the door, and with a nice smile asked me in. The room I entered had the usual wooden bed with a photograph of a fisherman above it. She introduced me to her husband, who was having his dinner on a little table in the window. I told her how much I admired her guernsey in London, and that her special award was well earned. It was lovely work, with an all-over tree and diamond pattern, and is now in the Northumberland W.I. Loan Collection of Needle-work (figure 75).

Mrs Laidlaw came from Eyemouth, over the Border, when she married, and knew no other good knitters about Seahouses. I turned to speak to her husband, who was quietly finishing his dinner; he was wearing a guernsey worked in a different tree pattern—seeing my eyes on it, he offered to take it off for me! But I wouldn't disturb him and studied it on his back. She and I had a long knitting talk, and she promised to send me samples of her patterns, one called 'Triple Wave' I was very anxious to have.

Before crossing into Scotland I visited Holy Island, but according to the hotelkeeper where I stayed in Berwick it was a tricky place to get to. I had the names of two knitters living there, so decided to go, and as the local bus driver was the brother of my landlord, he said he would find out what time I ought to start. The information was forthcoming and I had to be at a garage on the main road at 10.30 a.m. to be right for the tide, and he'd get me a car from the garage. But, I said, what about a boat? Oh, no, a car took one across.

Next morning at 10.30 I met my car, at least thirty years old and covered with rust and sand, and driven by a boy of about sixteen. I got in and off we went, up a hill past the church, and then I saw the sea and Holy Island. A vast stretch of water lay between us and the island, and as we drew up on the water's edge the boy said we must wait a few minutes for the tide. Tall stakes marked a way across, and after about five minutes we plunged into the sea and chugged through the water, with a sort of tidal wave at each side.

He suddenly called out, 'There's a bit of a ditch in a minute—look out.'
'But the water's through the floorboards,' I said.

'Well, put yer feet on the seat'—which I did, and I'm sure we were swimming for some time! Then it got shallower and we approached the low sandy shore, and drove at breakneck speed along the sands for about a mile, finally reaching the little grey stone village. He told me he'd fetch me at 3.30 p.m., and I was left to wander where I chose.

Another brother fetched me later, and we went back along the shore, all sand now between the island and the mainland except for large pools of water which we rushed through, and I had to pull up the windows to keep dry. I asked if the stakes marked a road, and he said, yes, but no one bothered with it, and they used to climb up if the tide came in too quickly.

I enjoyed my day though I learnt nothing, but the beach of Holy Island when the tide was high was wonderful, no sound but the larks, and an occasional wave breaking on the shore.

I read not long ago that a causeway is to be made across to the island—I wish it could be left as it was; and the boy with the car will be sorry, as he made a fairly stiff charge for my swim, as he said I wasn't a 'party' and he usually took five.

SEAHOUSES PATTERN I
Mrs. Laidlaw's Pattern

Figure 75

1st row K5, p3, k1, p1, k2, p1, k2, p3, k27, p3, k1.
2nd row K6, p2, k1, p1, k2, p1, k2, p2, k13, p1, k1, p1, k13, p2, k1.
3rd row K7, p1, (k2, p1) twice, k1, p1, k13, p2, k1, p2, k13, p1, k1.
4th row K6, p2, (k2, p1) twice, k1, p2, k11, p2, k3, p2, k11, p2, k1.
5th row K5, p3, k1, p1, k2, p1, k2, p3, k9, p2, k5, p2, k9, p3, k1.
6th row K4, p4, k1, p1, k2, p1, k2, p4, k7, p2, k2, p1, k1, p1, k2, p2, k7, p4, k1.
7th row K3, p5, (k2, p1) twice, k1, p5, k5, p2, k2, p2, k1, p2, k2, p2, k5, p5, k1.
8th row K2, p6, (k2, p1) twice, k1, p6, k3, p2, k2, p2, k3, p2, k2, p2, k3, p6, k1.
9th row K1, p7, k1, p1, k2, p1, k2, p7, k1, p2, k2, p2, k5, p2, k2, p2, k1, p7, k1.
10th row K2, p6, k1, p1, k2, p1, k2, p6, k2, p1, k2, p2, k2, p1, k1, p1, k2, p2, k2, p1, k2, p6, k1.
11th row K3, p5, (k2, p1) twice, k1, p5, k5, p2, k2, p2, k1, p2, k2, p2, k5, p5, k1.
12th row K4, p4, (k2, p1) twice, k1, p4, k5, p2, k2, p2, k3, p2, k2, p2, k5, p4, k1.
13th row K5, p3, k1, p1, k2, p1, k2, p3, k6, p1, k2, p2, k5, p2, k2, p1, k6, p3, k1.
14th row K6, p2, k1, p1, k2, p1, k2, p2, k9, p2, k2, p1, k1, p1, k2, p2, k9, p2, k1.
15th row K7, p1, (k2, p1) twice, k1, p1, k9, p2, k2, p2, k1, p2, k2, p2, k9, p1, k1.
16th row K6, p2, (k2, p1) twice, k1, p2, k8, p1, k2, p2, k3, p2, k2, p1, k8, p2, k1.
17th row K5, p3, k1, p1, k2, p1, k2, p3, k9, p2, k5, p2, k9, p3, k1.
18th row K4, p4, k1, p1, k2, p1, k2, p4, k7, p2, k2, p1, k1, p1, k2, p2, k7, p4, k1.
19th row K3, p5, (k2, p1) twice, k1, p5, k6, p1, k2, p2, k1, p2, k2, p1, k6, p5, k1.

20th row K2, p6, (k2, p1) twice, k1, p6, k7, p2, k3, p2, k7, p6, k1.
21st row K1, p7, k1, (p1, k2) twice, p7, k5, (p2, k5) twice, p7, k1.
22nd row K2, p6, k1, (p1, k2) twice, p6, k6, p1, k2, p1, k1, p1, k2, p1, k6, p6, k1.
23rd row K3, p5, (k2, p1) twice, k1, p5, k9, p2, k1, p2, k9, p5, k1.
24th row K4, p4, (k2, p1) twice, k1, p4, k9, p2, k3, p2, k9, p4, k1.
25th row K5, p3, k1, (p1, k2) twice, p3, k10, p1, k5, p1, k10, p3, k1.
26th row K6, p2, k1, (p1, k2) twice, p2, k13, p1, k1, p1, k13, p2, k1.
27th row K7, p1, (k2, p1) twice, k1, p1, k13, p2, k1, p2, k13, p1, k1.
28th row K6, p2, (k2, p1) twice, k1, p2, k11, p2, k3, p2, k11, p2, k1.
29th row K5, p3, k1, (p1, k2) twice, p3, k10, p1, k5, p1, k10, p3, k1.
30th row K4, p4, k1, (p1, k2) twice, p4, k9, p2, k3, p2, k9, p4, k1.
31st row K3, p5, (k2, p1) twice, k1, p5, k9, p2, k1, p2, k9, p5, k1.
32nd row K2, p6, (k2, p1) twice, k1, p6, k9, p1, k1, p1, k9, p6, k1.
33rd row K1, p7, k1, (p1, k2) twice, p7, k19, p7, k1.
34th row K2, p6, k1, (p1, k2) twice, p6, k9, p1, k1, p1, k9, p6, k1.
35th row K3, p5, (k2, p1) twice, k1, p5, k9, p2, k1, p2, k9, p5, k1.
36th row K4, p4, (k2, p1) twice, k1, p4, k9, p2, k3, p2, k9, p4, k1.
37th row K5, p3, k1, (p1, k2) twice, p3, k9, p2, k5, p2, k9, p3, k1.
38th row K6, p2, k1, (p1, k2) twice, p2, k9, p2, k2, p1, k1, p1, k2, p2, k9, p2, k1.

39th row K7, p1, (k2, p1) twice, k1, p1, k9, p2, k2, p2, k1, p2, k2, p2, k9, p1, k1.

40th row K6, p2, (k2, p1) twice, k1, p2, k7, p2, k2, p2, k3, p2, k2, p2, k7, p2, k1.

41st row K5, p3, k1, (p1, k1) twice, p3, (k5, p2, k2, p2) twice, k5, p3, k1.

42nd row K4, p4, k1, (p1, k1) twice, p4, k4, p1, k2, p2, k2, p1, k1, p1, k2, p2, k2, p1, k4, p4, k1.

43rd row K3, p5, (k2, p1) twice, k1, p5, k5, p2, k2, p2, k1, p2, k2, p2, k5, p5, k1.

44th row K2, p6, (k2, p1) twice, k1, p6, k3, p2, k2, p2, k3, p2, k2, p2, k3, p6, k1.

45th row K1, p7, k1, (p1, k2) twice, p7, k2, p1, k2, p2, k5, p2, k2, p1, k2, p7, k1.

46th row K2, p6, k1, (p1, k2) twice, p6, k5, p2, k2, p1, k1, p1, k2, p2, k5, p6, k1.

75

SEAHOUSES PATTERN II

Triple Wave

Multiple of 15

1st row (K1, p3) twice, k8, p3, k1, p3.
2nd row (K1, p1) 4 times, k1, p2, k2, p2, (k1, p1) 4 times.
3rd row (K1, p3) twice, k3, p2, k3, p3, k1, p3.
4th row (K1, p1) 4 times, k8, (p1, k1) 3 times, p1.
5th row (K1, p3) twice, k1, p2, k2, p2, k1, (p3, k1) twice.
6th row (K1, p1) 4 times, k3, p2, k3, (p1, k1) 3 times, p1.

Repeat from row 1.

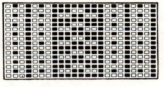

76

SEAHOUSES PATTERN III

Multiple of 22

1st row (K1, p7) twice, k1, (p1, k2) twice.
2nd row K1, p6, k3, p6, k1, (p1, k2) twice.
3rd row K1, p5, k5, p5, (k2, p1) twice, k1.
4th row K1, p4, k7, p4, (k2, p1) twice, k1.
5th row K1, p3, k9, p3, k1, (p1, k2) twice.
6th row K1, p2, k11, p2, k1, (p1, k2) twice.
7th row K1, p1, k13, p1, (k2, p1) twice, k1.
8th row K1, p2, k11, p2, (k2, p1) twice, k1.
9th row K1, p3, k9, p3, k1, (p1, k2) twice.
10th row K1, p4, k7, p4, k1, (p1, k2) twice.
11th row K1, p5, k5, p5, (k2, p1) twice, k1.
12th row K1, p6, k3, p6, (k2, p1) twice, k1.
13th row Repeat from row 1.

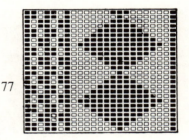

77

SEAHOUSES PATTERN IV

Turtle Neck

Materials
30 oz Listers Double Six.
1 pair 'A' needles (see tension note).
1 pair 'B' needles (see tension note).
1 set of 'B' needles with points at both ends.

Size
To fit 38 in. chest.

Measurements
Length at centre back=26 in.
Width across pattern at underarm=20 in.
Side seam=16½ in.
Sleeve seam=20 in.

Description
A long turtle neck sweater with a low set in sleeve. Gussets are worked at underarm. Main part of garment is worked in a tree pattern panel separated by a diamond and moss panel. Welts, cuffs and turtle neck worked in k2, p2, rib. The sleeves are picked up at the top and worked in pattern for a third of the way, then continued in stocking stitch to the cuff.

Tension
5 stitches to 1 in., measured over stocking stitch, using 'A' needles.

70

To test the tension

Use a portion of the wool and No. 7 needles. Cast on 15 stitches and work 12 rows of stocking stitch. Cast off, but do not press.

Now measure the tension

If you have more than 5 stitches to 1 in., work another sample using No. 6 needles. If, however, the first sample had less than 5 stitches to the inch, test again using No. 8 needles. The needles used for your correct tension sample are termed 'A' needles in the pattern. You will need two sizes finer for 'B' needles.

It is essential that your tension is absolutely correct.

Abbreviations

k=knit; p=purl; st=stitch; sts=stitches; k2 tog =knit 2 together; k2 tog t.b.s.=knit 2 together through back of stitches; inc=increase; dec= decrease.

Back

**Using 'B' needles, cast on 92 stitches (Rope edge).

Work in k2, p2, rib thus:

1st row K3, *p2, k2. Repeat from * ending the last repeat k3.

2nd row K1, *p2, k2. Repeat from * ending the last repeat k1.

Repeat these 2 rows until work measures 3 in. from the cast-on edge, ending on a 1st row.

Next row Increase stitches to 101 thus: Rib 6, *increase 1 in next stitch, rib 9. Repeat from *ending the last repeat rib 5.

Change to 'A' needles and work in pattern stitch thus:

1st row K1, *k19, p7, (k2, p1) twice, k1, p7. Repeat from * once, k20.

2nd row K1, p8, *k1, p1, k1, p9, k6, (p2, k1) twice, p1, k6, p9. Repeat from * once, k1, p1, k1, p8, k1.

3rd row K8, *p2, k1, p2, k9, p5, k1, (p1, k2) twice, p5, k9. Repeat from * once, p2, k1, p2, k8.

4th row K1, p6, *k2, p3, k2, p9, k4, p1, (k1, p2) twice, k4, p9. Repeat from * once, k2, p3, k2, p6, k1.

5th row K6, *p2, k5, p2, k9, p3, (k2, p1) twice, k1, p3, k9. Repeat from * once, p2, k5, p2, k6.

6th row K1, p4, *k2, p2, k1, p1, k1, p2, k2, p9, k2, (p2, k1) twice, p1, k2, p9. Repeat from * once, k2, p2, k1, p1, k1, p2, k2, p4, k1.

7th row K4, *p2, k2, p2, k1, p2, k2, p2, k9, p1, k1, (p1, k2) twice, p1, k9. Repeat from * once, p2, k2, p2, k1, p2, k2, p2, k4.

8th row K1, p2, *k2, p2, k2, p3, k2, p2, k2, p7, k2, p1, (k1, p2) twice, k2, p7. Repeat from * once, k2, p2, k2, p3, k2, p2, k2, p2, k1.

9th row K2, *p2, k2, p2, k5, p2, k2, p2, k5, p3, (k2, p1) twice, k1, p3, k5. Repeat from * once, p2, k2, p2, k5, p2, k2, p2, k2.

10th row K1, *(k2, p2) twice, k1, p1, k1, (p2, k2) twice, p3, k4, (p2, k1) twice, p1, k4, p3. Repeat from * once, (k2, p2) twice, k1, p1, k1, (p2, k2) twice, k1.

11th row K1, *p1, (k2, p2) twice, k1, (p2, k2) twice, p1, k2, p5, k1, (p1, k2) twice, p5, k2. Repeat from * once, p1, (k2, p2) twice, k1, (p2, k2) twice, p1, k1.

12th row K1, p2, *k2, p2, k2, p3, k2, p2, k2, p3, k6, p1, (k1, p2) twice, k6, p3. Repeat from * once, k2, p2, k2, p3, k2, p2, k2, p2, k1.

13th row K1, *k1, p2, k2, p2, k5, p2, k2, p2, k1, p7, (k2, p1) twice, k1, p7. Repeat from * once, k1, p2, k2, p2, k5, p2, k2, p2, k2.

14th row K1, p1, *k1, p2, k2, p2, k1, p1, k1, p2, k2, p2, k1, p2, k6, (p2, k1) twice, p1, k6, p2. Repeat from * once, k1, p2, k2, p2, k1, p1, k1, p2, k2, p2, k1, p1, k1.

15th row K4, *p2, k2, p2, k1, p2, k2, p2, k5, p5, k1, (p1, k2) twice, p5, k5. Repeat from * once, p2, k2, p2, k1, p2, k2, p2, k4.

16th row K1, p2, *k2, p2, k2, p3, k2, p2, k2, p5, k4, p1, (k1, p2) twice, k4, p5. Repeat from * once, k2, p2, k2, p3, k2, p2, k2, p2, k1.

17th row K3, *p1, k2, p2, k5, p2, k2, p1, k6, p3, (k2, p1) twice, k1, p3, k6. Repeat from * once, p1, k2, p2, k5, p2, k2, p1, k3.

71

18th row K1, p4, *k2, p2, k1, p1, k1, p2, k2, p9, k2, (p2, k1) twice, p1, k2, p9. Repeat from * once, k2, p2, k1, p1, k1, p2, k2, p4, k1.

19th row K4, *p2, k2, p2, k1, p2, k2, p2, k9, p1, k1, (p1, k2) twice, p1, k9. Repeat from * once, p2, k2, p2, k1, p2, k2, p2, k4.

20th row K1, p3, *k1, p2, k2, p3, k2, p2, k1, p8, k2, p1, (k1, p2) twice, k2, p8. Repeat from * once, k1, p2, k2, p3, k2, p2, k1, p3, k1.

21st row K6, *p2, k5, p2, k9, p3, (k2, p1) twice, k1, p3, k9. Repeat from * once, p2, k5, p2, k6.

22nd row K1, p4, *k2, p2, k1, p1, k1, p2, k2, p7, k4, (p2, k1) twice, p1, k4, p7. Repeat from * once, k2, p2, k1, p1, k1, p2, k2, p4, k1.

23rd row K5, *p1, k2, p2, k1, p2, k2, p1, k6, p5, k1, (p1, k2) twice, p5, k6. Repeat from * once, p1, k2, p2, k1, p2, k2, p1, k5.

24th row K1, p6, *k2, p3, k2, p7, k6, p1, (k1, p2) twice, k6, p7. Repeat from * once, k2, p3, k2, p6, k1.

25th row K1, *k5, p2, k5, p2, k5, p7, (k2, p1) twice, k1, p7. Repeat from * once, k5, p2, k5, p2, k6.

26th row K1, p5, *k1, p2, k1, p1, k1, p2, k1, p6, k6, (p2, k1) twice, p1, k6, p6. Repeat from * once, k1, p2, k1, p1, k1, p2, k1, p5, k1.

27th row K8, *p2, k1, p2, k9, p5, k1, (p1, k2) twice, p5, k9. Repeat from * once, p2, k1, p2, k8.

28th row K1, p6, *k2, p3, k2, p9, k4, p1, (k1, p2) twice, k4, p9. Repeat from * once, k2, p3, k2, p6, k1.

29th row K7, *p1, k5, p1, k10, p3, (k2, p1) twice, k1, p3, k10. Repeat from * once, p1, k5, p1, k7.

30th row K1, p8, *k1, p1, k1, p13, k2, (p2, k1) twice, p1, k2, p13. Repeat from * once, k1, p1, k1, p8, k1.

31st row K8, *p2, k1, p2, k13, p1, k1, (p1, k2) twice, p1, k13. Repeat from * once, p2, k1, p2, k8.

32nd row K1, p6, *k2, p3, k2, p11, k2, p1, (k1, p2) twice, k2, p11. Repeat from * once, k2, p3, k2, p6, k1.

33rd row K7, *p1, k5, p1, k10, p3, (k2, p1) twice, k1, p3, k10. Repeat from * once, p1, k5, p1, k7.

34th row K1, p6, *k2, p3, k2, p9, k4, (p2, k1) twice, p1, k4, p9. Repeat from * once, k2, p3, k2, p6, k1.

35th row K8, *p2, k1, p2, k9, p5, k1, (p1, k2) twice, p5, k9. Repeat from * once, p2, k1, p2, k8.

36th row K1, p8, *k1, p1, k1, p9, k6, p1, (k1, p2) twice, k6, p9. Repeat from * once, k1, p1, k1, p8, k1.

These 36 rows complete one pattern and are repeated throughout.

Repeat rows 1 to 10 inclusive once.

Now continue in pattern on the centre 101 stitches but increase 1 stitch at each end of the next row and every following 4th row until 6 stitches have been added at each side, keeping these extra stitches in stocking stitch (i.e. knit on right side rows and purl on wrong side rows). 113 stitches on needle.

Continue in pattern, keeping the 6 stitches at each end in stocking stitch until work measures 16½ in. from the cast-on edge, ending on a wrong side row.

Next row K6, and slip these 6 stitches of gusset on to a safety pin, then pattern to last 6 stitches, turn and leave remaining 6 stitches on another safety pin.

Continue without shaping on the 101 stitches until 4 complete patterns have been worked, ending on a wrong side row.**

Work should measure approximately 24½ in. from the cast-on edge.

Yoke

Change to 'B' needles and continue in stocking stitch only until the yoke measures 2¼ in., ending on a wrong side row.

Cast off 31 stitches at the beginning of the next 2 rows.

Leave remaining 39 stitches on a spare needle to be used later for turtle neck.

Work as for back from ** to **.

Yoke and shape neck

Change to 'B' needles.

1st row Knit 39 stitches. Turn and leave remaining 62 stitches for the time being.

2nd row Cast off 3 stitches, purl to last stitch, k1.

3rd row Knit.

4th row Cast off 2 stitches, purl to last stitch, k1.

5th row Knit to last 2 stitches, k2 tog t.b.s.

6th row K1, purl to last stitch, k1.

Repeat the last 2 rows twice more.

Continue in stocking stitch without shaping until yoke measures 2¼ in., ending on a wrong side row.

Cast off remaining 31 stitches.

Slip the centre 23 stitches on to a stitch holder, rejoin wool to remaining 39 stitches and work this side to correspond.

Join shoulder seams by back-stitching on the wrong side as near to the edges as possible to ensure neat seams.

Sleeves

These are worked from the shoulders with the 6 gusset stitches added on at each end thus:

With right side of work facing, slip the 6 stitches of gusset at the beginning of sleeve on to a 'B' needle, then pick up neatly and knit 36 stitches along armhole edge to top of shoulder seam, pick up 1 stitch on the seam (i.e. centre of sleeve), then pick up evenly 36 stitches along other side of armhole to the 6 gusset stitches, then knit across these 6 stitches (85 stitches).

Change to 'A' needles and work in pattern thus:

1st row (Wrong side of work) K1, p12, k6, p1, (k1, p2) twice, k6, p9, k1, p1, k1, p9, k6, p1, (k1, p2) twice, k6, p12, k1.

2nd row K14, p5, k1, (p1, k2) twice, p5, k9, p2, k1, p2, k9, p5, k1, (p1, k2) twice, p5, k14.

3rd row K1, p14, k4, (p2, k1) twice, p1, k4, p9, k2, p3, k2, p9, k4, (p2, k1) twice, p1, k4, p14, k1.

4th row K16, p3, (k2, p1) twice, k1, p3, k10, p1, k5, p1, k10, p3, (k2, p1) twice, k1, p3, k16.

5th row K1, p16, k2, p1, (k1, p2) twice, k2, p11, k2, p3, k2, p11, k2, p1, (k1, p2) twice, k2, p16, k1.

6th row K18, p1, k1, (p1, k2) twice, p1, k13, p2, k1, p2, k13, p1, k1, (p1, k2) twice, p1, k18.

7th row K1, p16, k2, (p2, k1) twice, p1, k2, p13, k1, p1, k1, p13, k2, (p2, k1) twice, p1, k2, p16, k1.

8th row K2 tog, k14, p3, (k2, p1) twice, k1, p3, k10, p1, k5, p1, k10, p3, (k2, p1) twice, k1, p3, k14, k2 tog t.b.s.

9th row K1, p13, k4, p1, (k1, p2) twice, k4, p9, k2, p3, k2, p9, k4, p1, (k1, p2) twice, k4, p13, k1.

10th row K13, p5, k1, (p1, k2) twice, p5, k9, p2, k1, p2, k9, p5, k1, (p1, k2) twice, p5, k13.

11th row K1, p11, k6, (p2, k1) twice, p1, k6, p6, k1, p2, k1, p1, k1, p2, k1, p6, k6, (p2, k1) twice, p1, k6, p11, k1.

12th row K2 tog, k9, p7, (k2, p1) twice, k1, p7, k5, p2, k5, p2, k5, p7, (k2, p1) twice, k1, p7, k9, k2 tog t.b.s.

13th row K1, p10, k6, p1, (k1, p2) twice, k6, p7, k2, p3, k2, p7, k6, p1, (k1, p2) twice, k6, p10, k1.

14th row K12, p5, k1, (p1, k2) twice, p5, k6, p1, k2, p2, k1, p2, k2, p1, k6, p5, k1, (p1, k2) twice, p5, k12.

15th row K1, p12, k4, (p2, k1) twice, p1, k4, p7, k2, p2, k1, p1, k1, p2, k2, p7, k4, (p2, k1) twice, p1, k4, p12, k1.

16th row K2 tog, k12, p3, (k2, p1) twice, k1, p3, k9, p2, k5, p2, k9, p3, (k2, p1) twice, k1, p3, k12, k2 tog t.b.s.

17th row K1, p13, k2, p1, (k1, p2) twice, k2, p8, k1, p2, k2, p3, k2, p2, k1, p8, k2, p1, (k1, p2) twice, k2, p13, k1.

18th row K15, p1, k1, (p1, k2) twice, p1, k9, p2, k2, p2, k1, p2, k2, p2, k9, p1, k1, (p1, k2) twice, p1, k15.

19th row K1, p13, k2, (p2, k1) twice, p1, k2, p9, k2, p2, k1, p1, k1, p2, k2, p9, k2, (p2, k1) twice, p1, k2, p13, k1.

20th row K2 tog, k11, p3, (k2, p1) twice, k1, p3, k6, p1, k2, p2, k5, p2, k2, p1, k6, p3, (k2, p1) twice, k1, p3, k11, k2 tog t.b.s.

21st row K1, p10, k4, p1, (k1, p2) twice, k4, p5, k2, p2, k2, p3, k2, p2, k2, p5, k4, p1, (k1, p2) twice, k4, p10, k1.

22nd row K10, p5, k1, (p1, k2) twice, p5, k5, p2, k2, p2, k1, p2, k2, p2, k5, p5, k1, (p1, k2) twice, p5, k10.

23rd row K1, p8, k6, (p2, k1) twice, p1, k6, p2, k1, p2, k2, p2, k1, p1, k1, p2, k2, p2, k1, p2, k6, (p2, k1) twice, p1, k6, p8, k1.

24th row K2 tog, k6, p7, (k2, p1) twice, k1, p7, k1, p2, k2, p2, k5, p2, k2, p2, k1, p7, (k2, p1) twice, k1, p7, k6, k2 tog t.b.s.

25th row K1, p7, k6, p1, (k1, p2) twice, k6, p3, k2, p2, k2, p3, k2, p2, k2, p3, k6, p1, (k1, p2) twice, k6, p7, k1.

26th row K9, p5, k1, (p1, k2) twice, p5, k2, p1, (k2, p2) twice, k1, (p2, k2) twice, p1, k2, p5, k1, (p1, k2) twice, p5, k9.

27th row K1, p9, k4, (p2, k1) twice, p1, k4, p3, (k2, p2) twice, k1, p1, k1, (p2, k2) twice, p3, k4, (p2, k1) twice, p1, k4, p9, k1.

28th row K2 tog, k9, p3, (k2, p1) twice, k1, p3, k5, p2, k2, p2, k5, p2, k2, p2, k5, p3, (k2, p1) twice k1, p3, k9, k2 tog t.b.s.

29th row K1, p10, k2, p1, (k1, p2) twice, k2, p7, k2, p2, k2, p3, k2, p2, k2, p7, k2, p1, (k1, p2) twice, k2, p10, k1.

30th row K12, p1, k1, (p1, k2) twice, p1, k9, p2, k2, p2, k1, p2, k2, p2, k9, p1, k1, (p1, k2) twice, p1, k12.

31st row K1, p10, k2, (p2, k1) twice, p1, k2, p9, k2, p2, k1, p1, k1, p2, k2, p9, k2, (p2, k1) twice, p1, k2, p10, k1.

32nd row K2 tog, k8, p3, (k2, p1) twice, k1, p3, k9, p2, k5, p2, k9, p3, (k2, p1) twice, k1, p3, k8, k2 tog t.b.s.

33rd row K1, p7, k4, p1, (k1, p2) twice, k4, p9, k2, p3, k2, p9, k4, p1, (k1, p2) twice, k4, p7, k1.

34th row K7, p5, k1, (p1, k2) twice, p5, k9, p2, k1, p2, k9, p5, k1, (p1, k2) twice, p5, k7.

35th row K1, p5, k6, (p2, k1) twice, p1, k6, p9, k1, p1, k1, p9, k6, (p2, k1) twice, p1, k6, p5, k1.

36th row K5, p7, (k2, p1) twice, k1, p7, k19, p7, (k2, p1) twice, k1, p7, k5, (71 sts).

37th row K1, purl to last stitch, k1.

Now continue in stocking stitch only, decreasing 1 stitch at each end of the next row and every following 6th row until 57 stitches remain.

Continue without shaping until sleeve measures 15½ in. from the picked up stitches at armhole, ending on a knit row.

Next row P3, p2 tog, p4. Repeat from * to end (48 stitches).

Change to 'B' needles and work in k2, p2, rib as for back welt for 4½ in.

Cast off LOOSELY in rib.

Work a second sleeve in the same way.

Turtle collar

Using a set of 'B' needles and with right side of work facing, knit across the 39 stitches of back neck, pick up and knit 19 stitches along the side of neck, knit across the 23 stitches of front neck, pick up and knit 19 stitches along other side of neck. (100 stitches).

Work in rounds of k2, p2, rib for 6 in.

Cast off LOOSELY in rib.

Turn the collar inside to make a double 3 in. turtle and neatly slip stitch down to the lower edge of collar.

To make up

1 DO NOT PRESS.
2 Join the sleeve, gusset and side seam edges together by back-stitching on the wrong side of work ⅛ in. from edges to ensure neat seams. Weave together on the right side of work the ribbing on the welts and cuffs.

SEAHOUSES CARDIGAN

Materials

32 oz Listers Double Six.
1 pair 'A' needles (see tension note).
1 pair 'B' needles (see tension note).
1 pair 'C' needles (see tension note).

Size

16 to fit 38 in. bust.

Measurements

Length at centre back = 26 in.
Width across back at underarm = 20 in.
Sleeve seam = 16 in.
Side seam = 16 in.

Description

A classic shaped cardigan with long set in sleeves and a high round neck. Main part worked in Seahouses pattern stitch. Welts, cuffs and neck band worked in k1, p1, rib. Front borders worked in pattern stitch. An inset pocket on each front. Fastened with 7 buttons.

Tension

5 stitches to 1 in., measured over stocking stitch, using 'A' needles.

To test the tension

Use a portion of the wool and No. 7 needles. Cast on 15 stitches and work 12 rows of stocking stitch. Cast off, but do not press.

Now measure the tension

If you have more than 5 stitches to 1 in. work another sample using No. 6 needles. If, however, the first sample had less than 5 stitches to the in., test again using No. 8 needles. When you are satisfied that you have achieved the correct tension. The needles used for your correct tension sample are termed 'A' needles in the pattern. You will need two sizes finer for 'B' needles and two sizes finer still for 'C' needles.

It is essential that your tension is absolutely correct.

Abbreviations

k = knit; p = purl; st = stitch; sts = stitches; k2 tog = knit 2 together; k2 tog t.b.s. = knit 2 together through back of stitches; inc = increase; dec = decrease.

Back

Using 'B' needles, cast on 101 stitches (Rope edge). Work in k1, p1 rib thus:

1st row K2, *p1, k1. Repeat from * ending the last repeat k2.

2nd row K1, *p1, k1. Repeat from * to end.

Repeat the last 2 rows until work measures 1 in. from the cast-on edge, ending on a 2nd row.

Change to 'A' needles and work in pattern stitch thus:

1st row K4, *k17, p7, (k2, p1) twice, k1, p7. Repeat from * once, k21.

2nd row K1, p10, *k1, p1, k1, p8, k6, (p2, k1) twice, p1, k6, p8. Repeat from * once, k1, p1, k1, p10, k1.

3rd row K10, *p2, k1, p2, k8, p5, k1, (p1, k2) twice, p5, k8. Repeat from * once, p2, k1, p2, k10.

4th row K1, p8, *k2, p3, k2, p8, k4, p1, (k1, p2) twice, k4, p8. Repeat from * once, k2, p3, k2, p8, k1.

5th row *K8, p2, k5, p2, k8, p3, (k2, p1) twice, k1, p3. Repeat from * once, k8, p2, k5, p2, k8.

6th row K1, p6, *k2, p2, k1, p1, k1, p2, k2, p8, k2, (p2, k1) twice, p1, k2, p8. Repeat from * once, k2, p2, k1, p1, k1, p2, k2, p6, k1.

7th row K6, *p2, k2, p2, k1, p2, k2, p2, k8, p1, k1, (p1, k2) twice, p1, k8. Repeat from * once, p2, k2, p2, k1, p2, k2, p2, k6.

8th row K1, p4, *k2, p2, k2, p3, k2, p2, k2, p6, k2, p1, (k1, p2) twice, k2, p6. Repeat from * once, k2, p2, k2, p3, k2, p2, k2, p4, k1.

9th row *K4, p2, k2, p2, k5, p2, k2, p2, k4, p3, (k2, p1) twice, k1, p3. Repeat from * once, k4, p2, k2, p2, k5, p2, k2, p2, k4.

10th row K5, *p2, k2, p2, k1, p1, k1, p2, k2, p2, k1, p3, k4, p2, k1) twice, p1, k4, p3, k1. Repeat from * once, p2, k2, p2, k1, p1, k1, p2, k2, p2, k5.

11th row K6, *p2, k2, p2, k1, p2, k2, p2, k4, p5, k1, (p1, k2) twice, p5, k4. Repeat from * once, p2, k2, p2, k1, p2, k2, p2, k6.

12th row K1, p4, *k2, p2, k2, p3, k2, p2, k2, p2, k6, p1, (k1, p2) twice, k6, p2. Repeat from * once, k2, p2, k2, p3, k2, p2, k2, p4, k1.

13th row K4, p2, *k2, p2, k5, p2, k2, p9, (k2, p1) twice, k1, p9. Repeat from * once, k2, p2, k5, p2, k2, p2, k4.

14th row K1, p3, *k1, p2, k2, p2, k1, p1, k1, p2, k2, p2, k1, p1, k6, (p2, k1) twice, p1, k6, p1. Repeat from * once, k1, p2, k2, p2, k1, p1, k1, p2, k2, p2, k1, p3, k1.

15th row K6, *p2, k2, p2, k1, p2, k2, p2, k4, p5, k1, (p1, k2) twice, p5, k4. Repeat from * once, p2, k2, p2, k1, p2, k2, p2, k6.

16th row K1, *p4, k2, p2, k2, p3, k2, p2, k2, p4, k4, p1, (k1, p2) twice, k4. Repeat from * once, p4, k2, p2, k2, p3, k2, p2, k2, p4, k1.

17th row *K5, p1, k2, p2, k5, p2, k2, p1, k5, p3, (k2, p1) twice, k1, p3. Repeat from * once, k5, p1, k2, p2, k5, p2, k2, p1, k5.

18th row K1, p6, *k2, p2, k1, p1, k1, p2, k2, p8, k2, (p2, k1) twice, p1, k2, p8. Repeat from * once, k2, p2, k1, p1, k1, p2, k2, p6, k1.

19th row K6, *p2, k2, p2, k1, p2, k2, p2, k8, p1, k1, (p1, k2) twice, p1, k8. Repeat from * once, p2, k2, p2, k1, p2, k2, p2, k6.

20th row K1, p5, *k1, p2, k2, p3, k2, p2, k1, p7, k2, p1, (k1, p2) twice, k2, p7. Repeat from * once, k1, p2, k2, p3, k2, p2, k1, p5, k1.

21st row *K8, p2, k5, p2, k8, p3, (k2, p1) twice, k1, p3. Repeat from * once, k8, p2, k5, p2, k8.

22nd row K1, *p6, k2, p2, k1, p1, k1, p2, k2, p6, k4, (p2, k1) twice, p1, k4. Repeat from * once, p6, k2, p2, k1, p1, k1, p2, k2, p6, k1.

23rd row K7, *p1, k2, p2, k1, p2, k2, p1, k5, p5, k1, (p1, k2) twice, p5, k5. Repeat from * once, p1, k2, p2, k1, p2, k2, p1, k7.

24th row K1, p8, *k2, p3, k2, p6, k6, p1, (k1, p2) twice, k6, p6. Repeat from * once, k2, p3, k2, p8, k1.

25th row K8, *p2, k5, p2, k4, p7, (k2, p1) twice, k1, p7, k4. Repeat from * once, p2, k5, p2, k8.

26th row K1, p7, *k1, p2, k1, p1, k1, p2, k1, p5, k6, (p2, k1) twice, p1, k6, p5. Repeat from * once, k1, p2, k1, p1, k1, p2, k1, p7, k1.

27th row K10, *p2, k1, p2, k8, p5, k1, (p1, k2) twice, p5, k8. Repeat from * once, p2, k1, p2, k10.

28th row K1, *p8, k2, p3, k2, p8, k4, p1, (k1, p2) twice, k4. Repeat from * once, p8, k2, p3, k2, p8, k1.

29th row *K9, p1, k5, p1, k9, p3, (k2, p1) twice, k1, p3. Repeat from * once, k9, p1, k5, p1, k9.

30th row K1, p10, *k1, p1, k1, p12, k2, (p2, k1) twice, p1, k2, p12. Repeat from * once, k1, p1, k1, p10, k1.

31st row K10, *p2, k1, p2, k12, p1, k1, (p1, k2) twice, p1, k12. Repeat from * once, p2, k1, p2, k10.

32nd row K1, p8, *k2, p3, k2, p10, k2, p1, (k1, p2) twice, k2, p10. Repeat from * once, k2, p3, k2, p8, k1.

33rd row *K9, p1, k5, p1, k9, p3, (k2, p1) twice, k1, p3. Repeat from * once, k9, p1, k5, p1, k9.

34th row K1, *p8, k2, p3, k2, p8, k4, (p2, k1) twice, p1, k4. Repeat from * once, p8, k2, p3, k2, p8, k1.

35th row K10, *p2, k1, p2, k8, p5, k1, (p1, k2) twice, p5, k8. Repeat from * once, p2, k1, p2, k10.

36th row K1, p10, *k1, p!, k1, p8, k6, p1, (k1, p 2) twice, k6, p8. Repeat from * once, k1, p1, k1, p10, k1.

These 36 rows form the pattern.

Continue in pattern without shaping until work measures 16 in. from the cast-on edge, ending on a wrong side row.

Shape shoulders

Keep continuity of pattern stitch.

Cast off 5 stitches at the beginning of the next 2 rows.

Cast off 6 stitches at the beginning of the next 6 rows.

Leave remaining 31 stitches on a spare needle to be used later for neck band.

Shape armholes

Keep continuity of pattern stitch.

Cast off 3 stitches at the beginning of the next 2 rows.

Decrease 1 stitch at each end of the next row and every alternate row until 77 stitches remain.

Continue without shaping until 5 complete patterns have been worked from the commencement.

If necessary, continue without shaping until work measures 25 in. from the cast-on edge, working in pattern on the diamond and moss panels but in stocking stitch on the tree panel and ending on a wrong side row.

Left front
Pocket inset

Using 'A' needles, cast on 27 stitches (Rope edge).

Work in stocking stitch for 4½ in. ending on a purl row.

Next row K2, p2, k1, p2, k12, p1, k1, (p1, k2) twice.
Next row P1, (k1, p2) twice, k2, p10, k2, p3, k3.
Next row K1, p1, k5, p1, k9, p3, (k2, p1) twice, k1.
Next row (P2, k1) twice, p1, k4, p8, k2, p3, k3.
Next row K2, p2, k1, p2, k8, p5, k1, (p1, k2) twice.
Next row P1, (k1, p2) twice, k6, p8, k1, p1, k1, p2, k1.
Next row K13, p7, (k2, p1) twice, k1.

Leave these stitches for the time being: these end on a right side row.

Using 'B' needles, cast on 51 stitches (Rope edge).

Work in k1, p1, rib as for back welt for 1 in., ending on a 2nd row.

Change to 'A' needles and continue in pattern thus:

1st row K21, p7, (k2, p1) twice, k1, p7, k9.
2nd row P1, k1, p8, k6, (p2, k1) twice, p1, k6, p8, k1, p1, k1, p10, k1.
3rd row K10, p2, k1, p2, k8, p5, k1, (p1, k2) twice, p5, k8, p2, k1.
4th row P2, k2, p8, k4, p1, (k1, p2) twice, k4, p8, k2, p3, k2, p8, k1.
5th row K8, p2, k5, p2, k8, p3, (k2, p1) twice, k1, p3, k8, p2, k3.
6th row P1, k1, p2, k2, p8, k2, (p2, k1) twice, p1, k2, p8, k2, p2, k1, p1, k1, p2, k2, p6, k1.
7th row K6, p2, k2, p2, k1, p2, k2, p2, k8, p1, k1, (p1, k2) twice, p1, k8, p2, k2, p2, k1.
8th row P2, k2, p2, k2, p6, k2, p1, (k1, p2) twice, k2, p6, k2, p2, k2, p3, k2, p2, k2, p4, k1.
9th row K4, p2, k2, p2, k5, p2, k2, p2, k4, p3, (k2, p1) twice, k1, p3, k4, p2, k2, p2, k3.
10th row P1, k1, p2, k2, p2, k1, p3, k4, (p2, k1) twice, p1, k4, p3, k1, p2, k2, p2, k1, p1, k1, p2, k2, p2, k1, p3, k1.
11th row K6, p2, k2, p2, k1, p2, k2, p2, k4, p5, k1, (p1, k2) twice, p5, k4, p2, k2, p2, k1.
12th row P2, k2, p2, k2, p2, k6, p1, (k1, p2) twice, k6, p2, k2, p2, k2, p3, k2, p2, k2, p4, k1.
13th row K4, p2, k2, p2, k5, p2, k2, p9, (k2, p1) twice, k1, p9, k2, p2, k3.
14th row P1, k1, p2, k2, p2, k1, p1, k6, (p2, k1) twice, p1, k6, p1, k1, p2, k2, p2, k1, p1, k1, p2, k2, p1, p3, k1.
15th row K6, p2, k2, p2, k1, p2, k2, p2, k4, p5, k1, (p1, k2) twice, p5, k4, p2, k2, p2, k1.
16th row P2, k2, p2, k2, p4, k4, p1, (k1, p2) twice, k4, p4, k2, p2, k2, p3, k2, p2, k2, p4, k1.
17th row K5, p1, k2, p2, k5, p 2, k2, p1, k5, p3, (k2, p1) twice, k1, p3, k5, p1, k2, p2, k3.
18th row P1, k1, p2, k2, p8, k2, (p2, k1) twice, p1, k2, p8, k2, p2, k1, p1, k1, p2, k2, p6, k1.
19th row K6, p2, k2, p2, k1, p2, k2, p2, k8, p1, k1, (p1, k2) twice, p1, k8, p2, k2, p2, k1.

20th row P2, k2, p2, k1, p7, k2, p1, (k1, p2) twice, k2, p7, k1, p2, k2, p3, k2, p2, k1, p5, k1.

21st row K8, p2, k5, p2, k8, p3, (k2, p1) twice, k1, p3, k8, p2, k3.

22nd row P1, k1, p2, k2, p6, k4, (p2, k1) twice, p1, k4, p6, k2, p2, k1, p1, k1, p2, k2, p6, k1.

23rd row K7, p1, k2, p2, k1, p2, k2, p1, k5, p5, k1, (p1, k2) twice, p5, k5, p1, k2, p2, k1.

24th row P2, k2, p6, k6, p1, (k1, p2) twice, k6, p6, k2, p3, k2, p8, k1.

25th row K8, p2, k5, p2, k4, p7, (k2, p1) twice, k1, p7, k4, p2, k3.

26th row P1, k1, p2, k1, p5, k6, (p2, k1) twice, p1, k6, p5, k1, p2, k1, p1, k1, p2, k1, p7, k1.

27th row K10, p2, k1, p2, k8, p5, k1, (p1, k2) twice, p5, k8, p2, k1.

28th row P2, k2, p8, k4, p1, (k1, p2) twice, k4, p8, k2, p3, k2, p8, k1.

29th row K9, p1, k5, p1, k9, p3, (k2, p1) twice, k1, p3, k9, p1, k3.

Shape for pocket top

30th row P1, k1, p12, k2, (p2, k1) twice, p1, k2, p12, k1, p1, k1, p10, k1.

31st row K10, p2, k1, p2, k12, p1, k1, p1, k2, p1, k1, k1, p1, k12, p2, k1.

32nd row P2, k2, p10, k2, p1, (k1, p2) twice, k2, p10, k2, p3, k2, p8, k1.

33rd row K9, p1, k5, p1, k9, p3, (k2, p1) twice, k1, p3, k9, p1, k3.

34th row P2, k2, p8, k4, (p2, k1) twice, p1, k4, p8, k2, p3, k2, p8, k1.

35th row K10, p2, k1, p2, k8, p5, k1, p1, k2, p1, k2, p5, k8, p2, k1.

36th row P1, k1, p8, k6, p1, (k1, p2) twice, k6, p8, k1, p1, k1.

37th row K21, p7, (k2, p1) twice, k1 then slip the last 27 stitches just worked on to a stitch holder, p7, k9.

38th row P1, k1, p8, k6, then with wrong side of pocket inset facing and placed in front of work, pattern across the 27 stitches of inset thus: (p2, k1) twice, p1, k6, p8, k1, p1, k1, p3, then

p7, k1.

39th row As 3rd row.

Continue in pattern without shaping until work measures 16 in. from the cast-on edge, ending on a wrong side row and making sure that the same number of rows have been worked as on back so that the work teams up.

Shape armhole

Keep continuity of pattern stitch.

1st row Cast off 3 stitches, pattern to end.

2nd row Pattern to end.

3rd row K2 tog, pattern to end.

4th row Pattern to end.

Repeat the last 2 rows until 39 stitches remain. Continue without shaping until work measures 23 in. from the cast-on edge, ending on a right side row.

Shape neck

Cast off 6 stitches once, 2 stitches 3 times, and 1 stitch twice, on rows beginning at neck edge. (25 stitches).

Shape shoulder

Decrease 1 stitch twice more on rows beginning at neck edge, AT THE SAME TIME, cast off 5 stitches once, and 6 stitches 3 times on rows beginning at armhole edge.

Right front
Pocket inset

Work as for Left front pocket inset but reversing the pattern by reading the pattern rows backwards.

Using 'B' needles, cast on 51 stitches (Rope edge).

Work in k1, p1, rib as for back welt for 1 in., ending on a 2nd row.

Change to 'A' needles and work as for left front, but reversing the pattern by reading the rows backwards, and reversing all shapings.

Sleeves

Using 'B' needles, cast on 53 stitches (Rope edge).

Work in k1, p1, rib as for back welt for 2½ in., ending on a 1st row.

Next row Rib 5, * increase 1 in next stitch, rib 5. Repeat from * ending the last repeat rib 5. (61 stitches).

Change to 'A' needles and work in pattern stitch, increasing 1 stitch at each end of the 9th row and every following 8th row thus:

1st row K1, p7, (k2, p1) twice, k1, p7, k17, p7, (k2, p1) twice, k1, p7, k1.

2nd row K1, p1, k6, (p2, k1) twice, p1, k6, p8, k1, p1, k1, p8, k6, (p2, k1) twice, p1, k6, p1, k1.

3rd row K3, p5, k1, (p1, k2) twice, p5, k8, p2, k1, p2, k8, p5, k1, (p1, k2) twice, p5, k3.

4th row K1, p3, k4, p1, (k1, p2) twice, k4, p8, k2, p3, k2, p8, k4, p1, (k1, p2) twice, k4, p3, k1.

5th row K5, p3, (k2, p1) twice, k1, p3, k8, p2, k5, p2, k8, p3, (k2, p1) twice, k1, p3, k5.

6th row K1, p5, k2, (p2, k1) twice, p1, k2, p8, k2, p2, k1, p1, k1, p2, k2, p8, k2, (p2, k1) twice, p1, k2, p5, k1.

7th row K7, p1, k1, (p1, k2) twice, p1, k8, p2, k2, p2, k1, p2, k2, p2, k8, p1, k1, (p1, k2) twice, p1, k7.

8th row K1, p5, k2, p1, (k1, p2) twice, k2, p6, k2, p2, k2, p3, k2, p2, k2, p6, k2, p1, (k1, p2) twice, k2, p5, k1.

9th row Inc. 1 in first st., k4, p3, (k2, p1) twice, k1, p3, k4, p2, k2, p2, k5, p2, k2, p2, k4, p3, (k2, p1) twice, k1, p3, k4, inc. 1 in last st.

10th row K1, p4, k4, (p2, k1) twice, p1, k4, p3, k1, p2, k2, p2, k1, p1, k1, p2, k2, p2, k1, p3, k4, (p2, k1) twice, p1, k4, p4, k1.

11th row K4, p5, k1, (p1, k2) twice, p5, k4, p2, k2, p2, k1, p2, k2, p2, k4, p5, k1, (p1, k2) twice, p5, k4.

12th row K1, p2, k6, p1, (k1, p2) twice, k6, p2, k2, p2, k2, p3, k2, p2, k2, p2, k6, p1, (k1, p2) twice, k6, p1, k2.

13th row K2, p7, (k2, p1) twice, k1, p9, k2, p2, k5, p2, k2, p9, (k2, p1) twice, k1, p7, k2.

14th row K1, p2, k6, (p2, k1) twice, p1, k6, p1, k1, p2, k2, p2, k1, p1, k1, p2, k2, p2, k1, p1, k6, (p2, k1) twice, p1, k6, p2, k1.

15th row K4, p5, k1, (p1, k2) twice, p5, k4, p2, k2, p2, k1, p2, k2, p2, k4, p5, k1, (p1, k2) twice, p5, k4.

16th K1, p4, k4, p1, (k1, p2) twice, k4, p4, k2, p2, k2, p3, k2, p2, k2, p4, k4, p1, (k1, p2) twice, k4, p4, k1.

17th row Inc. 1 in first st., k5, p3, (k2, p1) twice, k1, p3, k5, p1, k2, p2, k5, p2, k2, p1, k5, p3, (k2, p1) twice, k1, p3, k5, inc. 1 in last st.

18th row K1, p7, k2, (p2, k1) twice, p1, k2, p8, k2, p2, k1, p1, k1, p2, k2, p8, k2, (p2, k1) twice, p1, k2, p7, k1.

19th row K9, p1, k1, (p1, k2) twice, p1, k8, p2, k2, p2, k1, p2, k2, p2, k8, p1, k1, (p1, k2) twice, p1, k9.

20th row K1, p7, k2, p1, (k1, p2) twice, k2, p7, k1, p2, k2, p3, k2, p2, k1, p7, k2, p1, (k1, p2) twice, k2, p7, k1.

21st row K7, p3, (k2, p1) twice, k1, p3, k8, p2, k5, p2, k8, p3, (k2, p1) twice, k1, p3, k7.

22nd row K1, p5, k4, (p2, k1) twice, p1, k4, p6, k2, p2, k1, p1, k1, p2, k2, p6, k4, (p2, k1) twice, p1, k4, p5, k1.

23rd row K5, p5, k1, (p1, k2) twice, p5, k5, p1, k2, p2, k1, p2, k2, p1, k5, p5, k1, (p1, k2) twice, p5, k5.

24th row K1, p3, k6, p1, (k1, p2) twice, k6, p6, k2, p3, k2, p6, k6, p1, (k1, p2) twice, k6, p3, k1.

25th row Inc. 1 in first st., k2, p7, (k2, p1) twice, k1, p7, k4, p2, k5, p2, k4, p7, (k2, p1) twice, k1, p7, k2, inc. 1 in last st.

26th row K1, p4, k6, (p2, k1) twice, p1, k6, p5, k1, p2, k1, p1, k1, p2, k1, p5, k6, (p2, k1) twice, p1, k6, p4, k1.

27th row K6, p5, k1, (p1, k2) twice, p5, k8, p2, k1, p2, k8, p5, k1, (p1, k2) twice, p5, k6.

28th row K1, p6, k4, p1, (k1, p2) twice, k4, p8, k2, p3, k2, p8, k4, p1, (k1, p2) twice, k4, p6, k1.

29th row K8, p3, (k2, p1) twice, k1, p3, k9, p1, k5, p1, k9, p3, (k2, p1) twice, k1, p3, k8.

30th row K1, p8, k2, (p2, k1) twice, p1, k2, p12, k1, p1, k1, p12, k2, (p2, k1) twice, p1, k2, p8, k1.

31st row K10, p1, k1, (p1, k2) twice, p1, k12, p2, k1, p2, k12, p1, k1, (p1, k2) twice, p1, k10.

32nd row K1, p8, k2, p1, (k1, p2) twice, k2, p10, k2, p3, k2, p10, k2, p1, (k1, p2) twice, k2, p8, k1.

33rd row Inc 1 in first st, k7, p3, (k2, p1) twice, k1, p3, k9, p1, k5, p1, k9, p3, (k2, p1) twice, k1, p3, k7, inc 1 in last st.

34th row K1, p7, k4, (p2, k1) twice, p1, k4, p8, k2, p3, k2, p8, k4, (p2, k1) twice, p1, k4, p7, k1.

35th row K7, p5, k1, (p1, k2) twice, p5, k8, p2, k1, p2, k8, p5, k1, (p1, k2) twice, p5, k7.

36th row K1, p5, k6, p1, (k1, p2) twice, k6, p8, k1, p1, k1, p8, k6, p1, (k1, p2) twice, k6, p5, k1.

Continue in pattern, still increasing 1 stitch at each end of every 8th row until there are 81 stitches on the needle, working the extra stitches into stocking stitch at each end so that the pattern finishes with k10 at each end.

Continue without shaping until work measures 16 in. from the cast-on edge, ending on a wrong side row.

Shape top

Keep continuity of pattern stitch.

Cast off 3 stitches at the beginning of the next 2 rows.

Decrease 1 stitch at each end of the next row and every alternate row until 49 stitches remain.

Cast off 2 stitches at the beginning of the next 8 rows.

Cast off 3 stitches at the beginning of the next 2 rows.

Cast off 4 stitches at the beginning of the next 4 rows.

Cast off remaining 11 stitches.

Work a second sleeve in the same way.

Left front border

Using 'C' needles, cast on 9 stitches (Rope edge).

Work in patterns thus:

1st row K3, p1, k2, p1, k2.
2nd row K1, p2, k1, p2, k1, p1, k1.
3rd row K2, p1, k2, p1, k3.
4th row K1, p1, k1, p2, k1, p2, k1.

Repeat these 4 rows until the border is long enough to reach from the cast-on edge of left front to neck edge, slightly stretching the border to ensure a firm edge. To ensure correct length, neatly tack border to left front edge, slightly stretching the border. Break wool and leave these stitches to be used later for neck band.

Right front border

Work as for left front border, but making 6 buttonholes. Use the left front border as a guide, and 6 pins to represent buttons. Place the first pin in the centre of welt (i.e. $\frac{1}{2}$ an inch up from the cast-on edge) and the 6th pin $3\frac{1}{4}$ in. below neck edge, then space the remaining 4 pins evenly between, approximately $3\frac{3}{4}$ in. apart. (The 7th buttonhole will be worked in the neck band).

Work buttonholes on right front border on rows to correspond with pins thus:

1st row Pattern 3, cast off 3, pattern 3.
2nd row Pattern 3, cast on 3, pattern 3.

When the right front border is completed, do not break wool: these stitches are then ready for neck band.

Neck band

Join shoulder seams by back-stitching on the wrong side of work approximately $\frac{1}{8}$ in. from edges to ensure neat seams.

Using 'C' needles and with right side of work facing, pattern across the 9 stitches of right front border, pick up and knit 17 stitches along neck edge to shoulder, knit across the 31 stitches at back of neck, then pick up and knit 17 stitches to left front border, then pattern across these 9 stitches (83 stitches).

1st row Pattern 8 stitches, *k1, p1. Repeat from *
    to last 9 stitches, k1, pattern 8.
2nd row Pattern 8, *p1, k1. Repeat from * to last
9 stitches, p1, pattern 8.

Repeat these 2 rows until neck band measures
$\frac{1}{2}$ in., ending on a 1st row.

Next 2 rows Make a buttonhole as before.

Continue in pattern and rib until neck band
measures 1 in.

Cast off LOOSELY in rib.

DO NOT PRESS OR MAKE UP, BUT DARN IN ALL ENDS.

Pocket tops

Slip the 27 stitches of pocket top to a 'B' needle
and work in k1, p1 rib for $\frac{3}{4}$ in.

Cast off loosely in rib.

Work the other pocket top in the same way.

78 The Old Stock 1901. *Left to right:* Ben Herrington, Ben Brown, Edward Palmer ('Shemo') and another Southwold fisherman surname Stanard. The three fishermen to the left are wearing Suffolk guernseys

Sheringham Guernsey

This is an attractive pattern made in Dunraven 3 ply.

200 stitches knitted on size 17 long needles on the front and 200 for the back. 1 in. 2 purl, 2 plain welt. 10 in. plain knitting, with seam stitch of 1 purl, 2 plain, 1 purl.

Yoke starts with 3 bands each of alternate plain and purl, 2 rounds of each, but continuing the seam stitch through these bands after which the gusset starts under each arm.

The stitches are divided equally on to 3 needles for the shoulders and neck, the shoulder stitches are knitted in 2 rows plain, 2 rows purl as at bottom yoke, these 4 rows repeated 4 times.

Charts 79–81 show how yoke stitches are divided into 3 patterns for each shoulder and 3 patterns to be picked up for neck.

176 stitches are picked up for sleeves, making 8 patterns, the 3 rows of plain and purl rib are used to start and finish pattern which measures $3\frac{1}{2}$ in.; the rest of the sleeve worked in stocking stitch, the seam stitch of k1, p2, k1, is continued through centre of gusset and sleeve length 19 in., decreasing in sleeve every 6 rows each side of seam stitch.

The back of guernsey is same as front, finishing at shoulder with the 5 double bands of plain and purl. Shoulders grafted—neck and shoulder stitches picked up together and worked in same rib as welt and cuffs. Cuff 3 in. decreased to 92 stitches.

Measurements

Length $22\frac{1}{2}$ in. to base of neckband. Welt 1 in., plain knitting $9\frac{3}{4}$ in. Pattern of yoke starts with 2 rows purl, 2 rows plain, repeat twice. 11 in. yoke pattern and underarm gusset knitted in, starting with yoke.

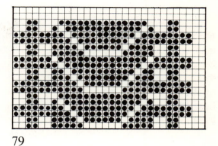

79

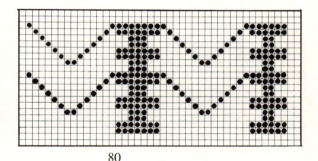

80

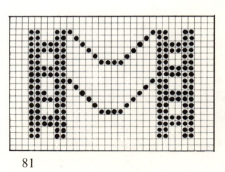

81

NORFOLK I, SHERINGHAM

Multiple of 28

This 'gansey' was knitted by Mrs Bishop of Sheringham about 1900 for her husband 'Tarr Bishop'. She always insisted on a tight fit, and when ganseys knitted for the children were pulled over their heads, they sometimes made the lobes of their ears bleed! She gave the family fittings, the first just before the pattern for correct width, the next for gussets, and then the arms.

The gansey could be re-knitted when worn thin, from practically any part, and made as new. She used 5 needles, see figure 82 and chart. It is wonderfully even in tension, and has worn to a lovely grey-blue through the action of sun, sea water, and time, and is really a Museum piece of fine knitting.

This is a repeat pattern of 16 rows, and is knitted in the round with seam stitches under the arms, from the welt and gussets, these are optional and give the wearer more room to work.

The same ridges start the pattern at the bottom, 3 in number consisting of 2 purl rounds and one plain round repeated twice, they are known as 'rigs' in Yorkshire, and the pattern called 'rig and fur' otherwise 'ridge and furrow' as in ploughing. The pattern is worked in purl stitch in these Norfolk jerseys.

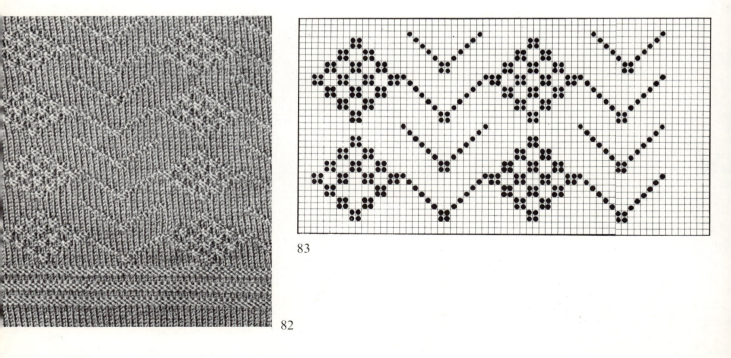

82

83

NORFOLK II, SHERINGHAM

400 stitches

Fisherman's gansey, in typical pattern worn by fishermen at Sheringham. This was knitted by Mrs Esther Nurse of Lower Bodham (a Sheringham lady) about 1950.

It was knitted in Patons 4-ply Behive fingering at a tension of 12 stitches and 20 rows to the inch. It took about ten to twelve weeks to knit.

Her father actually died wearing a gansey like this, it having to be cur off him as the gansey fitted like a glove.

Five needles were used in the making size 15 to 16.

Cast on in double wool for the welt k2, p2, for 2½ inches. Work 8 to 10 inches of stocking stitch (see figure 84) with a seam stitch up each side, under arm, dividing front and back. 3 ridges or rigs, as they are known in Norfolk, and 'rig and fur' ('ridge and furrow') in Yorkshire. All these Norfolk ganseys have these 3 ridges, 2 rounds purl, 2 rounds plain repeated twice. The body pattern follows, but seam stitch stops when pattern begins.

84

Work 3½ inches in pattern before stitches are divided equally for front and back, and worked separately to the shoulders where pattern finishes, and shoulders and neck stitches are divided into 3 equal quantities for the front and back. Each shoulder has 2 purl ridges, ending with 2 plain rows, this helps to shape neck. When both front shoulders are finished, work on back in same way, and cast off back and front shoulders together, forming another shoulder ridge. When the shoulders are joined, pick up neck and shoulder stitches about 148 to 150, and knit neck band in the round, and finish with 2 inches ribbing. Pick up stitches round armholes, they are 8½ inches deep, a 2 inch section of the pattern is worked round the top of the sleeves (see figure 84) with ribbing top and bottom. Continue sleeves on the round decreasing 1 stitch each side of seam stitch every 3 rows, until sleeve measures 15½ inches, knit a ribbed cuff. Full measure 18 inches.

86

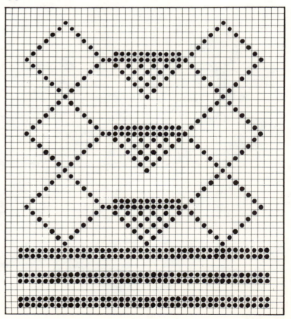

Figure 84 of the Sheringham gansey does not show the pattern clearly, but it gives the shape, and how the pattern is placed, and the shoulder ridges. Also the sleeve gusset ending in the sleeve pattern.

Length of gansey 24 inches.

Tension must be tested before starting to knit, as Norfolk ganseys are very finely knitted. If thicker wool and larger needles are used, fewer stitches will be needed.

87

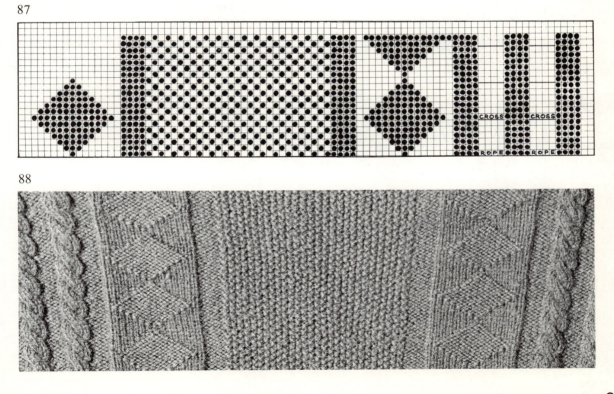

88

Caister, Lincolnshire

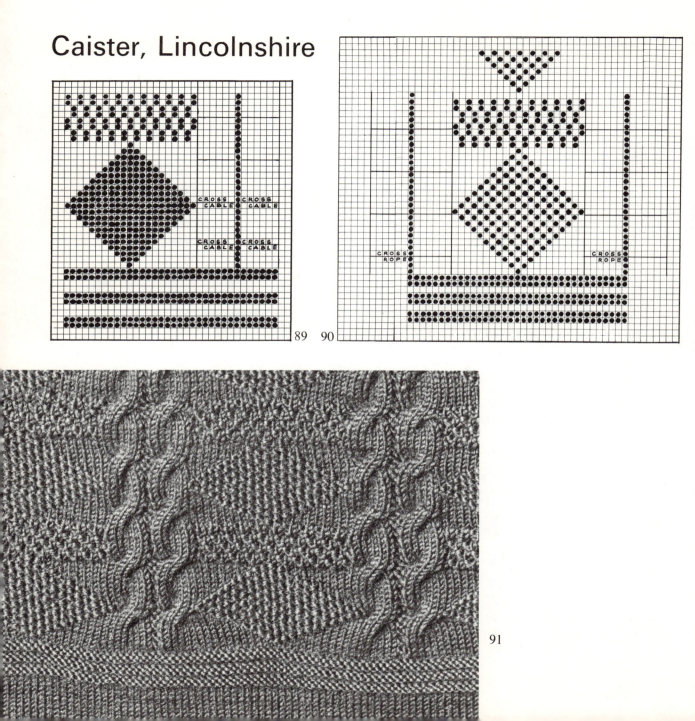

CROSS CABLE · CROSS CABLE

CROSS CABLE · CROSS CABLE

CROSS ROPE

CROSS ROPE

89 90

91

Musselburgh

On to Edinburgh from Berwick, passing Eyemouth—the home of a lovely guernsey, and I wondered how many patterns I was missing as we rushed past the tiny fishing villages in the train, but I was looking forward to finding some good material in Musselburgh.

Arriving at Fisherrow, a part of Musselburgh, I was directed down a side-street and the door was quickly opened by Mrs Williamson. Smiling and kind, she asked me in, and when she heard I had been sent by Lady Cecilia Howard I received a warm welcome, as he had knitted guernseys for her for years.

We talked about patterns, and I showed her all I had found amongst the Scottish fishermen. She told me my "knitten" was first class, and that I had all the patterns she knew, except one plait, and she showed me how that was knitted.

I asked her about the Musselburgh Festival, held once a year in September, and known as the 'Fishermen's Walk'. Mrs Williamson showed me newspaper cuttings and pictures. The following account describes the scene.

Fishermen Walk in the Sun Once More

The tradition among the townspeople of Musselburgh that rain never falls on the occasion of the annual Fishermen's Walk was borne out again this afternoon when hundreds of sightseers gathered to watch members of the fishing community take part in one of the burgh's most picturesque ceremonies. The Walk has been celebrated for more than 200 years to mark the end of the summer herring season at Fisherrow, and this afternoon, as in former years, there was a colourful scene as more than 400 fisherfolk in gala dress danced their way through streets gay with flags and bunting to the grounds of Pinkie House to hold their annual sports.

The women folk all wore gaily coloured shawls, many of them handed down in their families for generations, and the fisher doll banner and model boat all had a prominent part in the procession.

They were all so kind and friendly, and I had three offers of tea that afternoon in Musselburgh. The next day I went to Port Seton in the same bus and had a very dreary drive along the Forth side, only enlivened by seeing horses and jockeys lined up for the start of one of the Musselburgh races. I arrived at Port Seton to try to find someone to tell me about their Festival of the 'Burning of the Boats'—not a soul to be seen except a gang of workmen hacking up the road. I wandered down to the deserted harbour, containing only one half-submerged boat with two gulls asleep on the bows. I turned away, and at last found an old man who was quite willing to talk. He told me each autumn an old boat was burnt at their Festival and he thought this custom had been in vogue for hundreds of years.

It was probably one of the sacrifices of propitiation, to ensure a good yield from the sea. At Whitby the first fish caught each season is burnt, and at Musselburgh the first fish is given away to ensure good luck. These old Festivals and superstitions amongst the fisher people are most fascinating, and superstitions seems to abound along the coast.

SCOTTISH FLEET PATTERN I
Musselburgh

Multiple of 35

1st row (P1, k1) 3 times, p1, k6 for rope, (p1, k1) 3 times, (p1, k7) twice.

2nd row P3, k1, p3, k6, p3, k1, p3, k6, p1, k1, p1, k6.

3rd row (P1, k1) 3 times, p1, k6, (p1, k1) 3 times, p1, k5, p1, k3, p1, k5.

4th row P3, k1, p3, cross cable, p3, k1, p3, k4, (p1, k2) twice, p1, k4.

5th row (P1, k1) 3 times, p1, k6, (p1, k1) 3 times, p1, k3, p1, k2, p1, k1, p1, k2, p1, k3.

6th row P3, k1, p3, k6, p3, k1, p3, k2, p1, k2, p1, k3, (p1, k2) twice.

7th row (P1, k1) 3 times, p1, k6, (p1, k1) 4 times, (p1, k2) 4 times, p1, k1.

8th row P3, k1, p3, k6, p3, k1, p3, k3, p1, k2, p1, k1, p1, k2, p1, k3.

92

90

9th row (P1, k1) 3 times, p1, k6, (p1, k1) 3 times, (p1, k2) twice, p1, k3, (p1, k2) twice.

10th row P3, k1, p3, k6, p3, k1, p3, k4, (p1, k2) twice, p1, k4.

11th row (P1, k1) 3 times, p1, cross cable, (p1, k1) 3 times, p1, k3, p1, k2, p1, k1, p1, k2, p1, k3.

12th row P3, k1, p3, k6, p3, k1, p3, k5, p1, k3, p1, k5.

13th row (P1, k1) 3 times, p1, k6, (p1, k1) 3 times, p1, k4, (p1, k2) twice, p1, k4.

14th row P3, k1, p3, k6, p3, k1, p3, k6, p1, k1, p1, k6.

15th row (P1, k1) 3 times, p1, k6, (p1, k1) 3 times, p1, k5, p1, k3, p1, k5.

16th row P3, k1, p3, k6, p3, k1, p3, k7, p1, k7.

17th row (P1, k1) 3 times, p1, k6, (p1, k1) 3 times, p1, k6, p1, k1, p1, k6.

18th row P3, k1, p3, cross cable, p3, k1, p3, k15.

19th row (P1, k1) 3 times, p1, k6, (p1, k1) 3 times, (p1, k7) twice.

20th row P3, k1, p3, k6, p3, k1, p3, k15.

21st row (P1, k1) 3 times, p1, k6, (p1, k1) 3 times, p1, k15.

Continue pattern with chart to top of next tree, and when the two plain rows between tree patterns are finished, return to row 1.

This pattern is sometimes seen without the two plain rows between the trees; the top purl stitch of one tree coming next to the bottom purl stitch of tree above.

SCOTTISH FLEET PATTERN II
Musselburgh

Multiple of 48

1st row Moss 9 starting with k1, k8, p1, k8. Moss 9 starting p1, k6, p1, k6.

2nd row Moss 9, k7, p1, k1, p1, k7, moss 9, k5, p1, k1, p1, k5.

3rd row Moss 9, k6, m5, k6, m9, k4, p1, k3, p1, k4.

4th row M9, k5, m7, k5, m9, k3, (p1, k2) twice, p1, k3.

5th row (M9, k4) twice, m9, (k2, p1) twice, k1, p1, k2, p1, k2.

6th row M9, k3, m11, k3, m9, k1, p1, k2, p1, k3, p1, k2, p1, k1.

7th row M9, k2, m13, k2, m9, k3, p1, (k2, p1) twice, k3.

8th row M25, k1, m9, (k2, p1) twice, k1, p1, k2, p1, k2.

9th row M9, k2, m13, k2, m9, k4, p1, k3, p1, k4.

10th row M9, k3, m11, k3, m9, k3, (p1, k2) twice, p1, k3.

11th row (M9, k4) twice, m9, k5, p1, k1, p1, k5.

12th row M9, k5, m7, k5, m9, k4, p1, k3, p1, k4.

13th row M9, k6, m5, k6, m9, k6, p1, k6.

14th row M9, k7, m3, k7, m9, k5, p3, k5.

15th row M9, k8, p1, k8, m9, k6, p1, k6.

16th row M9, k8, p1, k8, m9, k13.

17th row As row 16.

Repeat from row 1.

93

SCOTTISH FLEET PATTERN III
Fisher Row

Multiple of 31

1st row (P1, k1) 3 times, p1, k6 for cable, (p1, k1) 3 times, p1, k11.

2nd row P3, k1, p3, k6, p3, k1, p3, k11.

3rd row (P1, k1) 3 times, p1, k6, (p1, k1) 3 times, (p1, k5) twice.

4th row P3, k1, k3, k6, p3, k1, p3, k5, p1, k5.

5th row (P1, k1) 3 times, p1, k6, (p1, k1) 3 times, p1, k4, p1, k1, p1, k4.

6th row P3, k1, p3, k6, p3, k1, p3, k4, p1, k1, p1, k4.

7th row (P1, k1) 3 times, p1, cross next 6 stitches for cable, (p1, k1) 3 times, p1, k3, (p1, k1) twice, p1, k3.

8th row P3, k1, p3, k6, p3, k1, p3, k3, (p1, k1) twice, p1, k3.

9th row (P1, k1) 3 times, p1, k6, (p1, k1) 3 times, p1, k2, (p1, k1) 3 times, p1, k2.

10th row P3, k1, p3, k6, p3, k1, p3, k2, (p1, k1) 3 times, p1, k2.

11th row (P1, k1) 3 times, p1, k6, (p1, k1) 9 times.

12th row P3, k1, p3, k6, p3, k1, p3, (k1, p1) 5 times, k1.

13th row (P1, k1) 3 times, p1, k6, (p1, k1) 3 times, p1, k2, (p1, k1), 3 times, p1, k2.

14th row P3, k1, p3, cross cable, p3, k1, p3, k2, (p1, k1) 3 times, p1, k2.

15th row (P1, k1) 3 times, p1, k6, (p1, k1) 3 times, p1, k3, (p1, k1) twice, p1, k3.

16th row P3, k1, p3, k6, p3, k1, p3, k3, (p1, k1) twice, p1, k3.

17th row (P1, k1) 3 times, p1, k6, (p1, k1) 3 times, p1, k4, p1, k1, p1, k4.

18th row P3, k1, p3, k6, p3, k1, p3, k4, p1, k1, p1, k4.

19th row (P1, k1) 3 times, p1, k6, (p1, k1) 3 times, (p1, k5) twice.

20th row P3, k1, p3, k6, p3, k1, p3, k5, p1, k5.

Repeat from row 1, crossing cable every 7th row.

94

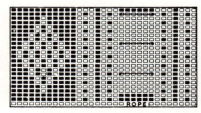

SCOTTISH FLEET PATTERN IV
Fisher Row

Multiple of 27

1st row (P1, k1) twice, p1, k6 for cable, (p1, k1) twice, p1, k11.

2nd row P5, k6, p5, k5, p1, k5.

3rd row (P1, k1) twice, p1, k6, (p1, k1) twice, p1, k4, p3, k4.

4th row P5, k6, p5, k3, p2, k1, p2, k3.

5th row (P1, k1) twice, p1, cross next 6 stitches for cable, (p1, k1) twice, p1, k2, p2, k3, p2, k2.

6th row P5, k6, p5, k1, p2, k5, p2, k1.

7th row (P1, k1) twice, p1, k6, (p1, k1) twice, p3, k7, p2.

8th row Same as row 6.

9th row Same as row 5, but do not cross cable.

10th row Same as row 4.

11th row Same as row 3.

12th row Same as row 2, crossing the cable, this must be done every 7th row.

Repeat from row 1.

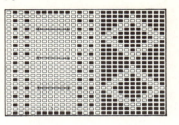

96   Scottish cables are often used on patterned backgrounds

SCOTTISH FLEET PATTERN V

Leith Diamond and Herring Bone

Multiple of 44

1st row (P1, k1) 3 times, p1, k4, (p1, k1) 3 times, p1, k4, (p1, k1) 4 times, (p1, k5) twice, p1, k1.

2nd row P3, k1, p3, k5, (p1, k1) twice, p1, k5, p3, k1, p3, k7, p1, k7.

3rd row (P1, k1) 3 times, p1, k5, (p1, k1) twice, p1, k5, (p1, k1) 3 times, p1, k5, (p1, k1) twice, p1, k5.

4th row P3, k1, p3, k6, p1, k1, p1, k6, p3, k1, p3, k4, p1, (k2, p1) twice, k4.

5th row (P1, k1) 3 times, p1, k6, p1, k1, p1, k6, (p1, k1) 3 times, p1, (k3, p1) 3 times, k3.

6th row P3, k1, p3, k7, p1, k7, p3, k1, p3, k2, p1, (k4, p1) twice, k2.

7th row (P1, k1) 3 times, (p1, k7) twice, (p1, k1) 3 times, p1, k1, (p1, k5) twice, p1, k1.

8th row P3, k1, p3, k6, p1, k1, p1, k6, p3, k1, p3, k7, p1, k7.

9th row (P1, k1) 3 times, p1, k6, p1, k1, p1, k6, (p1, k1) 3 times, p1, k5, (p1, k1) twice, p1, k5.

10th row P3, k1, p3, k5, (p1, k1) twice, p1, k5, p3, k1, p3, k4, (p1, k2) twice, p1, k4.

11th row (P1, k1) 3 times, p1, k5, (p1, k1) twice, p1, k5, (p1, k1) 3 times, p1, (k3, p1) 3 times, k3.

12th row P3, k1, p3, k4, (p1, k1) 3 times, p1, k4, p3, k1, p3, k2, p1, (k4, p1) twice, k2.

13th row (P1, k1) 3 times, p1, k4, (p1, k1) 3 times, p1, k4, (p1, k1) 3 times, p1, k1, p1, (k5, p1) twice, k1.

14th row P3, k1, p3, k3, (p1, k1) 4 times, p1, k3, p3, k1, p3, k7, p1, k7.

15th row (P1, k1) 3 times, p1, k3, (p1, k1) 4 times, p1, k3, (p1, k1) 3 times, p1, k5, (p1, k1) twice, p1, k5.

16th row P3, k1, p3, k2, (p1, k1) 5 times, p1, k2, p3, k1, p3, k4, (p1, k2) twice, p1, k4.

17th row (P1, k1) 3 times, p1, k2, (p1, k1) 5 times, p1, k2, (p1, k1) 3 times, p1, (k3, p1) 3 times, k3.

18th row P3, k1, p3, (k1, p1) 7 times, (k1, p3) twice, k2, p1, (k4, p1) twice, k2.

19th row (P1, k1) 15 times, (p1, k5) twice, p1, k1.

97

20th row P3, k1, p3, k2, (p1, k1) 5 times, p1, k2, p3, k1, p3, k7, p1, k7.

21st row (P1, k1) 3 times, p1, k2, (p1, k1) 5 times, p1, k2, (p1, k1) 3 times, p1, k5, (p1, k1) twice, p1, k5.

22nd row P3, k1, p3, k3, (p1, k1) 4 times, p1, k3, p3, k1, p3, k4, (p1, k2) twice, p1, k4.

23rd row (P1, k1) 3 times, p1, k3, (p1, k1) 4 times, p1, k3, (p1, k1) 3 times, (p1, k3) 4 times.

24th row P3, k1, p3, k4, (p1, k1) 3 times, p1, k4, p3, k1, p3, k2, (p1, k4) twice, p1, k2.

Repeat from row 1.

Fife

Travelling up North, I stayed at Upper Largo with the late Miss Rintoul, a great authority on bird life. She was also a keen gardener, and although we'd never met before we found we had many interests in common.

I went over to Anstruther in a gale of wind with frequent snowstorms. There is a quiet charm about the place, especially down by the harbourside. I called in at Mr Duncan's store and was able to buy some 6-ply black guernsey wool, and he was full of information, and said before the war he had women knitting for him the whole year round. He told me of a fisherman's wife who'd won a big knitting competition, and rather dubiously I set out to find her.

Passing the harbour, I noticed a fisherman varnishing a small boat, so I went across. He was wearing a very finely knitted guernsey with unusual shoulder straps—I asked him if he came south with the herring fleet, and he said 'yes', and was going to Whitby next year. I said I often went there, and he laughed and said we'd better meet and told me his boat was registered at Kirkcaldy, pronounced 'Kirkcoddy'—I said I'd look out for him! He went on varnishing, and I took down the pattern whilst he worked. The sleeves and cuffs were all worked in pattern, and it was a lovely piece of work, very finely knitted.

He sent me up to see his wife, but she was out, so I continued my search for the competition winner. At last I found the house, and she was delighted to show me her knitting. The prize piece was a lovely grey jersey, not a guernsey, but beautifully worked, and very fine. She told me she knitted all the guernseys for her husband and sons, who were away at sea. The kitchen was the real Scottish kind, warm and cosy, with a large double box-bed in the corner, painted yellowy brown.

After talking patterns for some time, she said would I like to see 'Granny in the attic', as she had been a great knitter in her time, and was eighty; so up we went, two flights of steep stairs, and she threw open a door at the top. I went in, and found the attic ran the full length of the house, and hanging from the rafters in all directions were fishing nets, and on the floor, coils of rope and beautifully made creels.

Granny was standing by a window at the far end, repairing a net. Yards and yards of net—she'd a netting shuttle in her right hand, and a small pair of scissors in her left. She worked at a tremendous pace—her hands flashing in and out, snipping and netting and talking at the same time, she spoke so fast I could hardly understand her.

She kept all the family nets repaired and at busy times worked in the attic the entire day—I was really sorry to say good-bye, but it was nearly their dinner time.

SCOTTISH FLEET PATTERN VI
Kirkcaldy

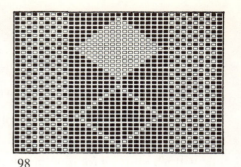

98

Multiple of 26

1st row K2, (p1, k1) 3 times, p1, k17, (p1, k1) 3 times, p1, k2.

2nd row (K1, p1) 4 times, k9, p1, k9, (p1, k1) 4 times.

3rd row K2, (p1, k1) 3 times, p1, k7, p1, k1, p1, k7, (p1, k1) 3 times, p1, k2.

4th row (K1, p1) 4 times, k7, p1, k3, p1, k7, (p1, k1) 4 times.

5th row K2, (p1, k1) 3 times, (p1, k5) 3 times, (p1, k1) 3 times, p1, k2.

6th row (K1, p1) 4 times, k5, p1, k7, p1, k5, (p1, k1) 4 times.

7th row K2, (p1, k1) 3 times, p1, k3, p1, k9, p1, k3, (p1, k1) 3 times, p1, k2.

8th row (K1, p1) 4 times, k3, p1, k11, p1, k3, (p1, k1) 4 times.

9th row K2, (p1, k1) 3 times, p1, k1, p1, k13, (p1, k1) 4 times, p1, k2.

10th row Same as row 8.
11th row Same as row 9.
12th row Same as row 8.
13th row Same as row 7.
14th row Same as row 6.
15th row Same as row 5.
16th row Same as row 4.
17th row Same as row 3.
18th row Same as row 2.

This diamond is knitted entirely in purl stitch. Follow chart till diamond is completed, then repeat from row 1.

SCOTTISH FLEET PATTERN VII
Anstruther

Multiple of 26

1st row P1, k1, p1, k13.
2nd row P3, k6, p1, k6.
3rd row P1, k1, p1, k5, p1, k1, p1, k5.
4th row P3, k4, (p1, k1) twice, p1, k4.
5th row P1, k1, p1, k3, (p1, k1) 3 times, p1, k3.
6th row P3, k2, (p1, k1) 4 times, p1, k2.
7th row (P1, k1) 8 times.
8th row Same as row 6.

9th row Same as row 5.
10th row Same as row 4.
11th row Same as row 3.
12th row Same as row 2.
13th row Same as row 1.
14th row P3, k13.
15th row P1, k1, p1, k13.

Repeat from row 2.

96

SCOTTISH FLEET PATTERN VIII
Anstruther (Mr Richie)

Multiple of 10

1st row *(K1, p1) twice, (k2, p1) twice, repeat from
*, (k1, p1) twice, k1.

2nd row K1, p3, k1, (p1, k2) twice, p3, k1, (p1, k2)
twice, p3, k1.

Repeat rows 1 and 2. These two rows form the
pattern.

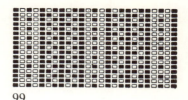

99

100

SCOTTISH FLEET PATTERN IX
Anstruther (Mr Richie)

Shoulder strap

Figure 101

1st row K25.

2nd row K1, p1, (k3, p1) 5 times, k3.

3rd row K2, p1, (k3, p1) 5 times, k2.

4th row (K3, p1) 6 times, k1.

5th row P1, k3, p1, (k3, p1) 5 times.

6th row Repeat from row 2. These 5 rows make up
the pattern.

19 rows are shown in the chart, but the shoulder
strap would have to be longer.

These directions are to show how to work the
pattern. In the Yorkshire guernseys, about 54
stitches are allowed for the shoulder strap—25
stitches are worked in pattern here, so another 29
or 30 stitches would be needed for a man's shoulder
strap.

Mr Ritchie's sleeves were worked in pattern
throughout to the cuff edge. They looked very nice.

A plait pattern was also seen at Anstruther
worked on a moss background. See Filey XI for
plait pattern.

101   Shoulder-strap pattern

SCOTTISH FLEET PATTERN X
Fife Jerseys

Figures 102–110

The following notes and diagrams were the work of the late Mrs Anstruther, who gave permission for them to be reproduced. They appeared in the *Scottish Country Woman*.

These diagrams give some of the traditional patterns worn by Fife fishermen. To be effective, the knitting should be very firm, 6-ply wool is generally used, and No. 13 or 14 pins. The wool is of a special navy blue dye that withstands salt water. The result is a garment rather like armour-plating, guaranteed to protect against wind and weather. The jerseys knitted by the good knitters in the fishing villages are wonderful pieces of work. The "setting in" of the sleeve, and the gusset under the arm, and the decreasing towards the cuff should all be studied by those who appreciate first-class knitting.

Notes on the diagrams

102 A simple counter-change pattern. The rib shown in   may also be used with this panel with good effect.

103 The diamond can either be used isolated as shown, or in a continuous criss-cross, or with smaller diamonds between the large ones.

104 This herring-bone pattern looks equally well the other way up, and is often used in Yorkshire in this way.

105 A neat cross-bar that looks effective in the finished garment.

106 Anchor pattern. A space equal to the length of the anchor should be left between the repeats.

107 The well-known kilt or flag pattern, which can also be used with a rib between the triangles. (See figure 114).

107 The zigzag can be used in various ways, this double line is known as 'Marriage Lines', or 'Ups and Downs'.

109 Heart-pattern can either be used by itslef, or interchanged with other patterns, such as the diamonds.

110 This triple cross-bar makes an interesting broken line right across the work.

In the diagrams the rib has been put in on each side of a panel, the better to show it up. Cable pattern is occasionally used, but it does not wear as well as the others on account of the crossing over of stitches, which puts a strain on the wool.

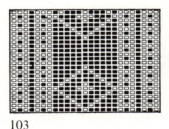

102

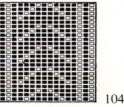

103

104

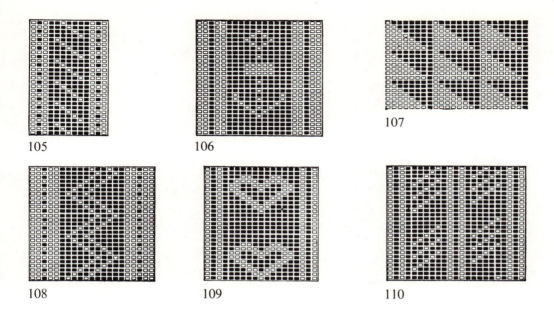

105   106   107

108   109   110

FISHERMAN'S JERSEY

Among the fishing fleets of Britain, the traditional clothing includes a heavy jersey knitted in thick wool on fine pins so that it becomes windproof and waterproof. There are traditional patterns for the different fishing fleets and anyone well versed in the subject can tell where a fisherman comes from by the pattern on his jersey. Here we give instructions for knitting a jersey with the anchor design worn by Fife fishermen. The sleeves are knitted from the top downwards so that when the wrists and elbows become worn they can be easily repaired. A gusset below the arm gives room and makes for easy movement. It is believed that this is the first time one of the traditional patterns for a fisherman's jersey has been written in book form. Hitherto, the women in the fishing villages have learned to knit these jerseys simply by being taught by word of mouth—one generation passing on the knowledge to another. The chart given at the end of the instructions shows some other designs of the Scottish fishing fleet which could be followed by expert knitters. We are indebted to Miss Sutherland, who is a professional designer of knitwear and a former member of the S.W.R.I., for translating these instructions from an actual fisherman's jersey.

Materials

24 oz 3-ply wool (used double throughout); four No. 13 knitting needles (points at both ends); two buttons.

Measurements

Chest, 42 in.; Length, 25 in.; Sleeve, 19 in. Tension: 1 pattern (18 stitches)=2½ in.

Abbreviations

K, knit; p, purl; st or sts, stitch or stitches; patt, pattern; cont, continue; stst, stocking stitch; dec, decrease(ing); inc, increase(ing); rep, repeat; beg, beginning.

NOTE. For 40 in. chest size use No. 14 knitting needles and work at tension of 1 pattern (18 stitches) to 2¼ in.

1st round *K13, p2, k1, p2. Repeat from * to end of round.

2nd round *K13, p5. Repeat from * to end of round.

3rd round *K6, p1, k6, p2, k1, p2. Repeat from * to end of round.

4th round *K5, p1, k1, p1, k5, p5. Repeat from * to end of round.

5th round *K4, p1, k1, p1, k1, p1, k4, p2, k1, p2. Repeat from * to end of round.

6th round *K3, p1, k5, p1, k3, p5. Repeat from * to end of round.

7th round *K2, p1, k3, p1, k3, p1, k2, p2, k1, p2. Repeat from * to end of round.

8th round *K1, p2, k7, p2, k1, p5. Repeat from * to end of round.

9th round *K1, p2, k3, p1, k3, p2, k1, p2, k1, p2. Repeat from * to end of round.

10th round *K1, p1, k9, p1, k1, p5. Repeat from * to end of round.

11th round *K6, p1, k6, p2, k1, p2. Repeat from * to end of round.

12th round As 2nd round.

13th round As 3rd round

Repeat last two rounds once more.

16th round As 2nd round.

17th round *K4, p5, k4, p2, k1, p2. Repeat from * to end of round.

18th round *K4, p5, k4, p5. Repeat from * to end of round.

19th round *K13, p2, k1, p2. Repeat from * to end of round.

20th round *K6, p1, k6, p5. Repeat from * to end of round.

21st round *K5, p1, k1, p1, k5, p2, k1, p2. Repeat from * to end of round.

22nd round As 20th round.

Repeat 1st and 2nd rounds once.

These 24 rounds form the pattern.

Front and back

Using wood double cast on 308 stitches and work in rounds of k2, p2 rib for 5 in.

Next round *Rib 18, increase in next stitch. Repeat from * to last 4 stitches, rib 4. (324 stitches).

Now continue in pattern until work measures 12 in. from beg.

Increase for underarm gusset

Work twice into centre rib stitch, work 9 patterns then increase again on centre rib stitch, work 9 more patterns to end of round.

Work three rounds keeping 2 stitches in stocking stitch above increase at each side and all other stitches in pattern.

Next round Work twice into each stocking stitch at either side and continue to keep all other stitches in pattern.

Work three rounds. (There will now be 4 stitches in stocking stitch at either side.)

Continue in this way increasing four more stitches on every 4th round and always increase on the stocking stitch edge next to rib until there are 26 stitches worked in stocking stitch for gusset.

Now at each side slip 26 gusset stitches worked in stocking stitch and 2 rib stitches at either side on to separate stitch holders. (30 stitches at each side.)

There will now be 157 stitches left on each side for front and back and from here each side is worked separately.

Front

Continue with front working in rows and keeping pattern correct until work measures 23½ in, ending inside of work facing.

Next row P52, turn.
*Next row Knit.
Next row Knit.
Next row Purl.
Next row Purl*.

Repeat from * to * six times.

Leave these 52 stitches to be grafted to back shoulder.

Return to remaining stitches, slip 53 centre stitches on to a stitch holder then work ridge pattern on remaining 52 stitches to correspond with opposite side.

Leave these 52 stitches to be grafted to back shoulder.

Back

Continue in pattern as for Front until work measures 23½ in. from beginning. Graft 52 stitches at each end to front shoulder and leave centre 53 stitches on a stitch holder.

Sleeves

Using wool double pick up and k52 stitches from pattern edge of front, 17 from shoulder edge and 52 from pattern edge of back, then work across the 30 stitches left at underarm. (151 stitches).

Arrange stitches evenly on three needles.

Using the rib stitches at either side of gusset as a guide to pattern, continue in pattern as for main part of Jersey on all stitches except gusset stitches which should still be worked in stocking stitch.

Decrease at each side of gusset on every 6th row until all gusset stitches are worked off. Continue in pattern until sleeve measures 16 in. or required length to cuff measured straight. (NOTE Last decrease on gusset will be on stitch only leaving even number of stitches). Then continue to decrease as before on either side of rib stitch until 90 stitches remain.

Next round *K7, k2 tog. Repeat from * to end of round. (80 stitches).

Continue in k2, p2, rib for 3 in.
Cast off in rib.

Neck band

Using wool double pick up and k8 stitches from centre left shoulder, work over the 53 stitches left at centre front in k2, p2 rib, pick up and k17 across right shoulder work across 53 stitches left at centre back then pick up and k9 stitches to centre left shoulder. Turn and cast on 8 stitches for underlap, rib across all stitches to last 8 stitches, k8. Work in rows and continue in rib but keeping 8 stitches in garter stitch at each end of row for 2½ in. At the same time make two buttonholes at front edge, one after ½-in. has been worked and another after 2 in. have been worked thus:

K3, cast off 4, work to end of row.

In next row cast on 4 stitches above those cast off in previous row.

Cast off. Sew on buttons to correspond with buttonholes.

NOTE This jersey should not be pressed.

Scottish Patterns

It has been a great pleasure collecting these patterns, and most of them were seen at Whitby and Scarborough during the East Coast herring season.

The pattern seen in figure 101 was taken from a lovely jersey shown at the Living Traditions Exhibition of Scottish Architecture and Crafts held in Edinburgh in 1951. It was a wonderfully planned and well-staged show, with a fishing village at one end, complete to a fisherman mending and making nets. He offered to teach me, but I already knew his craft, instead I asked him if I might have his guernsey pattern whilst he went on netting. This pattern is shown under Arbroath (figure 123). I found two others of interest. The first from Mallaig knitted by Mrs Wilson (figure 124), with the same shoulder strap as figure 123. When I got home I wrote to Mrs Wilson, asking her if she would lend me her guernsey for an illustration. Unfortunately the photograph did not do justice to her lovely work, as black wool is very difficult to portray and patterns do not show up, so I knitted the pattern in white, and it is shown in figure 124. This black 6-ply wool is lovely to knit, and much softer than English wool. Nearly all Scottish guernseys fasten with buttons on the shoulder and neck band, ensuring a much better shape when worn. They look so trim and smart when worn by the fishermen as best guernseys, and can be seen on Sundays, as the men gather in groups near the harbour, smoking and talking.

Another one seen at the Exhibition was shown by Catherine Gillies of Inverness, who kindly sent me the following notes on guernseys worn at Barra in the Hebrides.

'The complicated designs on fisherman's dark-blue jerseys round the British coast are not just haphazard, or worked in from whim. The Symbols have conveyed messages for several hundred years. In the Hebrides, for instance, the fishermen wear jerseys with a distinctive yoke.

The fancy is that the yoke represents the house or home. In the middle is an open diamond, representing a window. If the diamond has a heart inside it, that means 'the heart is in the home'. Closed diamonds, or 'nets', flank the central design with a double plait, meaning 'hoof prints in the sand'.

The yoke of the Hebrides jersey is defined by several rows of purl knitting, called 'poor man's wealth'—because it is so difficult to count. 'Steps' (to the house) lead up the middle of the lower part of the jersey. Double zigzags mean 'marriage lines' (ups and downs) and parallel zigzags the waves on which the fishermen sail. The double moss stitch panels represent 'sands'.

East Coast Scottish fishermen wear jerseys with designs running straight up and down. The designs, interspersed with cable (representing rope) or purl stitches, sometimes include the tree or 'fern' motif, as it is known, or the anchor symbol.

It is interesting to note that some of the Scottish patterns are circular instead of vertical, as in figure 127. The one shown is probably copied from those worn by members of the herring fleet. Another version is shown in figure 57, and in Scotland I have come across several other circular patterns. Figure 129 shows single moss stitch worked alternately with the Whitby pattern. The last one (figure 130) took me a long time to absorb, and I chased the man up and down the harbour side. I was only able to remember 4 different panels when he darted into The Fishermen's Inn, and I was not brave enough to follow!

SCOTTISH FLEET PATTERN XI
Zigzag pattern

Multiple of 14

1st row (P1, k1) twice, p1, k9.
2nd row P3, k2, p1, k8.
3rd row P1, k1, p1, k3, p1, k7.
4th row P3, k4, p1, k6.
5th row P1, k1, (p1, k5) twice.
6th row P3, k6, p1, k4.
7th row P1, k1, p1, k7, p1, k3.
8th row P3, k8, p1, k2.
9th row P1, k1, p1, k9, p1, k1.
10th row Same as row 8.
11th row Same as row 7.
12th row As row 6.
13th row As row 5.
14th row As row 4.
15th row As row 3.
16th row As row 2.
17th row Repeat from row 1.

111

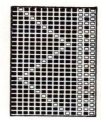

SCOTTISH FLEET PATTERN XII

Multiple of 12
1st row P2, k2, p2, k6, for cable. Repeat.
2nd row As row 1.
3rd row K2, p2, k2, k6, for cable.
4th row As row 3.
5th row Repeat from row 1; cross cable in this row
    and every 7th row.

112

113

SCOTTISH FLEET PATTERN XIII

Flag

1st row (P1, k1) 4 times,* p10, (k1, p1) 3 times, k1,*
    (this last stitch is not shown on the graph).
    Repeat between stars each row as needed.
2nd row P3, k1, p3, *k2, p11, k1, p3.*
3rd row (P1, k1) 3 times, p1, *k3, p8, (k1, p1) 3
    times.*
4th row P3, *k1, p3, k4, p9.*
5th row (P1, k1) 3 times, p1, *k5, p6, (k1, p1) 3
    times.*

6th row P3, *k1, p3, k6, p7.*
7th row (P1, k1) 3 times, p1, *k7, p4, (k1, p1) 3
    times.*
8th row P3, *k1, p3, k8, p5.*
9th row (P1, k1) 3 times, p1, *k9, p2, (k1, p1) 3
    times.*
10th row (P3, k1) twice, *p12, k1, p3, k1,* (this
    last stitch not shown on graph).
11th row (P1, k1) 3 times, p1, *k2, p9, (k1, p1) 3
    times.*
12th row P3, *k1, p3, k3, p10.*
13th row (P1, k1) 3 times, p1, *k4, p7, (k1, p1) 3
    times.*
14th row P3, *k1, p3, k5, p8.*
15th row (P1, k1) 3 times, p1, *k6, p5, (k1, p1) 3
    times.*
16th row P3, *k1, p3, k7, p6.*
17th row (P1, k1) 3 times, p1, *k8, p3, (k1, p1) 3
    times.*
18th row P3, *k1, p3, k9, p4.*

Repeat from row 1.

114   An elaborate version of Whitby flag

SCOTTISH FLEET PATTERN XIV

Figure 115

1st row **P2, k6, p2,* (k1, p1) 4 times, k6, p1, k5, p1, k7, p1, k5, p1, k6, (p1, k1) 4 times, p2, k6, p2.
Repeat from *.

2nd row P2, k6, p2, *(k1, p1) 4 times, (k5, p1) twice, k9, (p1, k5) twice, (p1, k1) 4 times, p2, k6, p2. Repeat.*

3rd row P2, k6, p2, *(k1, p1) 4 times, k4, p1, (k5, p1) 4 times, k4, (p1, k1) 4 times, p2, k6, p2. Repeat.*

4th row P2, k6, p2, *(k1, p1) 4 times, k3, p1, (k5, p1) twice, k1, (p1, k5) twice, p1, k3, (p1, k1) 4 times, p2, k6, p2. Repeat.*

5th row P2, cross cable, p2, *(k1, p1) 4 times, k2, p1, (k5, p1) twice, k3, (p1, k5) twice, p1, k2, (p1, k1) 4 times, p2, cross cable, p2. Repeat.*

6th row P2, k6, p2, *(k1, p1) 5 times, (k5, p1) 5 times, (k1, p1) 4 times, k1, p2, k6, p2. Repeat.*

These 6 rows make the pattern. Repeat from beginning of row 1** crossing the cables every 7th row. No graph given; it is the same pattern as for pattern XV, but centre pattern is worked singly.

115   Wide panels repeated round the guernsey

SCOTTISH FLEET PATTERN XV

Figure 118
Multiple of 68

1st row **P2, k6, p2, *(k1, p1) 4 times, k5, p2, (k8, p2) twice, k5, (p1, k1) 4 times, p2, k6, p2. Repeat from.*

2nd row P2, k6, p2, *(k1, p1) 4 times, k3, p2, k8, p2, k2, p2, k8, p2, k3, (p1, k1) 4 times, p2, k6, p2. Repeat from.*

3rd row P2, k6, p2, *(k1, p1) 4 times, k1, p2, k8,
p2, k6, p2, k8, p2, k1, (p1, k1) 4 times, p2, k6,
p2. Repeat.*

4th row P2, k6, p2, *(k1, p1) 4 times, k9, p2, k10,
p2, k9, (p1, k1) 4 times, p2, k6, p2. Repeat.*

5th row P2, k6, p2, *(k1, p1) 4 times, k7, p2, k14,
p2, k7, (p1, k1) 4 times, p2, k6, p2. Repeat.*

These 5 rows complete the pattern. Repeat from
row 1** crossing the cables in the next, and every
7th row afterwards.

116

SCOTTISH FLEET PATTERN XVI

Figure 118
Multiple of 36

117

1st row (P3, k1) twice, p2, k8, p3, k1, p3, k5, p1, k5.

2nd row (P1, k1) 4 times, p2, k8, (p1, k1) 3 times,
p1, k11.

3rd row P3, k1, p3, k2, p2, k7, p3, k1, p3, k5, p1, k5.

4th row (P1, k1) 3 times, p1, k3, p2, k6, (p1, k1) 3
times, p1, k4, p3, k4.

5th row P3, k1, p3, k4, p2, k5, p3, k1, p3, k3, p2,
k1, p2, k3.

6th row (P1, k1) 3 times, p1, k5, p2, k4, (p1, k1) 3
times, p1, k2. p2, k3, p2, k2.

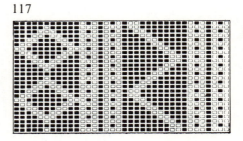

118   Zigzag and diamond pattern

7th row P3, k1, p3, k6, p2, k3, (p3, k1) twice, p2, k5, p2, k1.

8th row (P1, k1) 3 times, p1, k7, p2, k2, (p1, k1) 3 times, p3, k7, p2.

9th row P3, k1, p3, k8, p2, (k1, p3) twice, k1, p2, k5, p2, k1.

10th row (P1, k1) 3 times, p1, k8, p2, (k1, p1) 4 times, k2, p2, k3, p2, k2.

11th row P3, k1, p3, k7, p2, k2, p3, k1, p3, k3, p2, k1, p2, k3.

12th row (P1, k1) 3 times, p1, k6, p2, k3, (p1, k1) 3 times, p1, k4, p3, k4.

13th row P3, k1, p3, k5, p2, k4, p3, k1, p3, k5, p1, k5.

14th row (P1, k1) 3 times, p1, k4, p2, k5, (p1, k1) 3 times, p1, k11.

15th row P3, k1, p3, k3, p2, k6, p3, k1, p3, k5, p1, k5.

16th row (P1, k1) 3 times, p1, k2, p2, k7, (p1, k1) 3 times, p1, k4, p3, k4.

17th row (P3, k1) twice, k1, p2, k8, p3, k1, p3, k3, p2, k1, p2, k3.

18th row (P1, k1) 4 times, p2, k8, (p1, k1) 3 times, p1, k2, p2, k3, p2, k2.

19th row P3, k1, p3, k2, p2, k7, (p3, k1) twice, p2, k5, p2, k1.

20th row (P1, k1) 3 times, p1, k3, p2, k6, (p1, k1) 3 times, p3, k7, p2.

21st row P3, k1, p3, k4, p2, k5, (p3, k1) twice, p2, k5, p2, k1.

22nd row (P1, k1) 3 times, p1, k5, p2, k4, (p1, k1) 3 times, p1, k2, p2, k3, p2, k2.

23rd row P3, k1, p3, k6, p2, k3, p3, k1, p3, k3, p2, k1, p2, k3.

24th row (P1, k1) 3 times, p1, k7, p2, k2, (p1, k1) 3 times, p1, k4, p3, k4.

25th row P3, k1, p3, k8, p2, k1, p3, k1, p3, k5, p1, k5.

26th row (P1, k1) 3 times, p1, k8, p2, k1, (p1, k1) 3 times, p1, k11.

This pattern should now be clear to the knitter; it is not a repeat pattern as the diamonds do not work out accurately with the zigzag.

SCOTTISH FLEET PATTERN XVII
Garden Town, Banff

Multiple of 21

1st row P1, k2, for rope, p1, k8, p1, k8. Repeat.
2nd row P1, k2, p1, k7, p1, k1, p1, k7. Repeat.
3rd row P1, k2, p1, k6, p1, k3, p1, k6. Repeat.
4th row P1, cross cable, (1 over 1), (p1, k5) 3 times. Repeat.
5th row P1, k2, p1, k4, p1, k7, p1, k4. Repeat.
6th row P1, k2, p1, k3, p1, k9, p1, k3. Repeat.
7th row (P1, k2) twice, p1, k11, p1, k2. Repeat.
8th row P1, k2, p1, k1, p1, k13, p1, k1. Repeat.

Repeat from row 1, crossing rope every 4th row.

119

120   Herringbone and one-over-one cable

SCOTTISH FLEET PATTERN XVIII
Zigzag

Multiple of 16

1st row (K2, p2) twice, k1, p1, k6.
  Repeat each row as needed.
2nd row (K2, p2) twice, k2, p1, k5.
3rd row P2, k2, p2, k5, p1, k4.
4th row P2, k2, p2, k6, p1, k3.
5th row (K2, p2) twice, k5, p1, k2.
6th row (K2, p2) twice, k6, p1, k1.
7th row P2, k2, p2, k7, p1, k2.
8th row P2, k2, p2, k6, p1, k3.
9th row (K2, p2) twice, k3, p1, k4.
10th row (K2, p2) twice, k2, p1, k5.
11th row P2, k2, p2, k3, p1, k6.

  Repeat zigzag panel from row 2, but the double
moss must be followed in pattern from the graph
till the 21st row is reached, the moss stitch directions
are then the same as row 1.

121

SCOTTISH FLEET PATTERN XIX
Zigzag

Multiple of 16

1st row P2, k3, p2, k1, p2, k8. Repeat.
2nd row P7, k2, p2, k7. Repeat.
3rd row (P2, k3) twice, p2, k6. Repeat.
4th row P7, k4, p2, k5. Repeat.
5th row P2, k3, p2, k5, p2, k4. Repeat.
6th row P7, k6, p2, k3. Repeat.
7th row P2, k3, p2, k7, p2, k2. Repeat.
8th row P7, k8, p2, k1. Repeat.
9th row As row 7. Repeat.
10th row As row 6. Repeat.
11th row As row 5.
12th row As row 4.
13th row As row 3.
14th row As row 2.
15th row Repeat from row 1.

122

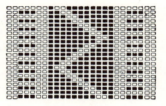

SCOTTISH FLEET PATTERN XX
Arbroath Marriage Lines

Multiple of 18

1st row P3, k9, p1, k3, p1, k1.
2nd row P1, k1, p1, k8, p1, k3, p1, k2.
3rd row P3, k7, (p1, k3) twice.
4th row P1, k1, p1, k6, p1, k3, p1, k4.
5th row P3, k5, p1, k3, p1, k5.
6th row P1, k1, p1, k4, p1, k3, p1, k6.
7th row P3, k3, p1, k3, p1, k7.
8th row P1, k1, p1, k2, p1, k3, p1, k8.
9th row P3, k1, p1, k3, p1, k9.
10th row As row 8.
11th row As row 7.
12th row As row 6.

13th row As row 5.
14th row As row 4.
15th row As row 3.
16th row As row 2.
17th row Repeat from row 1.

123

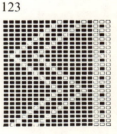

For shoulder strap chart and directions follow Scottish Fleet XI, Anstruther.

SCOTTISH FLEET PATTERN XXI
Mallaig

Figure 124
Multiple of 21

1st row P3, k2, p3, k6, p1, k6.
2nd row P1, k1, p1, k2, p1, k1, (p1, k6) twice.
3rd row P3, k2, p3, k5, p1, k1, p1, k5.
4th row P1, k1, p1, k2, p1, k1, p1, k5, p1, k1, p1, k5.
5th row P3, k2, p3, k4, (p1, k1) twice, p1, k4.
6th row P1, k1, p1, k2, p1, k1, p1, k4, (p1, k1) twice, p1, k4.
7th row P3, k2, p3, k3, (p1, k1) 3 times, p1, k3.

8th row P1, k1, p1, k2, p1, k1, p1, k3, (p1, k1) 3 times, p1, k3.
9th row (P3, k2) twice, p1, k1, p1, k3, p1, k1, p1, k2.
10th row (P1, k1, p1, k2) twice, p1, k1, p1, k3, p1, k1, p1, k2.
11th row P3, k2, p3, (k1, p1) twice, k5, (p1, k1) twice.
12th row P1, k1, p1, k2, (p1, k1) 3 times, p1, k5, (p1, k1) twice.
13th row (P3, k2) twice, p1, k1, p1, k3, p1, k1, p1, k2.
14th row (P1, k1, p1, k2) twice, p1, k1, p1, k3, p1, k1, p1, k2.
15th row P3, k2, p3, k3, (p1, k1) 3 times, p1, k3.
16th row P1, k1, p1, k2, p1, k1, p1, k3, (p1, k1) 3 times, p1, k3.
17th row P3, k2, p3, k4, (p1, k1) twice, p1, k4.
18th row P1, k1, p1, k2, p1, k1, p1, k4, (p1, k1) twice, p1, k4.
19th row P3, k2, p3, k5, p1, k1, p1, k5.
20th row P1, k1, p1, k2, p1, k1, p1, k5, p1, k1, p1, k5.

Repeat from row 1.

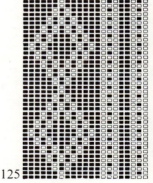

124 A very fine guernsey knitted in black wool by Mrs Wilson. It was shown at an Edinburgh exhibition

SCOTTISH FLEET PATTERN XXII
Diamond and Diagonal

Figure 127
Knit 2 rows. Purl 3 rows. Knit 3 rows. Purl 3 rows. Knit 2 rows.

1st row (P1, k19) twice, p1.
2nd row K1, p1, k17, p1, k1, p1, k17, p1.
3rd row K2, p1, k15, p1, k3, p1, k15, p1, k1.
4th row K3, p1, k13, p1, k5, p1, k13, p1, k2.

5th row K4, p1, k11, p1, k7, p1, k11, p1, k3.
6th row K5, (p1, k9) twice, p1, k4.
7th row K6, p1, k7, p1, k11, p1, k7, p1, k5.
8th row K7, p1, k5, p1, k13, p1, k5, p1, k6.
9th row K8, p1, k3, p1, k15, p1, k3, p1, k7.
10th row K9, p1, k1, p1, k17, p1, k1, p1, k8.
11th row K10, p1, k19, p1, k9.

126 Diamond and diagonal. The chart is worked in double stitch

127 The pattern is worked in single stitch

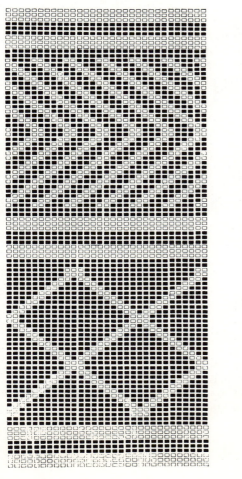

12th row As row 10.
13th row As row 9.
14th row As row 8.
15th row As row 7.
16th row K5, (p1, k9) 3 times, p1, k4.
17th row As row 5.
18th row As row 4.
19th row As row 3.
20th row As row 2.
21st row As row 1.
22nd row As row 2.
23rd row As row 3.
24th row As row 4.
25th row As row 5.
26th row K5, (p1, k9) 3 times, p1, k4.
27th row As row 7.
28th row As row 8.
29th row As row 9.
30th row As row 10.
31st row As row 11.

Knit 2 rows. Purl 3 rows. Knit 3 rows. Purl 3 rows. Knit 2 rows.

Diagonal panel
1st row K3, p1. Repeat as many times as needed.
2nd row K2, p1, *k3, p1,* Repeat.*
3rd row K1, p1, *k3, p1.* Repeat.*
4th row P1, *k3, p1.* Repeat.*

Repeat these 4 rows 4 times.

Second half of diagonal
1st row K1, p1, *k3, p1.* Repeat.*
2nd row K2, p1, *k3, p1.* Repeat.*
3rd row K3, p1. Repeat.
4th row P1, k3. Repeat.

Repeat these 4 rows 4 times, and start pattern again from *. These two panels are repeated alternately up the guernsey and the diamond pattern is worked round the sleeves half-way between shoulder and elbow.

Chart 126 shows this pattern worked double.

SCOTTISH FLEET PATTERN XXIII

Figure 126

A chart is given of this pattern from which the knitter can work; it is double instead of single as in figure 127 and looks very rich when finely knitted.

SCOTTISH FLEET PATTERN XXIV

Figure 129

This pattern is one of the exceptions, as the panels go round the guernsey instead of from the neck downwards. Two patterns only are used alternately, and if worked on fine needles it is most attractive. I found it on a broad fisherman, knitted in black wool, and it at once caught my eye.

Knit 3 rows. Purl 3 rows. Repeat these 6 rows twice, then knit 3 more rows.

Work a panel in moss stitch of 33 rows.

Knit 3 rows. Purl 3 rows. Repeat these 6 rows twice, then knit 3 more rows.

Second panel

1st row P2, k2, repeated.
2nd row Knit plain.
3rd row K2, p2, repeated.
4th row Knit plain.

Repeat these 4 rows 7 times. Continue in pattern for 1 more row, making 33 rows in all.

The pattern starts about 3 inches above the welt, leaving seam stitches at the sides, and working in gussets, as given in other directions. The pattern continues to neck band. The shoulders are worked in 2 rows purl, 2 rows plain, alternately.

Sleeves to elbow or wrist.

129   Another type of guernsey pattern

128

SCOTTISH FLEET PATTERN XXV

First panel

Figure 130(1)

Multiple of 30

Knit 2 rows. Purl 2 rows. Repeat once between stars. Knit 2 rows.

9th row P2, k2. Repeat.

10th row Same as row 9.

Knit next 2 rows.

Repeat last 4 rows 5 times.

Knit 2 rows. Purl 2 rows. Repeat once, Knit 2 rows.

Second panel

Figure 130 (2)

1st row P1, k1, p1, *k21, p1, k1, p1.* Repeat.

2nd row P3, k21, p3.

Repeat last two rows twice.

7th row P1, k1, p1, *k10, p1, k10, p1, k1, p1.*

8th row P3, (k9, p3) twice.* k1.

9th row P1, k1, p1, *k8, p2, k1, p2, k8, p1, k1, p1.

10th row P3, k7, p2, k3, p2, k7, p3.*

11th row P1, k1, p1, *k6, p2, k5, p2, k6, p1, k1, p1.*

12th row P3, k5, p2, k7, p2, k5, p3.*

13th row P1, k1, p1, *k4, p2, k9, p2, k4, p1, k1, p1.

14th row P3, *k3, p2, k11, p2, k3, p3.*

15th row P1, k1, p1, *k2, p2, k13, p2, k2, p1, k1, p1.

16th row P3, *k1, p2, k15, p2, k1, p3.*

17th row P1, k1, p1, *k2, p2, k13, p2, k2, p1, k1, p1.*

18th row P3, *k3, p2, k11, p2, k3, p3.*

19th row P1, k1, p1, *k4, p2, k9, p2, k4, p1, k1, p1.*

20th row P3, *k5, p2, k7, p2, k5, p3.*

21st row P1, k1, p1, *k6, p2, k5, p2, k6, p1, k1, p1.*

22nd row P3, k7, p2, k3, p2, k7, p3.*

23rd row P1, k1, p1, *k8, p2, k1, p2, k8, p1, k1, p1.*

24th row P3, *(k9, p3) twice.*

25th row P1, k1, p1, *k10, p1, k10, p1, k1, p1.*

26th row P3, *k21, p3.*

27th row P1, k1, p1, *k21, p1, k1, p1.

Repeat last two rows twice.

Knit 2 rows. Purl 2 rows. Repeat last 4 rows once. Knit 2 rows.

130   The six panels are worked round the guernsey

3

2

1

Third panel

Figure 130 (3)

1st row *K4, p2.* Repeat between stars.
2nd row K3, p2, *k4, p2.* Repeat.
3rd row K2, p2, *k4, p2.* Repeat.
4th row K1, p2, *k4, p2.*
5th row *P2, k4.* Repeat.
6th row P1, k4, *p2, k4.* Repeat.

Pattern now repeats from row 1. Continue until 26 rows have been completed.
Knit 2 rows. Purl 2 rows. Repeat these 4 rows once. Knit 2 rows.

Fourth panel

Figure 130 (4)

1st row *(K1, p1) twice, k1, moss 20, (k1, p1) twice.*
2nd row *K1, p3, k1, moss 20, k1, p3.*

Repeat these 2 rows 13 times.
Knit 2 rows. Purl 2 rows. Repeat these 4 rows once. Knit 4 rows.

Fifth panel

Figure 130 (5)

1st row (K6, p2) 4 times. Repeat as often as needed.
2nd row K5, p2, (k6, p2) 3 times, k1.
3rd row K4, p2, (k6, p2) 3 times, k2.
4th row K3, p2, (k6, p2) 3 times, k3.
5th row K2, p2, (k6, p2) 3 times, k4.
6th row K1, p2, (k6, p2) 3 times, k5.
7th row (P2, k6) 4 times.
8th row P1, (k6, p2) 4 times, k6, p1.
9th row (K6, p2) 4 times.
10th row K5, p2, (k6, p2) 3 times, k1.
11th row Knit.
13th and 14th rows Purl.
14th row Knit.
15th row K5, p2, (k6, p2) 3 times.
16th row (K6, p2) 3 times, k6, p1.
17th row P1, (k6, p2) 3 times, k6.
18th row (P2, k6) 3 times, p2, k5.
19th row K1, (p2, k6) 3 times, p2, k4.
20th row K2, (p2, k6) 3 times, p2, k3.
21st row K3, (p2, k6) 3 times, p2, k2.
22nd row K4, (p2, k6) 3 times, p2, k1.
23rd row K5, (p2, k6) 3 times, p2.
24th row (K6, p2) 4 times.

Knit 4 rows. *Purl 2 rows. Knit 2 rows.* Repeat* once.

Sixth panel

Figure 130 (6)

1st row *(K1, p1) twice, k1, (p2, k2) 5 times, (k1, p1) twice.*

115

2nd row *K1, p3, k22, p3.*

3rd row (K1, p1) twice, k3, (p2, k2) 4 times, p2, (k1, p1) twice.

4th row Same as row 2. Repeat these 4 rows six times.

Knit 2 rows. Purl 2 rows. Repeat last 4 rows once. Knit 2 rows.

If more panels are needed, the two at the bottom can be repeated, and one of the panels used as decoration on the sleeves between shoulder and elbow. The shoulders should be worked alternately in 2 plain rows, 2 purl rows, to match the dividing lines between the panels.

The welt should also be worked in this way, and is also used in the Staithes guernsey, figure 68.

SCOTTISH FLEET PATTERN XXVI
Tree and Bars

Figure 131

Multiple of 39

1st row P1, k1, p1, k6, p1, k1, p1, k5, (p1, k1) twice, p1, k5, p1, k1, p1, k6, p1, k1, p1.

2nd row (M3, k6) twice, p3, (k6, m3) twice.

3rd row M3, k6, m3, k7, p1, k7, m3, k6, m3.

4th row Repeat row 3 once.

5th row M3, k6, m3, k15, m3, k6, m3.

Repeat row 5 twice, crossing cables in row 7, and in every 7th row afterwards.

8th row *M3, k6, m3, k1, p13, k1, m3, k6, m3.

Repeat row 8 twice.

11th row M3, k6, m3, k15, m3, k6, m3.

Repeat last row twice.

14th row M3, cross cable, m3, k1, p13, k1, m3, cross cable, m3.

Repeat last row twice without crossing cables.

17th row M3, k6, m3, k15, m3, k6, m3.

Repeat last row twice.

20th row M3, k6, m3, k7, p1, k7, m3, k6, m3.

21st row M3, cross cable, m3, k6, p3, k6, m3, cross cable, m3.

22nd row M3, k6, m3, k5, (p1, k1) twice, p1, k5, m3, k6, m3.

23rd row M3, k6, m3, k4, (p1, k2) twice, p1, k4, m3, k6, m3.

24th row M3, k6, m3, k3, p1, k2, p3, k2, p1, k3, m3, k6, m3.

25th row M3, k6, m3, (k2, p1) twice, k1, p1, k1, (p1, k2) twice, m3, k6, m3.

26th row M3, k6, m3, k1, p1, (k2, p1) 4 times, k1, m3, k6, m3.

27th row M3, k6, m3, k3, p1, k2, p3, k2, p1, k3, m3, k6, m3.

28th row M3, cross cable, m3, (k2, p1) twice, k1, p1, k1, (p1, k2) twice, m3, cross cable, m3.

29th row M3, k6, m3, k4, p1, (k2, p1) twice, k4, m3, k6, m3.

30th row M3, k6, m3, k3, p1, k2, p3, k2, p1, k3, m3, k6, m3.

31st row M3, k6, m3, k5, (p1, k1) twice, p1, k5, m3, k6, m3.

32nd row M3, k6, m3, k4, p1, k2, p1, k4, m3, k6, m3.

33rd row (M3, k6) twice, p3, (k6, m3) twice.

34th row M3, k6, m3, k5, (p1, k1) twice, p1, k5, m3, k6, m3.

35th row M3, cross cable, m3, k6, p3, k6, m3, cross cable, m3.

36th row M3, k6, m3, k7, p1, k7, m3, k6, m3.

Repeat last row once.

38th row M3, k6, m3, k15, m3, k6, m3.

Repeat this row twice.
Repeat pattern from row 8.*

131

SCOTTISH FLEET PATTERN XXVII
Flag and Bar

Figure 133

1st row *K17, (p1, k1) 4 times, p13, (k1, p1) 3 times. Repeat pattern in each row as needed.

2nd row K17, p3, k1, p3, k3, p13, k1, p3.

3rd row K17, (p1, k1) 3 times, p1, k5, p9, (k1, p1) 3 times.

4th row K2, p13, k2, p3, k1, p3, k7, p9, k1, p3.

5th row K17, (p1, k1) 3 times, p1, k9, p5, (k1, p1) 3 times.

6th row K17, p3, k1, p3, k11, p5, k1, p3.

7th row K17, (p1, k1) 3 times, p1, k13, (p1, k1) 3 times, p1.

8th row K2, p13, k2, (p3, k1) twice, p15, k1, p3.

9th row K17, (p1, k1) 3 times, p1, k3, p11, (k1, p1) 3 times.

10th row K17, p3, k1, p3, k5, p11, k1, p3.

11th row K17, (p1, k1) 3 times, p1, k7, p7, (k1, p1) 3 times.

12th row K2, p13, k2, p3, k1, p3, k9, p7, k1, p1.

13th row K17, (p1, k1) 3 times, p1, k11, p3, (k1, p1) 3 times.

14th row K17, p3, k1, p3, k13, p3, k1, p3.

Repeat from row 1.

The purl bar of 13 stitches does not repeat correctly—this bar is worked every 4th row and can be followed from the chart.

132

133

SCOTTISH FLEET PATTERN XXVIII

This pattern was worn by a Scottish fisherman, but the cable and Betty Martin stitch are seen at Whitby, and the diamond is often used at Flamborough. It can be worked from the Whitby graph figure 62. The diamond is shown in Flamborough V and directions for knitting are given with that pattern.

134

The Isles of Aran

A fisherman's guernsey in cable
and cross-over patterns

These islands lie off the west coast of Ireland on the outer edge of Galway Bay. There are three main islands, Inishmore, Inishmaan or Middle Island, and Inisheer.

The people of Aran have lived here for centuries and have made their living by the cultivation of the land, entailing really hard work as there is only a thin covering of soil over the rock surface, and often no soil at all. Great use is made of the seaweed to enrich and manure their crops.

They also trade with the mainland in cattle, and many difficulties arise in getting them into the small boats, the cattle swimming out and then being hauled aboard with ropes.

The islanders live in an unspoilt world of their own, carrying on their work without hindrance in an atmosphere of peace, very unusual nowadays. Communication with the mainland is often cut off by heavy Atlantic seas, and the difficulty of transferring passengers and baggage from the steamer to a coracle in a heavy swell is, in fact, often an impossible feat. But in fine weather, summer visitors are a source of income.

The island women weave their own tweed and make a type of belt called a 'criss' which is woven over the foot, in very bright colours and most attractive patterns.

The women are justly famous for their knitting, and Aran jerseys are unique and fascinating in design. They are like other generations of guernsey knitters in our islands, as the patterns are never written down, but handed on in families.

The highly skilled knitters turn out lovely work, but sometimes, with a true Irish touch of 'nothing really matters', their knitting shows mistakes, always found in the simple patterns, and a careless nonchalance in the crossing of their cables!

The more intricate the pattern, the more perfect the knitting, and their best work is of the highest standard. Some of the interlaced or plaited patterns seen to have originated from the designs found on Irish stones and crosses—the latter are most impressive and rich in their decoration.

Other patterns used are:
Cables, representing fishing ropes.
Diamonds, the shape of the fishing net mesh.
Honeycomb, which is a tribute to the hard-working bee.
Moss Stitch, represents local mosses, sometimes called 'Poor Man's Wealth'.
Trellis, shows small fields fenced with stone.
Zigzag, forked lightning, or cliff paths.
Marriage Lines, depict the ups and downs of married life.
Tree of Life, or Fern Stitch, have great importance attached to them, and with Trinity Stitch they have a religious significance as well.

The original Aran knitting wools were spun, and dyed locally. Green from the mosses, brown from the seaweed, and grey and cream colour from the stones and pebbles.

Wool and knitting leaflets can be obtained from:

STAR WOOL STORES
8 Donaghadee Road, 16 Central Avenue,
Bangor, County Down, Northern Ireland.

CASH & CO.
Patrick Street, Cork.

A.N.I. Ltd.
7 St Michael's Mansions, Ship Street, Oxford.

These Aran knitters group their patterns very cleverly and use the travelling stitch, both plain and crossed, singly or in pairs and trebles, running across the surface of the knitting, and also use it in crossovers. Cable stitch is worked in with great effect among the other patterns.

Some of the knitters embellish their work with 'bobbles', knitted in as the work progresses; they certainly add a richness and character, but many are distinctly over-bobbled, thus detracting from the pattern and making it fussy and tiresome. These jerseys have caused me many sleepless nights, working out the patterns from pictures and drawings, and even from tracings of pictures! They are too lovely to be lost, and some record must be kept before they become a forgotten craft.

The following directions have been worked in sections, and in no case is the whole Guernsey pattern given. Experienced knitters can follow these directions and apply them as they wish. Nearly all the patterns repeat across the front and back, but in some cases the fronts and backs are different. They are not knitted on the round on fine needles, as in our guernseys, but two needles are used and the back and front are joined up the seams afterwards. There is a certain amount of shaping under the arms, and of course in the sleeves; and the latter are carried out in the same pattern as the body, though often in a smaller version, or part of the pattern is left out, to fit the shape of the sleeves. In nearly all the elaborate jerseys the welts show decoration in relation to the patterns used.

A circular needle can be used for knitting the body, changing to a set of needles at the armholes and for the sleeves.

Some of the simple patterns are charming for children's jerseys.

The Aran cap, shown in figure 160, would be lovely for a child—full directions are given for knitting this cap. When I took it to be photographed I left it with an assistant; it was described in her notes as 'Mrs Thompson's tea cosy'!

Abbreviations used in Aran patterns

m1: make a stitch.

s1: slip a stitch.

s1f or ssf: slip 1 stitch on to a spare needle and drop to front of work.

s2f: slip 2 in same manner, up to 6 stitches.

s1b or ssb: slip 1 stitch on to a spare needle and drop to back of work.

s2b or more stitches are slipped in same way.

kss: knit slip stitch.

k2ss: knit 2 slip stitches, or more.

pss: purl slip stitch.

p2ss: purl 2 stitches.

k1b: knit through the back of the stitch, or k2b (or more), through the back of the stitches.

p1b up to p6b: purl through the back of the stitches —working through the backs of the stitches gives a very rich, raised effect, and is known as cross stitch.

kssb: knit a slip stitch through the back. K6ssb. This may be found under cables, and is worked the same way.

k 1st ssb: knit first slip stitch through back of stitch.

p 2nd ss: purl second slip stitch, on spare needle.

Two different methods of making bobbles are given under Aran VIII and IX, the other method, Aran, XII.

( ): Brackets usually mean a repeat of pattern inside the brackets. The number of repeats follows the brackets.

*: Stars denote repetition of pattern.

twist or tw: knit into second stitch on left-hand needle, then into the first stitch, slip both stitches off needle together. Used in Aran VIII.

moss or m3, 4 or 5: work in moss stitch.

wf: wool forward.

psso: pass slip stitch over.

ARAN PATTERN I

Figure 136

This pattern shows a good use of cables and double moss stitch dia'onds. It is interesting to note the way this diamond is worked by Aran knitters with an outline stitch on a purl background. In English and Scottish guernseys it is knitted on a plain background, as shown in Leith, figure 97. The cable shown on the right of the picture and in the sleeve varies its point of crossing. The same fault is seen in the single crossover pattern.

Single cross-over pattern
Seen each side of centre panel.

Multiple of 8

1st row (P2, k1) twice, p2.
2nd row (K2, p1) twice, k2.

Repeat these two rows 4 times.

11th row P2, s1f, p1, kss, s1b, k1, pss, p2.
12th row K3, p2, k3.
13th row P3, s1f, k1, kss, p3.
14th row K3, p2, k3.
15th row P2, s1b, k1, pss, s1f, p1, kss, p2.
16th row Same as row 2.

Repeat these 16 rows.

Centre panel

Multiple of 35

1st row P2, k9, p5, k1, p1, k1, p5, k9, p2.
2nd row *K2, p9, k5, p1, k1, p1, k5, p9, k2.
3rd row P2, s3b, k1, k3ss, k1, s1f, k3, kss, p4, s1b, k1, pss, k1, s1f, p1, kss, p4, s3b, k1, k3ss, k1, s1f, k3, kss, p2.
4th row K2, p9, k4, (p1, k1) twice, p1, k4, p9, k2.
5th row P2, k9, p3, s1b, k1, pss, k1, p1, k1, s1f, p1, kss, p3, k9, p2.
6th row K2, p9, k3, p1, (k1, p1) 3 times, k3, p9, k2.
7th row P2, s3b, k1, k3ss, k1, s1f, k3, kss, p2, s1b, k1, pss, (k1, p1) twice, k1, s1f, p1, kss, p2, s3b, k1, k3ss, k1, s1f, k3, kss, p2.

8th row K2, p9, k2, (p1, k1) 4 times, p1, k2, p9, k2.
9th row P2, k9, p1, s1b, k1, pss, (k1, p1) 3 times, k1, s1f, p1, kss, p1, k9, p2.
10th row K2, p9, (k1, p1) 6 times, k1, p9, k2.
11th row P2, cross cable, (as in rows 3 and 7), s1b, k1, pss, (k1, p1) 4 times, k1, s1f, p1, kss, cross cable, p2.
12th row K2, p10, (k1, p1) 5 times, k1, p10, k2.
13th row P2, k9, s1f, p1, kss, (p1, k1) 4 times, p1, s1b, k1, pss, k9, p2.
14th row K2, p9, (k1, p1) 6 times, k1, p9, k2.
15th row P2, cross cable, p1, s1f, p1, kss, (p1, k1) 3 times, p1, s1b, k1, pss, p1, cross cable, p2.
16th row K2, p9, k2, (p1, k1) 4 times, p1, k2, p9, k2.
17th row P2, k9, p2, s1f, p1, kss, (p1, k1) twice, p1, s1b, k1, pss, p2, k9, p2.
18th row K2, p9, k3, (p1, k1) 3 times, p1, k3, p9, k2.
19th row P2, cross cable, p3, s1f, p1, kss, p1, k1, p1, s1b, k1, pss, p3, cross cable, p2.
20th row K2, p9, k4, (p1, k1) twice, p1, k4, p9, k2.
21st row P2, k9, p4, s1f, p1, kss, p1, s1b, k1, pss, p4, k9, p2.
22nd row K2, p9, k5, p1, k1, p1, k5, p9, k2.
23rd row P2, cross cable, p5, s2f, k1, knit 1st stitch on spare needle, purl 2nd stitch, p5, cross cable, p2.
24th row K2, p9, k6, p2, k5, p9, k2.
25th row P2, k9, p5, k1, s1f, p1, kss, p5, k9, p2.

Repeat pattern from row 2*.

Repeat single cross-over pattern and diamond as on right side of figure

124

ARAN JERSEY PATTERN II

Centre panel

Figure 137

18 stitches

1st row K1b, p5, k1b, p1, (k1b) twice, p1, k1b, p5, k1b.

2nd row P1b, k5, p1b, k1, (p1b) twice, k1, p1b, k5, p1b.

3rd row *K1b, p4, (s1b, k1b, pss) twice, (ssf, p1, kssb) twice, p4, k1b.

4th row P1b, k4, p1b, k1, p1b, k2, p1b, k1, p1b, k4, p1b.

5th row K1b, p3, (s1b, k1b, pss) twice, p2, (s1f, p1, kssb) twice, p3, k1b.

6th row P1b, k3, p1b, k1, p1b, k4, p1b, k1, p1b, k3, p1b.

7th row K1b, p2, s1b, k1b, pss, s1b, k1b, kss, p4, s1f, k1b, kssb, s1f, p1, kssb, p2, k1b.

8th row P1b, k2, p1b, k1, (p1b) twice, k4, (p1b) twice, k1, p1b, k2, p1b.

9th row K1b, p1, (s1b, k1b, pss) twice, s1f, p1, kssb, p2, s1b, k1b, pss, (s1f, p1, kssb) twice, p1, k1b.

10th row (P1b, k1) twice, p1b, (k2, p1b) 3 times, k1, p1b, k1, p1b, k1, p16.

11th row K1b, (s1b, k1b, pss) twice, p2, s1f, p1, kssb, s1b, k1b, pss, p2, (ssf, p1, kssb) twice, k1b.

137　Cross-over cross-stitch patterns

12th row (P1b) twice, k1, p1b, k4, s1f, p1b, pssb, k4, p1b, k1, (p1b) twice.

13th row K1b, (s1f, p1, kssb) twice, p2, s1b, k1b, pss, s1f, p1, kssb, p2, (s1b, k1b, pss) twice, k1b.

14th row (P1b, k1) twice, p1b, (k2, p1b) 3 times, (k1, p1b) twice.

15th row K1b, p1, (s1f, p1, kssb) twice, s1b, k1b, pss, p2, s1f, p1, kssb, (s1b, k1b, pss) twice, p1, k1b.

16th row P1b, k2, p1b, k1, (p1b) twice, k4, (p1b) twice, k1, p1b, k2, p1b.

17th row K1b, p2, s1f, p1, kssb, s1f, purl next knit stitch, kssb, p4, (s1b, k1b, pss) twice, p2, k1b.

18th row P1b, k3, p1b, k1, p1b, k4, p1b, k1, p1b, k3, p1b.

19th row K1b, p3, (s1f, p1, k1b) twice, p2, (s1b, k1b, pss) twice, p3, k1b.

20th row P1b, k4, p1b, k1, p1b, k2, p1b, k1, p1b, k4, p1b.

21st row K1b, p4, (s1f, p1, kssb) twice, (s1b, k1b, pss) twice, p4, k1b.

22nd row P1b, k5, p1b, k1, s1f, p1b, pssb, k1, p1b, k5, p1b.

Repeat pattern from row 3.

138

Side panel

42 stitches

1st row *P2, (k1b, p1) 3 times, k1b, p2, k1b, p1, k1b, p4, k1b, p1, k1b.*

Repeat once between stars.

2nd row ** *P1b, k1, p1b, k4, p1b, k1, p1b, k2, (p1b, k1) 3 times, p1b, k2.*

3rd row *P2, (k1b, p1) 3 times, k1b, p2, k1b, p1, s1f, p1, kssb, p2, ssb, k1b, pss, p1, k1b.*

4th row *(P1b, k2) 4 times, (p1b, k1) 3 times, p1b, k2.*

5th row *P2, (k1b, p1) 3 times, (k1b, p2) twice, s1f, p1, kssb, s1b, k1b, pss, p2, k1b.*

6th row *P1b, k3, p2b, k3, p1b, k2, (p1b, k1) 3 times, p1b, k2.*

7th row *P2, (k1b, p1) 3 times, k1b, p2, k1b, p3, s1f, k1b, kssb, p3, k1b.*

8th row *P1b, k3, (p1b) twice, k3, p1b, k2, (p1b, k1) 3 times, p1b, k2.*

9th row *P2, (k1b, p1) 3 times, (k1b, p2) twice, s1b, k1b, pss, s1f, p1, kssb, p2, k1b.*

10th row *(P1b, k2) 4 times, (p1b, k1) 3 times, p1b, k2.*

11th row *P2, slip 3 stitches on to spare needle, drop to front, knit into back of next purl stitch, purl next knit stitch, knit into back of next purl stitch, purl next stitch, knit into back of first stitch on spare needle, purl next stitch, knit into back of 3rd stitch, p2, k1b, p1, s1b, k1b, pss, p2, s1f, p1, kssb, p1, k1b.*

12th row *P1b, k1, p1b, k4, p1b, k1, p1b, k2, (p1b, k1) 3 times, p1b, k2.*

13th row *P2, (k1b, p1) 3 times, k1b, p2, k1b, s1b, k1b, pss, p4, s1f, p1, kssb, k1b.*

14th row *(P1b) twice, k6, (p1b) twice, k2, (p1b, k1) 3 times, p1b, k2.*

15th row *P2, (k1b, p1) 3 times, k1b, p2, k1b, s1f, p1, kssb, p4, s1b, k1b, pss, k1b.*

Repeat from row 2**.

ARAN PATTERN III

(1) Pattern and Moss Stitch at each side

Cast on about 140 stitches for front.

11 stitches

1st row P1, k1b, p1, k1, p1, k5, p1.

2nd row K1, p5, k1, p1, k1, p1b, k1.

3rd row *P1, k1b, p1, k1, m1, p1, s1, k1, psso, k3, p1.

4th row K1, p4, k1, p2, k1, p1b, k1.

5th row P1, k1b, p1, k1, m1, k1, p1, s1, k1, psso, k2, p1.

6th row (K1, p3) twice, k1, p1b, k1.

7th row P1, k1b, p1, k1, m1, k2, p1, s1, k1, psso, k1, p1.

8th row K1, p2, k1, p4, k1, p1b, k1.

9th row P1, k1b, p1, k1, m1, k3, p1, s1, psso, p1.

10th row K1, p1, k1, p5, k1, p1b, k1.

11th row P1, k1b, p1, s1, k1, psso, k3, p1, k1, m1, p1.

12th row K1, p2, k1, p4, k1, p1b, k1.

13th row P1, k1b, p1, s1, k1, psso, k2, p1, k1, m1, k1, p1.

14th row (K1, p3) twice, k1, p1b, k1.

15th row P1, k1b, p1, s1, k1, psso, k1, p1, k1, m1, k2, p1.

16th row K1, p4, k1, p2, k1, p1b, k1.

17th row P1, k1b, p1, s1, k1, psso, p1, k1, m1, k3, p1.

18th row K1, p5, k1, p1, k1, p1b, k1.

Repeat from 3rd row.*

(2) Cross-over side panels

20 stitches

1st row K1b, (p1, k2) twice, p1, k1b, p3, s2f, k2ss, p3, k1b.

2nd row P1b, p2, s1f, p2, kss, s2b, k1, p2ss, k2, p1b, (k1, p2) twice, k1, p1b.

3rd row K1b, p1, (k2, p1) twice, k1b, (p2, k2) twice, p2, k1b.

4th row P1b, (k2, p2) twice, k2, p1b, (k1, p2) twice, k1, p1b.

5th row K1b, p1, s2f, p1, k2, k2ss, p1, k1b, (p2, k2) twice, p2, k1b.

6th row P1b, (k2, p2) twice, k2, p1b, k1, s1f, p2, kss, p2, k1, p1b.

7th row K1b, (p1, k2) twice, p1, k1b, (p2, k2) twice, p2, k1b.

8th row P1b, (k2, p2) twice, k2, p1b, (k1, p2) twice, k1, p1b.

9th row *K1b, (p1, k2) twice, p1, k1b, p2, s3f, p1, k2, k2ss, pss, (on spare needle), p2, k1b.

10th row P1b, k3, p4, k3, p1b, (k1, p2) twice, k1, p1b.

11th row K1b, (p1, k2) twice, p1, k1b, p2, s1b, k2, pss, s2f, p1, k2ss, p2, k1b.

12th row P1b, (k2, p2) twice, k2, p1b, (k1, p2) twice, k1, p1b.

13th row K1b, p1, s2f, p1, k2, k2ss, p1, k1b, (p2, k2) twice, p2, k1b.

14th row P1b, (k2, p2) twice, k2, p1b, k1, p4, k2, p1b.

15th row K1b, p1, s1b, k2, pss, k2, p1, k1b, (p2, k2) twice, p2, k1b.

16th row P1b, (k2, p2) twice, k2, p1b, (k1, p2) twice, k1, p1b.

Repeat from row 9*.

(3) Side panel

18 stitches

1st row K1b, p6, s2f, k2, k2ss, p6, k1b.

2nd row P1b, k6, p4, k6, p1b.

3rd row *K1b, p5, s1b, k2, pss, s2f, p1, k2ss, p5, k1b.

4th row P1b, k5, p2, k2, p2, k5, p1b.

5th row K1b, p4, s1b, k2, pss, p2, s2f, p1, k2ss, p4, k1b.

6th row P1b, k4, (p2, k4) twice, p1b.

7th row K1b, p3, s1b, k2, pss, k4, s2f, p1, k2ss, p3, k1b.

8th row P1b, k3, p2, k1, p4, k1, p2, k3, p1b.

9th row K1b, p2, s1b, k2, pss, s1b, k2, kss, s2f, k1, k2ss, s2f, p1, k2ss, p2, k1b.

10th row P1b, k2, p2, k1, p6, k1, p2, k2, p1b.

11th row K1b, p1, s1b, k2, pss, s1b, k2, kss, k2, s2f, k1, k2ss, s2f, p1, k2ss, p1, k1b.

12th row P1b, k1, p2, k1, p8, k1, p2, k1, p1b.

13th row K1b, p1, k1, s1f, p1, kss, s2f, p1, k2ss, k2, s1b, k2, pss, s1b, k1, pss, k1, p1, k1b.

14th row P1b, (k1, p2) twice, k1, p6, (k1, p1) twice, k1, p1b.

15th row K1b, p1, k1, p1, s1f, p1, kss, s2f, p1, k2ss, s1b, k2, pss, s1b, k1, pss, p1, k1, p1, k1b.

16th row P1b, k1, p1, k1, p1, k1, p4, k1, p1, k2, p1, k1, p1b.

17th row K1b, p1, s1f, p1, kss, s1b, k1, pss, p1, s2f, k2, k2ss, p1, s1f, p1, kss, s1b, k1, pss, p1, k1b.

18th row P1b, k2, s1b, k1, kss, k2, p4, k2, s1f, k1, kss, k2, p1b.

After row 18 is finished, repeat from row 3.*

(4) Waved ribbon pattern each side of centre

8 stitches

1st row P2, k4, p2.

2nd row K2, p4, k2.

Repeat these 2 rows once.

5th row P2, s2b, k2, k2ss, p2.

6th row K2, p4, k2.

Repeat first 4 rows once.

11th row P2, s2f, k2, k2ss, p2.

12th row K2, p4, k2.

Repeat from row 1.

The rib is crossed alternately from right to left, then left to right; the same ridge always on top.

Centre panel

(5) Trellis

Figure 140

24 stitches

1st row P1, k1b, p3, k2, (p4, k2) twice, p3, k1b, p1.

2nd row K1, p1b, k3, s1f, p1, pss, (k4, s1f, p1, pss) twice, k3, p1b, k1.

3rd row P1, k1b, p2, (s1b, k1b, pss, s1f, p1, kss, p2) 3 times, k1b, p1.

4th row K1, p1b, (k2, p1) 6 times, k2, p1b, k1.

5th row P1, k1b, p1, (s1b, k1, pss, p2, s1f, p1, kssb) 3 times, p1, k1b, p1.

6th row K1, p1b, k1, p1, (k4, s1f, p1, pss) twice, k4, p1, k1, p1b, k1.

7th row P1, k1b, p1, s1f, p1, kssb, (p2, s1b, k1b, pss, s1f, p1, kssb) twice, p2, s1b, k1b, pss, p1, k1b, p1.

8th row K1, p1b, (k2, p1) 6 times, k2, p1b, k1.

9th row P1, k1b, (p2, s1f, p1, kss, s1b, k1, pss) 3 times, p2, k1b, p1.

Repeat from row 2.

139

140   Trellis pattern, cable and ribbon stitch

ARAN PATTERN IV

142 Back of the same guernsey. In trellis with figure-of-eight centres, double cross-overs and plait welts and collar in 'Tree of Life'

Tree pattern

Figures 141 and 142

(1) Welt pattern

13 stitches

1st row K4, p3, k3b, p3.

2nd row K3, p3b, k3, p4.

3rd row K4, p2, s1b, k1b, pss, k1b, s1f, p1, kssb, ps.

4th row *K2, (p1b, k1) twice, p1b, k2, p4.

5th row K4, p1, s1b, k1b, pss, p1, k1b, p1, s1f, p1, kssb, p1.

6th row K1, p1b, k2, p1b, k2, p1b, k1, p4.

7th row K4, s1b, k1b, pss, p1, k3b, p1, s1f, p1, kssb.

8th row P1b, k2, p3b, k2, p1b, k4.

9th row K4, p2, s1b, k1b, pss, k1b, s1f, p1, kssb, p2.

Repeat from row 4.* This pattern forms welt, cuffs and collar. Pattern for latter must be worked on the inside, to show when turned over.

When the welt is finished work one row of purl across from right to left starting row 1 of body pattern on the inside. The directions are given in sequence: 3 moss stitches (1) side panel. (2) centre panel. (3) side panel. 3 moss. Increase as needed at side in moss. Irish moss is described in Filey pattern VII figure 29.

Front side pattern

(2) Cross-overs and Cable Stitch

32 stitches

Used back and front

1st row *K2, (p1b, k1, p1b, k2) twice, p8, k2, (p1b, k1, p1b, k2) twice.

2nd row P2, (k1b, p1, k1b, p2) twice, k8, p2, (k1b, p1, k1b, p2) twice.

3rd row K2, (p1b, k1, p1b, k2) twice, p8, k2, (p1b, k1, p1b, k2) twice.

4th row P2, (k1b, p1, k1b, p2) twice, s2b, k2, k2ss, s2f, k2, k2ss, p2, (k1b, p1, k1b, p2) twice.

5th row K2, (p1b, k1, p1b, k2) twice, p8, k2, (p1b, k1, p1b, k2) twice.

6th row P2, (k1b, p1, k1b, p2) twice, k8, p2, (k1b, p1, k1b, p2) twice.

Repeat last two rows once.

9th row K2, (p1b, k1, p1b, k2) twice, s2f, p2, p2ss, s2b, p2, p2ss, k2, (p1b, k1, p1b, k2) twice.

10th row P2 (slip next 3 stitches on to spare needle and drop to the front, decrease next 2 purl stitches by slipping one stitch over the other, knit into the back of this purl stitch, purl the next stitch, knit into the back of the next purl stitch, and purl next stitch. Then knit into the back of the first stitch on spare needle, purl the next, knit into the back of the third stitch, P2, K8, P2.

Repeat once between brackets, the pattern, finishing on P2. This row crosses the pattern, and is repeated every 15th row.

After row 4 the cable is crossed every 5th row.

11th row K2, (p1b, k1) 3 times, p1b, k2, p8, k2, (p1b, k1) 3 times, p1b, k2.

12th row P2, k1b, p1, k1b, increase one by lifting, purl this increase and the next stitch, k1b, p1, k1b, p2, k8, p2, k1b, p1, k1b, increase one by lifting, purl this increase and the next stitch, k1b, p1, k1b, p2.

Repeat from row 1.*

(3) Centre front panel

35 stitches

Purl one row and start pattern next row on the inside.

1st row P5, k1, (p1b) 3 times, k1, p11, k1, p11, k1, p1, k1, (p1b) 3 times, k1, p5.

2nd row K5, k1b, p1, (k1b) 3 times, p1, k1b, k11, k1b, p1, (k1b) 3 times, p1, k1b, k5.

3rd row P5, p1b, k1, (p1b) 3 times, k1, p1b, p11, p1b, k1, (p1b) 3 times, k1, p1b, p5.

4th row K4, (s1b, k1b, pss) twice, k1b, (s1f, p1, kssb) twice, k9, (s1b, k1b, pss) twice, k1b, (s1f, p1, kssb) twice, k4.

5th row P4, (p1b, k1) 4 times, p1b, p9, (p1b, k1) 4 times, p1b, p4.

6th row K3, (s1b, k1b, p22) twice, (k1b 3 times, (s1f, p1, kssb) twice, k7, (s1b, k1b, pss) twice, (k1b) 3 times, (s1f, p1, kssb) twice, k3.

7th row P3, (p1b, k1) twice, (p1b) 3 times, (k1, p1b) twice, p7, (p1b, k1) twice, (p1b) 3 times, (k1, p1b) twice, p3.

8th row K2, (s1b, k1b, pss) 3 times, k1b, (s1f, p1, kssb) 3 times, k5, (s1b, k1b, pss) 3 times, k1b, (s1f, p1, kssb) 3 times, k2.

9th row P2, (p1b, k1) 6 times, p1b, p5, (p1b, k1) 6 times, p1b, p2.

10th row K1, (s1b, k1b, pss) 3 times, (k1b) 3 times, (s1f, p1, kssb) 3 times, k3, (s1b, k1b, pss) 3 times, (k1b) 3 times, (s1f, p1, kssb) 3 times, k1.

11th row P1, (p1b, k1) 3 times, (p1b) 3 times, (k1, p1b) 3 times, p3, (p1b, k1) 3 times, (p1b) 3 times, (k1, p1b) 3 times, p1.

12th row *(S1b, k1b, pss) 4 times, k1b, (s1f, p1, kssb) 4 times, k1b.

13th row (P1b, k1) 8 times, (p1b) 3 times, (k1, p1b) 8 times.

14th row S1f, k1, kssb, (s1f, p1, kssb) 3 times, k1b, (s1b, k1b, pss) 4 times, k1b, (s1f, p1, kssb) 4 times, k1b, (s1b, k1b, pss) 3 times, s1b, k1b, kss.

15th row P1, (p1b, k1) 3 times, (p1b) 3 times, (k1, p1b) 8 times, (p1b) twice, (k1, p1b) 3 times, p1.

16th row K1, s1f, k1, kssb, (s1f, p1, kssb) twice, p1, k1b, p1, (s1b, k1b, pss) 3 times, (k1b) 3 times, (s1f, p1, kssb) 3 times, p1, k1b, p1, (s1b, k1b, pss) twice, s1b, k1b, kss, k1.

17th row P2, (p1b, k1) 7 times, (p1b) 3 times, (k1, p1b) 7 times, p2.

18th row K2, s1f, k1, kssb, (s1f, p1, kssb) twice, k1b, (s1b, k1b, pss) 4 times, k1b, (s1f, p1, kssb) 4 times, k1b, (s1b, k1b, pss) twice, s1b, k1b, kss, k2.

19th row P3, (p1b, k1) twice, (p1b) 3 times, (k1, p1b) 8 times, (p1b) twice, (k1, p1b) twice, p3.

20th row K3, s1f, k1, kssb, s1f, p1, kssb, p1, k1b, p1, (s1b, k1b, pss) 3 times, (k1b) 3 times, (s1f, p1, kssb) 3 times, p1, k1b, p1, s1b, k1b, pss, s1b, k1b, kss, k3.

21st row P4, (p1b, k1) 6 times, (k1b) 3 times, (k1, p1b) 6 times, p4.

22nd row K4, s1f, k1, kssb, s1f, p1, kssb, k1b, (s1b, k1b, pss) 4 times, k1b, (s1f, p1, kssb) 4 times, k1b, s1b, k1b, pss, s1b, k1b, kss, k4.

23rd row P5, p1b, k1, (p1b) 3 times, (k1, p1b) 8 times, (p1b) twice, k1, p1b, p5.

24th row K5, s1f, k1, kssb, p1, k1b, p1, (s1b, k1b, pss) 3 times, (k1b) 3 times, (s1f, p1, kssb) 3 times, p1, k1b, p1, s1b, k1b, kss, k5.

25th row P6, (p1b, k1) 5 times, (p1b) 3 times, (k1, p1b) 5 times, p6.

26th row K6, s1f, k1, kssb, k1b, (s1b, k1b, pss) 4 times, k1b, (s1f, p1, kssb) 4 times, k1b, s1b, k1b, kss, k6.

27th row P7, (p1b) 3 times, (k1, p1b) 7 times, k1, (p1b) 3 times, p7.

28th row K6, s1b, k1b, pss, k1b, s1f, p1, kssb, purl next knit stitch, (s1b, k1b, pss) twice, (k1b) 3 times, (s1f, p1, kssb) twice, purl next knit stitch, s1b, k1b, pss, k1b, s1f, p1, kssb, k6.

29th row P6, (p1b, k1) 5 times, (p1b) 3 times, (k1, p1b) 5 times, p6.

30th row K5, s1b, k1b, pss, (k1b) 3 times, s1f, p1, kssb, p1, (s1b, k1b, pss) twice, k1b, (s1f, p1, kssb) twice, p1, s1b, k1b, pss, (k1b) 3 times, s1f, p1, kssb, k5.

31st row P5, p1b, k1, (p1b) 3 times, (k1, p1b) 7 times, k1, (p1b) 3 times, k1, p1b, p5.

Repeat from row 12.

32nd row K4, (s1b, k1b, pss) twice, k1b, (s1f, p1, kssb) twice, p1, s1b, k1b, pss, (k1b) 3 times, s1f, p1, kssb, p1, (s1b, k1b, pss) twice, k1b, (s1f, p1, kssb) twice, k4.

33rd row P4, (p1b, k1) 6 times, (p1b) 3 times, k1, (p1b) 6 times, p4.

34th row K3, (s1b, k1b, pss) twice, (k1b) 3 times, (s1f, p1, kssb) twice, p1, s1b, k1b, pss, k1b, s1f, p1, kssb, s1f, p1 and slip stitch on spare needle to back, knit next stitch back, purl stitch on spare needle, s1b, k1b, pss, (k1b) 3 times, (s1f, p1, kssb) twice, k3.

35th row P3, (p1b, k1) twice, (p1b) 3 times, (k1, p1b) 8 times, (p1b) twice, (k1, p1b) twice, p3.

36th row K2, (s1b, k1b, pss) 3 times, k1b, (s1f, p1, kssb) 3 times, p2, k1b, p2, (s1b, k1b, pss) 3 times, k1b, (s1f, p1, kssb) 3 times, k2.

37th row P2, (p1b, k1) 6 times, (p1b, k2) twice, (p1b, k1) 6 times, p1b, p2.

38th row K1, (s1b, k1b, pss) 3 times, (k1b) 3 times, (s1f, p1, kssb) 3 times, p1, k1b, p1, (s1b, k1b, pss) 3 times, (k1b) 3 times, (s1f, p1, kssb) 3 times, k1.

39th row P1, (p1b, k1) 3 times, (p1b) 3 times, (k1, p1b) 3 times, k1, (p1b, k1) twice, (k1, p1b) 3 times, k1, (p1b) 3 times, (k1, p1b) 3 times, p1.

Repeat from row 12.

ARAN PATTERN V OPENWORK

Trinity Stitch

Next armhole

Multiple of 24

Cast on stitches divisible by 4, plus 4 edge stitches. First row is knitted on wrong side.

1st row K2*, (k1, p1, k1) into the next stitch, making 3, pass wool in front of work and purl 3 together. Pass wool to back * repeat between stars ending row k2.

2nd row Purl.

3rd row K2 *Purl 3 together (k1, p1, k1) into the next stitch.* Repeat between stars ending row k2.

4th row Purl.

Repeat from row 1.* 4 rows make the pattern.

Front side panel

Cross-over pattern

24 stitches

1st row P4, k4b, p8, k4b, p4.

2nd row K4, p4b, k8, p4b, k4.

3rd row P3, s1b, k2b, pss, s2f, p1, k2ssb, p6, s1b, k2b, pss, s2f, p1, k2ssb, p3.

4th row K3, p2b, k2, p2b, k6, p2b, k2, p2b, k3.

5th row P2, *s1b, k2b, pss, p2, s2f, p1, k2ssb,* p4, repeat between * and * once; finish row p2.

6th row K2, (p2b, k4) 3 times, p2b, k2.

7th row P1, *s1b, k2b, pss, p4, s2f, p1, k2ssb, p2*, repeat once, finish p1.

8th row K1, p2b, k6, p2b, k2, p2b, k6, p2b, k1.

9th row S1b, k2b, pss, p6, s2f, p1, k2ssb, s1b, k2b, pss, p6, s2f, p1, k2ssb.

10th row P2b, k8, s2f, p2b, p2ssb, k8, p2b.

11th row S2f, p1, k2b, p6, s1b, k2b, pss, s2f, p1, k2ssb, p6, s1b, k2b, pss.

12th row K1, p2b, k6, p2b, k2, p2b, k6, p2b, k1.

13th row P1, s2f, p1, k2ssb, p4, s1b, k2b, pss, p2, s2f, p1, k2ssb, p4, s1b, k2b, pss, p1.

14th row K2, (p2b, k4) 3 times, p2b, k2.

15th row P2, s2f, p1, k2ssb, p2, s1b, k2b, pss, p4, s2f, p1, k2ssb, p2, s1b, k2b, pss, p2.

16th row K3, p2b, k2, p2b, k6, p2b, k2, p2b, k3.

17th row P3, s2f, p1, k2ssb, s1b, k2b, pss, p6, s2f, p1, k2ssb, s1b, k2b, pss, p3.

18th row K4, s2f, p2b, p2ssb, k8, s2f, p2b, p2ssb, k4.

Repeat from row 3.*

143   Front view, knitted in heavy wool.
Trellis openwork pattern and bobbles

Centre panel front

Figure 143
22 stitches

1st row ***K**8, k2 tog, wf, k2, wf, s1, k1, psso, k8.
2nd row Purl every even row.
3rd row K7, (k2 tog, wf) twice, s1, k1, psso, wf, s1, k1, psso, k7.
5th row K6, (k2 tog, wf) twice, k1, (wf, s1, k1, psso) twice, k6.
7th row K5, (k2 tog, wf) twice, k3, (wf, s1, k1, psso) twice, k5.
9th row K4, (k2 tog, wf) twice, k5, (wf, s1, k1, psso) twice, k4.
11th row K3, (k2 tog, wf) twice, k2, make bobble (see page 146), k3, (wf, s1, k1, psso) twice, k3.
13th row K2, (k2 tog, wf) twice, k9, (wf, s1, k1, psso) twice, k2.
15th row K1, (k2 tog, wf) twice, k11, (wf, s1, k1, psso) twice, k1.

Knit and purl 4 rows alternately then repeat from row 1.

ARAN PATTERN VI

The heavy back pattern of the same guernsey with side panel worked in 'Marriage Lines'

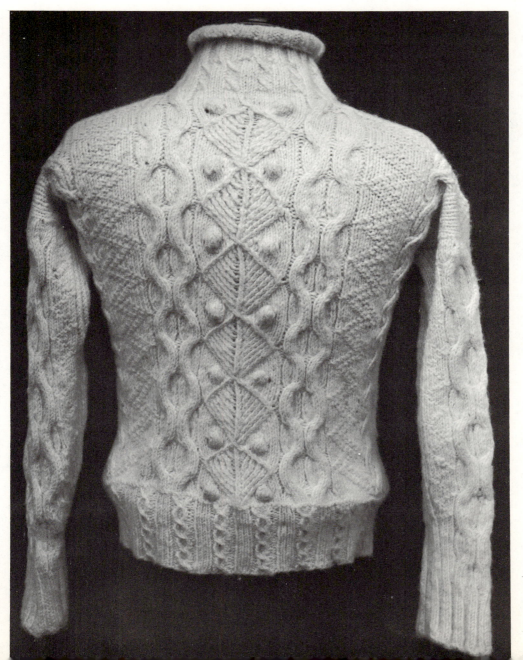

Figure 144

This back shows the waved ribbon pattern page 130 used in double form of 8 stitches for each ribbon, divided by 1 purl stitch, which is also used at each side of the ribbon, easily seen in figure 144. The directions are for a simple waved ribbon so pattern has to be repeated.

The centre panel is not given as it is difficult to keep it even. The front centre could be used instead (Aran V), panels of Marriage Lines are used at the sides, directions for working on page 158 and are given with this pattern.

Marriage Lines

Cast on 15 stitches

1st row P1, k1, p1, k12.
2nd row *P11, (k1, p1) twice.
3rd row K2, p1, k1, p1, k10.
4th row P9, k1, p1, k1, p3.
5th row K4, p1, k1, p1, k8.

6th row P7, k1, p1, k1, p5.
7th row K6, p1, k1, p1, k6.
8th row P5, k1, p1, k1, p7.
9th row K8, p1, k1, p1, k4.
10th row P3, k1, p1, k1, p9.
11th row K10, p1, k1, p1, k2.
12th row (P1, k1) twice, p11.
13th row K12, p1, k1, p1.
14th row (P1, k1) twice, p11.
15th row K10, p1, k1, p1, k2.
16th row P3, k1, p1, k1, p9.
17th row K8, p1, k1, p1, k4.
18th row P5, k1, p1, k1, p7.
19th row K6, p1, k1, p1, k6.
20th row P7, k1, p1, k1, p5.
21st row K4, p1, k1, p1, k8.
22nd row P9, k1, p1, k1, p3.
23rd row K2, p1, k1, p1, k10.
24th row P11, (k1, p1) twice.

Repeat from row 2.*

ARAN PATTERN VII

Welt pattern

Figure 146

Knitted in rib of 4 plain, 3 purl, with single cross travelling stitch on purl ribs.

1st row *K4, k1b, p2* repeat.
2nd row *K2, p1b, p4* repeat.
3rd row *K4, slip next stitch on to spare needle to front, p1, k1b, off spare needle, p1.*
4th row *K1, p1b, k1, p4.*

5th row *K4, p1, slip next stitch on to spare needle to front, p1, kssb.*
6th row *P1b, k2, p4.*
7th row *K4, p1, slip next stitch on to spare needle to back, k1b, pss.*
8th row *K1, p1b, k1, p4.*
9th row *K4, ssb, k1b, pss, p1.

Repeat from row 2. These 9 rows make up welt pattern. One purl row divides the welt from the next pattern.

Pattern above welt

30 stitches

1st row K1, *m1, s1, k1, psso, k10, k2 tog, m1, k1, m1, s1, k1, psso, k10, k2 tog, m1, k1.* Repeat.

2nd and alternate rows Purl.

3rd row K2, *m1, s1, k1, psso, k8, k2 tog, m1, k3,* repeat. Row ends k2.

5th row K3, *m1, s1, k1, psso, k6, k2 tog, m1, k5,* repeat. Row ends k3.

7th row K4, *m1, s1, k1, psso, k4, k2 tog, m1, k7,* repeat. Row ends k4.

9th row K5, *m1, s1, k1, psso, k2, k2 tog, m1, k9,* repeat. Row ends k5.

10th row Purl.

Another row of purl knitting divides this pattern from the next. These 10 rows make the pattern.

Centre panel front

27 stitches

1st row P5, k5, p7, k5, p5.

Next, and each alternate row Purl.

3rd row P3, p2 tog, k2, wf, k1, wf, k2, p2, p3 tog, p2, k2, wf, k1, wf, k2, p2 tog, p3.

5th row P2, p2 tog, k2, wf, k3, wf, k2, p1, p3 tog, p1, k2, wf, k3, wf, k2, p2 tog, p2.

7th row P1, p2 tog, k2, wf, k5, wf, k2, p3 tog, k2, wf, k5, wf, k2, p2 tog, p1.

8th row Purl. Repeat from row 1.

Front left side section

32 stitches

1st row P1, k1b, p2, k1b, p1, k1, m1, s1, k1, psso, moss 7, p1, k4, p1, k4, p6.

2nd row K6, p4, k1, p4, k1, moss 7, p3, k1, p1b, k2, p1b, k1.

3rd row P1, k1b, p2, k1b, p1, k2, m1, s1, k1, psso, moss 6, p1, k4, p1, k4, p1, k5.

4th row P5, k1, p4, k1, p4, k1, moss 6, p4, k1, p1b, k2, p1b, k1.

5th row P1, k1b, p2, k1b, p1, k3, m1, s1, k1, psso, moss 5, p1, k4, p1, k4, p1, k1, m1, k2 tog,-m1, k2 tog.

6th row P5, k1, p4, k1, p4, k1, moss 5, p5, k1, p1b, k2, p1b, k1.

7th row P1, k1b, p2, k1b, p1, k4, m1, s1, k1, psso, moss 4, p1. Slip 2 stitches on to spare needle, to front, k2, k2 on spare needle, p1. Repeat from * to * once, k5.

8th row K6, p4, k1, p4, k1, moss 4, p6, k1, p1b, k2, p1b, k1.

145   Detail of the above also showing crossover in travelling cross stitch

146   A finely knitted guernsey in openwork moss and zigzag pattern

9th row P1, slip next stitch onto spare needle to front, p1, kssb, put next stitch on spare needle to back, purl stitch on spare needle, p1, k5, m1, s1, k1, psso, moss 3, p1, k4, p1, k4, p6.

10th row P5, k1, p4, k1, p4, k1, moss 3, p7, k2, p2b, k2.

11th row P2, slip 1 onto spare needle to front, k1b, k1b on spare, p2, k6, m1, s1, k1, psso, moss 2, p1, k4, p1, k4, p1, k1, m1, k2 tog, m1, k2 tog.

12th row P5, k1, p4, k1, p4, k1, moss 2, p8, k1, s1f, kss, s1b, k1, p1b, k1.

13th row P1, k1b, p2, k1b, p1, k7, m1, s1, k1, psso, p2, k4, p1, k4, p1, k5.

14th row K6, slip 2 st on spare needle to front, p2, p2 on spare needle, k1, sl 2 st on spare needle to front, p2, p2 on spare needle, k1.

These cable twists are made every 7th row. P10, k1, p1b, k2, p1b, k1.

15th row P1, k1b, p2, k1b, p1, k8, m1, sl 1, k1, psso, p1, k4, p1, k4, p6.

16th row P5, k1, p4, k1, p4, k1, p10, k1, p1b, k2, p1b, k1.

17th row P1, k1b, p2, k1b, p1, k8, k2 tog, m1, p1, k4, p1, k4, p1, k1, m1, k2 tog, m1, k2 tog.

18th row P5, k1, p4, k1, p4, k1, p2, moss 8, k1, p1b, k2, p1b, k1.

19th row P1, k1b, p2, k1b, p1, moss 7, k2 tog, m1, k1, p1, k4, p1, k4, p1, k5.

20th row K6, p4, k1, p4, k1, p3, moss 7, k1, p1b, k2, p1b, k1.

21st row P1, k1b, p2, k1b, p1, moss 6, k2 tog, m1, k2, p1, cross cable, p1, cross cable, p6.

22nd row P5, k1, p4, k1, p4, k1, p5, moss 5, k1, p1b, k2, p1b, k1.

23rd row P1, slip next stitch to front, p1, kss, sl stitch to back, k1b, p sl stitch, p1, moss 5, k2 tog, m1, k3, p1, k4, p1, k4, p1, k1, m1, k2 tog, m1, k2 tog.

24th row P5, k1, p4, k1, p4, k1, p4, moss 5, k2, p2b, k2.

25th row P2, slip next stitch to front, k1b, kssb, p2, moss 4, k2 tog, m1, (k4, p1) 3 times, k5.

26th row K6, p4, k1, p4, k1, p7 moss 3, k1, ssf, p1b, kss, ssb, k1, pssb, k1.

27th row P1, k1b, p2, k1b, p2, k1, p1, k2 tog, m1, k5, p1, k4, p1, k4, p6.

28th row P5, k1, twist cable, k1, twist cable, k1, p7, moss 3, k1, p1b, k2, p1b, k1.

29th row P1, k1b, p2, k1b, p1, moss 2, k2 tog, m1, k6, p1, k4, p1, k4, p1, k1, m1, k2 tog, m1, k2 tog.

30th row P5, k1, p4, k1, p4, k1, p8, k1, p1, k1, p1b, k2, p1b, k1.

31st row P1, k1b, p2, k1b, p2, k2 tog, m1, k7, p1, k4, p1, k4, p1, k5.

32nd row K6, p4, k1, p4, k1, p10, k1, p1b, k2, p1b, k1.

33rd row P1, k1b, p2, k1b, p1, k2 tog, m1, k8, p1, k4, p1, k4, p6.

Repeat from row 1.

If used as a repeat pattern the single cross stitch and double cable patterns have to be counted separately and crossed at correct intervals.

Centre panel back

Figure 148

39 stitches

1st row *P1, k3, p7, k3, p1,* k4, p1, k4, *repeat pattern once, in every row except 10 and 12.

2nd row *K1, p5, s1, p2 tog, psso, p5, k1,* p4, k1, p4.

3rd row *P1, k1, m1, k2, p5, k2, m1, k1, p1,* k4, p1, k4, end row with k2.

4th row *K1, p5, s1, k2 tog, psso, p5, k1,* p4, k1, p4.

5th row *P1, k2, m1, k2, p3, k2, m1, k2, p1,* k4, p1, k4.

6th row *K1, p5, s1, k2 tog, psso, p5, k1,* p4, k1, p4.

7th row *P1, k3, m1, k5, m1, k3, p1,* slip 2 stitches to front, k2, k2 slipped stitches, p1, sl 2 front, k2, k2ss.

8th row *K1, p13, k1,* p4, k1, p4.

9th row *P5, k2, m1, k1, m1, k2, p5,* k4, p1, k4.

10th row K1, p15, (k1, p4) twice, k1, p15, k1. No repeat in this row.

11th row *P3, p2 tog, k2, m1, k3, m1, k2, p2 tog, p3* k4, p1, k4.

12th row K1, p15, (k1, p4) twice, k1, p15, k1, no repeat.

13th row *P2, p2 tog, k2, m1, k5, m1, k2, p2 tog, p2*, k4, p1, k4.

14th row *K1, p15, k1, s2f, p2, p2ss, k1, s2f, p2, p2ss.

15th row *P1, p2 tog, k2, p7, k2, p2 tog, p1,* k4, p1, k4.

16th row *K1, p5, s1, p2 tog, psso, p5, k1,* p4, k1, p4.

17th row *P1, k1, m1, k2, p5, k2, m1, k1, p1,* k4, p1, k4.

18th row *K1, p5, s1, p2 tog, psso, p5, k1,* p4, k1, p4.

19th row *P1, k2, m1, k2, p3, k2, m1, k2, p1,* k4, p1, k4.

20th row *K1, p5, s1, p2 tog, psso, p5, k1,* p4, k1, p4.

21st row *P1, k3, m1, k5, m1, k3, p1,* cross cables as in rows 7 and 14.

Repeat from row 8.

Side panel back

Figure 148

30 stitches

1st row K2, p5, k2, p1, k1, p4, m1, s1, k1, psso, (p1, k1) 5 times, p1, k2 tog, m1.

2nd row P2, (k1, p1) 5 times, k1, p2, k4, p1, k1, p2, k5, p2.

3rd row K9, p1, ssf, p1, kss, p3, k1, m1, s1, k1, psso, (k1, p1) 4 times, k1, k2 tog, m1, k1.

4th row P4, (k1, p1) 3 times, k1, p4, k3, p1, k2, p9.

5th row K2, p5, ssf, k1, kss, p2, ssf, p1, kss, p2, k2, m1, s1, k1, psso, (p1, k1) 3 times, p1, k2 tog, m1, k2.

6th row P4, (k1, p1) 3 times, k1, p4, k2, p1, k3, p2, k5, p2.

7th row K9, p3, ssf, p1, kss, p1, k3, m1, s1, k1, psso, (k1, p1) twice, k1, k2 tog, m1, k3.

8th row P6, k1, p1, k1, p6, k1, p1, k4, p9.

9th row K2, p5, ssf, k1, kss, p4, ssf, p1, kss, k4, m1, s1, k1, psso, p1, k1, p1, k2 tog, m1, k4.

10th row P6, k1, p1, k1, p7, k5, p2, k5, p2.

11th row K9, p4, s1b, k1, pss, k5, m1, s1, k1, psso, k1, k2 tog, m1, k5.

12th row P15, k1, p1, k4, p9.

148   Back of guernsey. Openwork diamonds are used instead of zigzag

13th row K2, p5, ssf, k1, kss, p3, ssb, k1, pss, p1, k5, k2 tog, m1, k1, m1, s1, k1, psso, k5.

14th row P15, k2, p1, k3, p2, k5, p2.

15th row K9, p2, ssb, k1, pss, p2, k4, k2 tog, m1, p1, k1, p1, m1, s1, k1, psso, k4.

16th row P6, k1, p1, k1, p6, k3, p1, k2, p9.

17th row K2, p5, ssf, k1, kss, p1, ssb, k1, pss, p3, k3, k2 tog, m1, (k1, p1) twice, k1, m1, s1, k1, psso, k3.

18th row P6, k1, p1, k1, p6, k4, p1, k1, p2, k5, p2.

19th row K9, s1b, k1, pss, p4, k2, k2 tog, m1, (p1, k1) 3 times, p1, m1, s1, psso, k2.

20th row P4, (k1, p1) 3 times, k1, p4, k5, p10.

21st row K2, p5, ssf, k1, kss, s1 to front, p1, kss, p4, k1, k2 tog, m1, (k1, p1) 4 times, k1, m1, s1, k1, psso, k1.

22nd row P4, (k1, p1) 3 times, k1, p4, k4, p1, k1, p2, k5, p2.

23rd row K9, p1, ss front, p1, kss, p3, k2 tog, m1, (p1, k1) 5 times, p1, m1, s1, k1, psso.

24th row P2, (k1, p1) 5 times, k1, p2, k3, p1, k2, p9.

25th row K2, p5, ssf, k1, kss, p2, ssf, p1, kss, p2, m1, s1, k1, psso, (p1, k1) 5 times, p1, k2 tog, m1.

26th row P2, (k1, p1) 5 times, k1, p2, k2, p1, k3, p2, k5, p2.

27th row K9, p3, s1f, p1, kss, p1, k1, m1, s1, k1, psso, (k1, p1) 4 times, k1, k2 tog, m1, k1.

28th row P4, (k1, p1) 3 times, k1, p4, k1, p1, k4, p9.

29th row K2, p5, ssf, k1, kss, p4, ssf, p1, kss, k2, m1, s1, k1, psso, (p1, k1) 3 times, p1, k2 tog, m1, k2.

30th row P4, (k1, p1) 3 times, k1, p5, (k5, p2) twice.

31st row K9, p4, ssb, k1, pss, k3, m1, s1, k1, psso, (k1, p1) twice, k1, k2 tog, m1, k3.

32nd row P6, k1, p1, k1, p6, k1, p1, k4, p9.

33rd row K2, p5, ssf, k1, kss, p3, ssb, k1, pss, p1, k4, m1, s1, k1, psso, p1, k1, p1, k2 tog, m1, k4.

34th row P6, k1, p1, k1, p6, k2, p1, k3, p2, k5, p2.

35th row K9, p2, ssb, k1, pss, p2, k5, m1, s1, k1, psso, k1, k2 tog, m1, k5.

36th row P15, k3, p1, k2, p9.

Repeat diamond pattern from row 13, step pattern, small rope, and travelling stitch do not repeat evenly with pattern, but are quite easy to follow.

ARAN PATTERN VIII

Figure 149

33 stitches

1st row K6, p1, k4, (k1, p1) 5 times, k1b, k4, p1, k6.

2nd row P6, k1, p4, (p1, k1) 5 times, p1b, p4, k1, p6.

3rd row K6, p1, k3, (s1b, k1b, pss) 3 times, k1, (ssf, p1, kssb) 3 times, k3, p1, k6.

4th row P6, k1, p3, (p1b, k1) 3 times, p1, k1, (p1b, k1) twice, p1b, p3, k1, p6.

5th row K2, make bobble as follows, knit into the front, back, front, back and front of the next stitch, making 5 stitches out of one stitch, knit next stitch, turn and purl 5, turn and knit 5, turn and purl 5. Next slip 2nd, 3rd, 4th and 5th stitches over the 1st stitch and knit into the back of bobble stitch—this completes the bobble. K2, p1, k2, (s1b, k1b, pss) 3 times, k1, p1, k1, (ssf, p1, kssb) 3 times, k2, p1, k2, make another bobble, k2.

6th row P6, k1, p2, (p1b, k1) 3 times, (p1, k1) twice, p1, (p1b, k1) twice, p2, k1, p6.

7th row K6, p1, k1, (s1b, k1b, pss) 3 times, (k1, p1) twice, k1, (ssf, p1, kssb) 3 times, k1, p1, k6.

8th row P6, k1, p1, (p1b, k1) 3 times, (p1, k1) 3 times, (p1b, k1) twice, p1b, p1, k1, p6.

149   Good centre pattern outlined with bobbles

9th row K6, p1, (s1b, k1b, pss) 3 times, (k1, p1) 3 times, k1, (s1f, p1, kssb) 3 times, p1, k6.

10th row P6, k1, (p1b, k1) 3 times, (p1, k1) 4 times, (p1b, k1) twice, p1b, k1, p6.

11th row K6, p1, s1f, k1, kssb, (s1f, p1, kssb) twice, (p1, k1) 3 times, p1, (ssb, k1b, pss) twice, s1b, k1b, kss, p1, k6.

12th row P6, k1, p1, (p1b, k1) 3 times, (p1, k1) 3 times, (p1b, k1) twice, p1b, p1, k1, p6.

13th row K2, make bobble, k2, p1, k1, s1f, k1, kssb, (ssf, p1, kssb) twice, (p1, k1) twice, p1, (ssb, k1b, pss) twice, ssb, k1b, kss, k1, p1, k2. Make bobble, k2.

14th row P6, k1, p2, (p1b, k1) 3 times, (p1, k1) twice, (p1b, k1) twice, p1b, p2, k1, p6.

15th row K6, p1, k2, s1f, k1, kssb, (ssf, p1, kssb) twice, p1, k1, p1, (ssb, k1b, pss) twice, ssb, k1b, kss, k2, p1, k6.

16th row P6, k1, p3, (p1b, k1) 3 times, p1, k1, (p1b, k1) twice, p1b, p3, k1, p6.

17th row K6, p1, k3, ssf, k1, kssb, (ssf, p1, kssb) twice, p1, (ssb, k1b, pss) twice, ssb, k1b, kss, k3, p1, k6.

18th row Same as row 2. These 17 rows form this repeat pattern.

Side panels

This is a repeat pattern of 21 rows.

28 stitches

1st row K8, p1, knit into 2nd stitch on left hand needle, then into the 1st stitch, slip both stitches off needle together, p1, k1, p1, k5 *s1b, k1, pss, s1f, p1, kss, k1, p1, tw2 (as in directions above).

2nd row K1, p2, k1, p2, k2, p6, k1, p1, k1, p2, k1, p8.

3rd row K8, p1, tw2, p1, (k1, p1) twice, k3, s1f, k1, kss, s1b, k1, kss, k1, p1, tw2, p1.

4th row K1, p2, k1, p8, (k1, p1) twice, k1, p2, k1, p8.

5th row S2b, k2, k2ss, s2f, k2, kss, p1, tw2, p1, (k1, p1) 3 times, k6, p1, tw2, p1.

6th row K1, p2, k1, p6, (k1, p1) 3 times, k1, p2, k1, p8.

7th row K8, p1, tw2, (k1, p1) 4 times, k4, p1, tw2, p1.

8th row K1, p2, k1, p4, (k1, p1) 4 times, k1, p2, k1, p8.

9th row S2b, k2, k2ss, s2f, k2, k2ss, p1, tw2, p1, (k1, p1) 5 times, k2, p1, tw2, p1.

10th row (K1, p2) twice, (k1, p1) 5 times, k1, p2, k1, p8.

150   Close-up of pattern knitted in fine wool

11th row K8, p1, tw2, p1, (k1, p1) 6 times, p1, tw2, p1.

12th row K1, p2, k1, (k1, p1) 6 times, k1, p2, k1, p8.

13th row S2b, k2, k2ss, s2f, k2, k2ss, p1, tw2, p1, (k1, p1) 5 times, k2, p1, tw2, p1.

14th row K1, p2, k1, p2, (k1, p1) 5 times, k1, p2, k1, p8.

15th row K8, p1, tw2, p1, (k1, p1) 4 times, k4, p1, tw2, p1.

16th row K1, p2, k1, p4, (k1, p1) 4 times, k1, p2, k1, p8.

17th row S2b, k2, kss, s2f, k2, kss, p1, tw2, p1, (k1, p1) 3 times, k6, p1, tw2, p1.

18th row K1, p2, k1, p6, (k1, p1) 3 times, k1, p2, k1, p8.

19th row K8, p1, tw2, p1, (k1, p1) twice, k8, p1, tw2, p1.

20th row K1, p2, k1, p8, (k1, p1) twice, k1, p2, k1, p8.

21st row S2b, k2, kss, s2f, k2, kss, p1, tw2, p1, k1. p1, k5, repeat from * in row 1.

Welt

Cast on multiple of 10

1st row *K3, p2, k1b, p1, k1b, p2,* repeat.

2nd row *K2, p1b, k1, p1b, k2, p3,* repeat.

Repeat these two rows once. Every 5th row work as follows:

5th row K3, p2, slip next two stitches on to spare needle to back k1b, p1 (the 2nd stitch on spare needle), k1b (off spare needle), p2.* Repeat.

ARAN PATTERN IX

Figure 151

47 stitches

1st row K9, p1, (k1b, p1) twice, (k2, p1) 6 times, k1, p1, k1b, p1, k1b, p1, k9.

2nd row P9, k1, p1b, k1, p1b, k1, p1, k1, (p2, k1) 6 times, p1b, k1, p1b, k1, p9.

3rd row K9, p1, k1b, p1, k1b, p1, (k2, p1) 6 times, k1, p1, k1b, p1, k1b, p1, k9.

4th row P9, k1, p1b, k1, p1b, k1, p1, k1, (p2, k1) 6 times, p1b, k1, p1b, k1, p9.

5th row S2f, k2, kss, k1, s2b, k2, kss, p1, slip next 2 stitches to front, k1b, p1, (the purl stitch on spare needle), k1b, (off spare needle, p1, k1, (ssf, p1, kss, k1) 6 times, p1, s2f; k1b, p1, (the purl stitch on spare needle), k1b, (off spare needle), p1, s2f, k2, kss, k1, s2b, k2, kss.

6th row P9, k1, p1b, k1, p1b, k1, (p2, k1) 6 times, p1, k1, p1b, k1, p1b, k1, p9.

7th row K9, p1, k1b, p1, k1b, p1, k1, p1, (k2, p1) 6 times, k1b, p1, k1b, p1, k9.

8th row P9, k1, p1b, k1, p1b, k1, (p2, k1) 6 times, p1, k1, p1b, k1, p1b, k1, p9.

9th row K9, p1, k1b, p1, k1b, p1, k1, p1, (k2, p1) 6 times, k1b, p1, k1b, p1, k9.

10th row S2b, p2, p2ss, p1, s2f, p2, p2ss, k1, s2f, p1b, k 2nd, ss, p1ssb, k1, p1, (s1b, k1, pss, p1) 6 times, k1, s2f, p1b, k 2nd, ss, p1ssb, k1, s2b, p2, p2ss, p1, s2f, p2, p2ss.

11th row K9, p1, k1b, p1, k1b, p1, (k2, p1) 6 times, k1, p1, k1b, p1, k1b, p1, k9.

12th row P9, k1, p1b, k1, p1b, k1, p1, k1, (p2, k1) 6 times, p1b, k1, p1b, k1, p9.

13th row K9, p1, k1b, p1, k1b, p1, (k2, p1) 6 times, k1, p1, k1b, p1, k1b, p1, k9.

14th row P9, k1, p1b, k1, p1b, k1, p1, k1, (p2, k1) 6 times, p1b, k1, p1b, k1, p9.

Repeat from row 5.

151 A very rich pattern. Welts and centre in the same stitch. The wide cables are most effective

Side panel
Tree and Bobble

15 stitches

1st row K6, k1b, p2, k3b, p2, k1b.
2nd row K3, p3b, k3, p6.
3rd row K6, p2, s1b, k1b, pss, k1b, ssf, p1, kss, p2.
4th row K2, p1b, k1, p1b, k1, p1b, k2, p6.
5th row K2. Make bobble as follows: Knit into next stitch front, back, front, back, front, making 5 stitches out of one. Knit the next stitch.

Turn, purl 5, turn, knit 5, turn, purl 5, turn, slip 2nd, 3rd, 4th and 5th stitches over the 1st stitch. Knit into the back of the bobble stitch, k2, p1, s1b, k1b, pss, p1, k1b, p1, ssf, p1, kssb, p1.
6th row K1, p1b, k2, p1b, k2, p1b, k1, p6.
7th row K6, s1b, k1b, pss, p1, k3b, p1, s1f, p1, kssb.
8th row K3, p3b, k3, p6.
9th row K6, p2, ssb, k1b, pss, k1b, ssf, p1, kss, p2.
10th row K2, p1b, k1, p1b, k1, p1b, k2.
11th row Repeat from row 5, making another bobble and continuing in pattern.

152   Detail of centre

153   A fine guernsey showing the good use of bobbles

ARAN PATTERN X

Welt

Figure 153

Multiple of 8

1st row *K3, (p1, k1b) twice, p1.* Repeat.
2nd row *(K1, p1b) twice, k1, p3.* Repeat.

Repeat these two rows twice. Knit every 7th row as follows.

7th row *K3, p1, s2f, k1b, p1, (the purl stitch from the needle slipped to the front) K1b, (the other slipped stitch), p1.* Repeat.

8th row As row 2.

Repeat these 8 rows as many times as needed.

Jersey

Centre openwork and bobble pattern with panel of 3 cross stitch travelling stitches, each side. Also plain panel with bobbles.

Multiple of 42

1st row K6, (k1b, p1) twice, k1b, p5, k1, make bobble, k2, k2 tog, wf, k1, p1, k1, make bobble, k2, k2 tog, wf, k1, p5, (k1b, p1) twice, k1b.

2nd row (P1b, k1) 3 times, k4, p7, k1, p8, k5, (p1b, k1) twice, p1b, p6.

3rd row K2, make bobble, k2, (slf, p1, kssb) 3 times, p4, k3, k2 tog, wf, k2, p1, k1, k3, k2 tog, wf, k2, p4, (s1b, k1b, pss) 3 times.

4th row *(K1, p1b) 3 times, k4, p7, k1, p8, k4, (p1b, k1) 3 times, p6.

5th row K6, p1, (s1f, p1, kssb) 3 times, p3, k2, k2 tog, wf, k3, p1, k3, k2 tog, wf, k3, p3, (s1b, k1b, pss) 3 times.

6th row K2, (p1b, k1) twice, p1b, k3, p7, k1, p8, k3, (p1b, k1) twice, p1b, k2, p6.

7th row K6, p2, (s1f, p1, kssb) 3 times, p2, k1, k2 tog, wf, k4, p1, k2, k2 tog, wf, k4, p2, (s1b, k1b, pss) 3 times, p2.

8th row K3, (p1b, k1) twice, p1b, k2, p7, k1, p8, k2, (p1b, k1) twice, p1b, k3, p6.

9th row K6, p3, (s1f, p1, kssb) 3 times, p1, k2 tog, wf, k5, p1, k1, k2 tog, wf, k5, p1, (s1b, k1b, pss) 3 times, p3.

154   Detail of centre

10th row K4, (p1b, k1) 3 times, p7, k1, p8, (k1, p1b) 3 times, k4, p6.

11th row K2, make bobble, k2, p4, (s1f, p1, k1b) 3 times, k1, wf, s1, k1, psso, make bobble, k2, p1, k2, wf, s1, k1, psso, make bobble, k2, (s1b, k1b, pss) 3 times, p4.

12th row K5, (p1b, k1) twice, p1b, p7, k1, p8, (p1b, k1) twice, p1b, k5, p6.

13th row K6, p4, (s1b, k1b, pss) 3 times, k2, wf, s1, k1, psso, k3, p1, k3, wf, s1, k1, psso, k3, (s1f, p1, kssb) 3 times, p4.

14th row K4, (p1b, k1) 3 times, p7, k1, p8, (k1, p1b) 3 times, k4, p6.

15th row K6, p3, (s1b, k1b, pss) 3 times, p1, k3, wf, s1, k1, psso, k2, p1, k4, wf, s1, k1, psso, k2, p1, (s1f, p1, kssb) 3 times, p3.

16th row K3, (p1b, k1) twice, p1b, k2, p7, k1, p8, k2, (p1b, k1) twice, p1b, k3, p6.

17th row K6, p2, (s1b, k1b, pss) 3 times, p2, k4, wf, s1, k1, psso, k1, p1, k5, wf, s1, k1, psso, k1, p2, (s1f, p1, kssb) 3 times, p2.

18th row K2, (p1b, k1) twice, p1b, k3, p7, k1, p8, k3, (p1b, k1) twice, p1b, k2, p6.

19th row K6, p1, (s1b, k1b, pss) 3 times, p3, k5, wf, s1, k1, psso, p1, k6, wf, s1, k1, psso, p3, (s1f, p1, kssb) 3 times, p1.

20th row K1, (p1b, k1) twice, p1b, k4, p7, k1, p8, k4, (p1b, k1) 3 times, p6.

21st row K2, make bobble, k2, (s1b, k1b, pss) 3 times, p4, k1, make bobble, k1, k2 tog, wf, k1, p1, k2, make bobble, k1, k2 tog, wf, k1, p4, (s1f, p1, kssb) 3 times.

22nd row (P1b, k1) 3 times, k4, p7, k1, p8, k5, (p1b, k1) twice, p1b, p6.

23rd row K6, (s1f, p1, kssb) 3 times, p4, k3, k2 tog, wf, k2, p1, k4, k2 tog, wf, k2, p3, (s1f, p1, kssb) 3 times, p1.

Repeat from row 4.*

Side panel

Side panels of waved ribbon pattern, cross over, miniature rib and diamond.

Multiple of 37

1st row Moss 3, k11, p1, k2, p3, k4b, p3, (k4, p1) twice.

2nd row K1, p9, k3, p4b, k3, p2, k1, p11, m3.

3rd row M3, (k5, p1) twice, s1f, k1, kss, p2, s1b, k2b, pss, s2f, p1, k2, ssb, p2, (k4, p1) twice.

4th row K1, p9, (k2, p2b) twice, k2, p2, (k1, p5) twice, m3.

5th row M3, k4, p1, k1, p1, k4, p1, k2, p1, s1b, k2b, pss, p2, s2f, p1, k2, ssb, p1, s2b, k2, k2ss, p1, s2f, k2, k2ss, p1.

6th row K1, p9, k1, p2b, k4, p2b, k1, p2, k1, p4, k1, p1, k1, p4, m3.

7th row M3, k3, (p1, k1) twice, p1, k3, p1, s1f, k1, kss, p1, (k2b, p1) 3 times, (k4, p1) twice.

8th row K1, p9, (k1, p2b) 3 times, k1, p2, k1, p3, (k1, p1) twice, k1, p3, m3.

9th row *M3, k2, (p1, k1) 3 times, (p1, k2) twice, p1, (k2b, p1) 3 times, (k4, p1) twice.

10th row K1, p9, (k1, p2b) 3 times, (k1, p2) twice, (k1, p1) 3 times, k1, p2, m3.

11th row M3, (k1, p1) 6 times, s1f, k1, kss, p1, k2b, p4, k2b, p1, (k4, p1) twice.

12th row K1, p9, k1, p2b, k4, p2b, k1, p2, k1, (p1, k1) 5 times, p1, m3.

13th row M3, (p1, k1) 5 times, p2, k2, p1, s2f, p1, k2, ssb, p2, s1b, k2b, pss, p1, s2f, k2, k2ss, p1, s2b, k2, k2ss, p1.

14th row K1, p9, k2, (p2b, k2) twice, p2, k2, (p1, k1) 5 times, m3.

15th row M3, (k1, p1) 5 times, k1, p1, s1f, k1, kss, p2, s2f, p1, k2, ssb, s1b, k2b, pss, p2, (k4, p1) twice.

16th row K1, p9, k3, p4b, k3, p2, (k1, p1) 6 times, m3.

17th row M3, k2, (p1, k1) 4 times, k1, p1, k2, p3, s2f, k2b, k2, ssb, p3, s2b, k2, k2ss, p1, s2f, k2, k2ssb, p1.

18th row K1, p9, k3, p4b, k3, (p2, k1) twice, (p1, k1) 3 times, p2, m3.

19th row M3, k3, (p1, k1) twice, p1, k3, p1, s1f, k1, kss, p2, s1b, k2b, pss, s2f, p1, k2, ssb, p2, (k4, p1) twice.

20th row K1, p9, (k2, p2b) twice, k2, p2, k1, p3, (k1, p1) twice, k1, p3, m3.

21st row M3, k4, p1, k1, p1, k4, p1, k2, p1, s1b, k2b, pss, p2, s2f, p1, k2, ssb, p1, (k4, p1) twice.

22nd row K1, p9, k1, p2b, k4, p2b, k1, p2, k1, p4, (k1, p1) twice, p3, m3.

23rd row M3, (k5, p1) twice, s1f, k1, kss, p1, (k2b, p1) 3 times (k4, p1) twice.

ARAN PATTERN XI

Centre diamond

Figure 155

23 stitches

1st row K6, (k1b, p1) 5 times, k1b, k6.

2nd row *P6, (p1b, k1) 5 times, p1b, p6.

3rd row K5, (s1b, k1b, pss) 3 times, k1, (s1f, p1, kssb) 3 times, k5.

4th row P5, (p1b, k1) 3 times, p1, (k1, p1b) 3 times, p5.

5th row K4, (s1b, k1b, pss) 3 times, k1, p1, k1, (s1f, p1, kssb) 3 times, k4.

6th row P4, (p1b, k1) 3 times, p1, k1, p1, (k1, p1b) 3 times, p4.

7th row P1, k3, (s1b, k1b, pss) 3 times, (k1, p1) twice, k1, (s1f, p1, kssb) 3 times, k3.

8th row P3, (p1b, k1) 3 times, (p1, k1) 3 times, (p1b, k1) twice, p1b, k3.

9th row K2, (s1b, k1b, pss) 3 times, (k1, p1) 3 times, k1, (s1f, p1, kssb) 3 times, k2.

10th row P2, (p1b, k1) 3 times, (p1, k1) 4 times, (p1b, k1) twice, p1b, p2.

11th row K1, (s1b, k1b, pss) 3 times, (k1, p1) 4 times, k1, (s1f, p1, kssb) 3 times, k1.

12th row P1, (p1b, k1) 3 times, (p1, k1) 5 times, (p1b, k1) twice, p1b, p1.

13th row (S1b, k1b, pss) 3 times, (k1, p1) 5 times, k1, (s1f, p1, kssb) 3 times.

14th row (P1b, k1) 3 times, (p1, k1) 6 times, (p1b, k1) twice, p1b.

15th row S1f, k1, kssb, (s1f, p1, kssb) twice, (p1, k1) 5 times, p1, (s1b, k1b, pss) twice, s1b, k1b, kss.

16th row P1, (p1b, k1) 3 times, (p1, k1) 5 times, (p1b, k1) twice, p1b, p1.

17th row K1, s1f, k1, kssb, (s1f, p1, kssb) twice, (p1, k1) 4 times, p1, (s1b, k1b, pss) twice, s1b, k1b, kss, k1.

18th row P2, (p1b, k1) 3 times, (p1, k1) 4 times, (p1b, k1) twice, p1b, p2.

19th row K2, s1f, k1, kssb, (s1f, p1, kssb) twice, (p1, k1) 3 times, p1, (s1b, k1b, pss) twice, s1b, k1b, kss, k2.

20th row P3, (p1b, k1) 3 times, (p1, k1) 3 times, (p1b, k1) twice, p1b, p3.

21st row K3, s1f, k1, kssb, (s1f, p1, kssb) twice, (p1, k1) twice, p1, (s1b, k1b, pss) twice, s1b, k1b, kss, k3.

22nd row P4, (p1b, k1) 3 times, (p1, k1) twice, (p1b, k1) twice, p1b, p4.

23rd row K4, s1f, k1, kssb, (s1f, p1, kssb) twice, p1, k1, p1, (s1b, k1b, pss) twice, s1b, k1b, kss, k4.

24th row P5, (p1b, k1) 3 times, p1, k1, (p1b, k1) twice, p1b, p5.

25th row K5, s1f, k1, kssb, (s1f, p1, kssb) twice, p1, (s1b, k1b, pss) twice, s1b, k1b, kss, k5.

Repeat from row 2.*

The side panels have to be reversed after the centre panel is knitted to make these patterns match to face each other.

155   The clarity of the pattern is lost through the use of very fine wool

Welt

Figure 156

Multiple of 6

1st row *K3, k1b, p2,* repeat.
2nd row *K2, p1b, p3,* repeat.
3rd row *K3, slf, p1, kssb, p1,* repeat.
4th row *K1, p1b, k1, p3,* repeat.
5th row *K3, p1, slf, p1, kssb,* repeat.
6th row *P1b, k2, p3,* repeat.

Repeat from row 1 till welt is correct length.

Side panel
Zigzag and Bobbles

Cast on 19 stitches

1st row (P1b, k1) 3 times, k7, p6.
2nd row K6, p7, (s1b, k1b, pss) 3 times.
3rd row K1, (p1b, k1) 3 times, k6, p6.
4th row K6, p1, (k1b, p1) twice, p1, (s1b, k1b, pss) 3 times, p1.
5th row K2, (p1b, k1) twice, p1b, k2, (p1b, k1) twice, p6.
6th row K2, make bobble (see page 149, side panel row 5), k2, (p1, k1b) twice, p1, (s1b, k1b, pss) 3 times, p2.
7th row K3, (p1b, k1) 5 times, p6.
8th row K6, p1, slf, p1, k1b, kssb, (s1b, k1b, pss) 3 times, p3.
9th row K4, (p1b, k1) 3 times, k3, p6.
10th row K6, p3, (s1b, k1b, pss) 3 times, p4.

11th row K5, (p1b, k1) twice, p1b, k3, p6.
12th row K6, p2, (s1b, k1b, pss) 3 times, p5.
13th row K6, (p1b, k1) 3 times, k1, p6.
14th row K2, make bobble, k2, p1, (s1b, k1b, pss) 3 times, p6.
15th row K2, p1b, k1, p1b, k2, (p1b, k1) 3 times, p6.
16th row K6, (s1b, k1b, pss) 3 times, p2, k1b, p1, k1b, p2.
17th row K2, p1b, k1, p1b, k3, (p1b, k1) twice, p1b, p6.
18th row K6, (slf, p1, kssb) 3 times, p2, slf, p1, k1b, kssb, p2.
19th row K7, (p1b, k1) 3 times, p6.
20th row K6, p1, (slf, p1, kssb) 3 times, p6.
21st row K6, (p1b, k1) twice, p1b, k2, p6.
22nd row K2, make bobble, k2, p2, (slf, p1, kssb) 3 times, p5.
23rd row K5, (p1b, k1) twice, p1b, k3, p6.
24th row K6, p3, (slf, p1, kssb) 3 times, p4.
25th row K4, (p1b, k1) twice, p1b, k4, p6.
26th row K6, p4, (slf, p1, kssb) 3 times, p3.
27th row K3, (p1b, k1) 3 times, k4, p6.
28th row K6, (p1, k1b) twice, p1, (slf, p1, kssb) 3 times, p2.
29th row K2, (p1b, k1) twice, p1b, k2, (p1b, k1) twice, p6.
30th row K2, make bobble, k2, (p1, k1b) twice, p2, (slf, p1, kssb) 3 times, p1.
31st row (K1, p1b) 3 times, k3, (p1b, k1) twice, p6.
32nd row K6, p1, slf, k1b, kssb, p3, (slf, p1, kssb) 3 times.

Repeat from row 1.

156   Detail of side patterns and centre diamond knitted in thicker wool

Marriage Lines and Tree

Cast on 30 stitches

1st row P6, k3b, p7, k1, p1, k12.
2nd row *P11, (k1, p1) twice, k6, p3b, k6.
3rd row P5, s1b, k1b, pss, k1b, s1f, p1, kssb, p5, k2, p1, k1, p1, k10.
4th row P9, k1, p1, k1, p3, k5, (p1b, k1) twice, p1b, k5.
5th row P4, s1b, k1b, pss, p1, k1b, p1, s1f, p1, kssb, p4, k4, p1, k1, p1, k8.
6th row P7, k1, p1, k1, p5, k4, (p1b, k2) twice, p1b, k4.
7th row P3, s1b, k1b, pss, p2, k1b, p2, s1f, p1, kssb, p3, k6, p1, k1, p1, k6.
8th row P5, k1, p1, k1, p7, k3, (p1b, k3) 3 times.
9th row P2, s1b, k1b, pss, p3, k1b, p3, s1f, p1, kssb, p2, k8, p1, k1, p1, k4.
10th row P3, k1, p1, k1, p9, k2, (p1b, k4) twice, p1b, k2.
11th row P1, s1b, k1b, pss, p4, k1b, p4, s1f, p1, kssb, p1, k10, p1, k1, p1, k2.
12th row (P1, k1) twice, p11, k1, (p1b, k5) twice, p1b, k1.

13th row S1b, k1b, pss, p4, k3b, p4, s1f, p1, kssb, k12, p1, k1, p1.
14th row (P1, k1) twice, p11, p1b, k5, p3b, k5, p1b.
15th row P5, s1b, k1b, pss, k1b, s1f, p1, kssb, p5, k10, p1, k1, p1, k2.
16th row P3, k1, p1, k1, p9, k5, (p1b, k1) twice, p1b, k5.
17th row P4, s1b, k1b, pss, p1, k1b, p1, s1f, p1, kssb, p4, k8, p1, k1, p1, k4.
18th row P5, k1, p1, k1, p7, k4, (p1b, k2) twice, p1b, k4.
19th row P3, s1b, k1b, pss, p2, k1b, p2, s1f, p1, kssb, p3, k6, p1, k1, p1, k6.
20th row P7, k1, p1, k1, p5, (k3, p1b) 3 times, k3.
21st row P2, s1b, k1b, pss, p3, k1b, p3, s1f, p1, kssb, p2, k4, p1, k1, p1, k8.
22nd row P9, k1, p1, k1, p3, k2, (p1b, k4) twice, p1b, k2.
23rd row P1, s1b, k1b, pss, p4, k1b, p4, s1f, p1, kssb, p1, k2, p1, k1, p1, k10.
24th row P11, (k1, p1) twice, k1, (p1b, k5) twice, p1b, k1.
25th row S1b, k1b, pss, p4, k3b, p4, s1f, p1, kssb, p1, k1, p1, k12.

Repeat from row 2*.

ARAN PATTERN XII
Creggiehaven

Centre panel bobbles

Figure 157

42 stitches

1st row K1b, p5, (k1b, p1) twice, (k1b) twice, (p1, k1b) twice, p10, (k1b, p1) twice, (k1b, twice, (p1, k1b) twice, p5, k1b.
2nd row *P1b, k5, (p1b, k1) twice, (p1b) twice, (k1, p1b) twice, k10, (p1b, k1) twice, (p1b) twice, (k1, p1b) twice, k5, p1b.

3rd row K1b, p5, k1b, p1, k1b. Make bobble as follows: Knit 4, turn, purl 4, work 6 rows on these 4 stitches. Join last stitch of final purl row to first stitch of bobble row by knitting them together, knit two, and join the 1st stitch of final purl row to the 4th stitch of first bobble row by knitting them together. Continue in pattern: k1b, p1, k1b, p10, k1b, p1, k1b. Make another bobble as above. K1b, p1, k1b, p5, k1b.

4th row P1b, k5, (p1b, k1) twice, (p1b) twice, (k1, p1b) twice, k10, (p1b, k1) twice, (p1b) twice, (k1, p1b) twice, k5, p1b.

5th row K1b, p4, (s1b, k1b, pss) 3 times, (s1f, p1, kssb) 3 times, p8, (s1b, k1b, pss) 3 times, (s1f, p1, kssb) 3 times, p4, k1b.

6th row P1b, k4, (p1b, k1) twice, p1b, k2, (p1b, k1) twice, p1b, k8, (p1b, k1) twice, p1b, k2, (p1b, k1) twice, p1b, k4, p1b.

7th row K1b, p3, (s1b, k1b, pss) 3 times, p2, (s1f, p1, kssb) 3 times, p6, (s1b, k1b, pss) 3 times, p2, (s1f, p1, kssb) 3 times, p3, k1b.

8th row P1b, k3, (p1b, k1) twice, p1b, k4, (p1b, k1) twice, p1b, k6, (p1b, k1) twice, p1b, k4, (p1b, k1) twice, p1b, k3, p1b.

9th row K1b, p2, (s1b, k1b, pss) 3 times, p4, (s1f, p1, kssb) 3 times, p4, (s1b, k1b, pss) 3 times, p4, (s1f, p1, kssb) 3 times, p2, k1b.

10th row P1b, k2, (p1b, k1) twice, p1b, k6, (p1b, k1) twice, p1b, k4, (p1b, k1) twice, p1b, k6, (p1b, k1) twice, p1b, k2, p1b.

11th row K1b, p1, (s1b, k1b, pss) 3 times, p6, (s1f, p1, kssb) 3 times, p2, (s1b, k1b, pss) 3 times, p6, (s1f, p1, kssb) 3 times, p1, k1b.

12th row (P1b, k1) 3 times, p1b, k8, (p1b, k1) 3 times, (k1, p1b) 3 times, k8, (p1b, k1) 3 times, p1b.

13th row K1b, (s1b, k1b, pss) 3 times, p8, (s1f, p1, kssb) 3 times, (s1b, k1b, pss) 3 times, p8, (s1f, p1, kssb) 3 times, k1b.

14th row (P1b) twice, (k1, p1b) twice, k10, (p1b, k1) twice, (p1b) twice, (k1, p1b) twice, k10, (p1b, k1) twice, (p1b) twice.

15th row K1b. Make bobble, as given in row 3, k1b, p10, k1b, p1, k1b. Make bobble. K1b, p1, k1b, p10, k1b. Make bobble, k1b.

16th row (P1b) twice, (k1, p1b) twice, k10, (p1b, k1) twice, (p1b) twice, (k1, p1b) twice, k10, (p1b, k1) twice, (p1b) twice.

17th row K1b, (s1f, p1, kssb) 3 times, p8, (s1b, k1b, pss) 3 times, (s1f, p1, kssb) 3 times, p8, (s1b, k1b, pss) 3 times, k1b.

157   A fine bold pattern

18th row (P1b, k1) 3 times, p1b, k8, (p1b, k1) twice, p1b, k2, (p1b, k1) twice, p1b, k8, (p1b, k1) 3 times, p1b.

19th row K1b, p1, (s1f, p1, kssb) 3 times, p6, (s1b, k1b, pss) 3 times, p2, (s1f, p1, kssb) 3 times, p6, (s1b, k1b, pss) 3 times, p1, k1b.

20th row P1b, k2, (p1b, k1) twice, p1b, k6, (p1b, k1) twice, p1b, k4, (p1b, k1) twice, p1b, k6, (p1b, k1) twice, p1b, k2, p1b.

21st row K1b, p2, (s1f, p1, kssb) 3 times, p4, (s1b, k1b, pss) 3 times, p4, (s1f, p1, kssb) 3 times, p4, (s1b, k1b, pss) 3 times, p2, k1b.

22nd row P1b, k3, (p1b, k1) twice, p1b, k4, (p1b, k1) twice, p1b, k6, (p1b, k1) twice, p1b, k4, (p1b, k1) twice, p1b, k3, p1b.

23rd row K1b, p3, (s1f, p1, kssb) 3 times, p2, (s1b, k1b, pss) 3 times, p6, (s1f, p1, kssb) 3 times, p2, (s1b, k1b, pss) 3 times, p3, k1b.

24th row P1b, k4, (p1b, k1) twice, p1b, k2, (p1b, k1) twice, p1b, k8, (p1b, k1) twice, p1b, k2, (p1b, k1) twice, p1b, k4, p1b.

25th row K1b, p4, (s1f, p1, kssb) 3 times, (s1b, k1b, pss) 3 times, p8, (s1f, p1, kssb) 3 times, (s1b, k1b, pss) 3 times, p4, k1b.

Repeat from row 2.*

Long zigzag pattern

1st row (K1b, p1) 5 times, k1b, (p1, k1) 3 times, p1.

2nd row (K1, p1) 3 times, k1, (p1b, k1) 5 times, p1b.

3rd row *(K1b, p1) 3 times, s1f, k1b, kssb, (s1f, p1, kssb) twice, (p1, k1) 3 times.

4th row (P1, k1) 3 times, (p1b, k1) twice, (p1b) twice, (k1, p1b) 3 times.

5th row (K1b, p1) 3 times, k1b, (s1f, p1, kssb) 3 times, (p1, k1) twice, p1.

6th row (K1, p1) twice, k1, (p1b, k1) 6 times, p1b.

7th row (K1b, p1) 4 times, s1f, k1b, kssb, (s1f, p1, kssb) twice, (p1, k1) twice.

8th row (P1, k1) twice, (p1b, k1) twice, (p1b) twice, (k1, p1b) 4 times.

9th row (K1b, p1) 4 times, k1b, (s1f, p1, kssb) 3 times, p1, k1, p1.

10th row K1, p1, k1, (p1b, k1) 7 times, p1b.

11th row (K1b, p1) 5 times, s1f, k1b, kssb, (s1f, p1, kssb) twice, p1, k1.

12th row P1, k1, (p1b, k1) twice, (p1b) twice, (k1, p1b) 5 times.

13th row (K1b, p1) 5 times, k1b, (s1f, p1, kssb) 3 times, p1.

13th row (K1b, p1) 5 times, k1b, (s1f, p1, kssb) 3 times, p1.

14th row (K1, p1b) 9 times.

15th row (K1b, p1) 6 times, s1f, k1b, kssb, (s1f, p1, kssb) twice.

16th row (P1b, k1) twice, (p1b) twice, (k1, p1b) 6 times.

17th row (K1b, p1) 6 times, (s1b, k1b, pss) 3 times.

18th row (K1, p1b) 9 times.

19th row (K1b, p1) 5 times, k1b, (s1b, k1b, pss) 3 times, k1.

20th row P1, k1, (p1b, k1) twice, (p1b) twice, (k1, p1b) 5 times.

21st row (K1b, p1) 5 times, (s1b, k1b, pss) 3 times, k1, p1.

22nd row K1, p1, k1, (p1b, k1) 7 times, p1b.

23rd row (K1b, p1) 4 times, k1b, (s1b, k1b, pss) 3 times, k1, p1, k1.

24th row (P1, k1) twice, (p1b, k1) twice, (p1b) twice, (k1, p1b) 4 times.

25th row (K1b, p1) 4 times, (s1b, k1b, pss) 3 times, (k1, p1) twice.

26th row (K1, p1) twice, k1, (p1b, k1) 6 times, p1b.

27th row (K1b, p1) 3 times, k1b, (s1b, k1b, pss) 3 times, (k1, p1) twice, k1.

28th row (P1, k1) 3 times, (p1b, k1) twice, (p1b) twice, (k1, p1b) 3 times.

29th row (K1b, p1) 3 times, (s1b, k1b, pss) 3 times, (k1, p1) 3 times.

30th row (K1, p1) 3 times, (k1, p1b) 6 times.

31st row (K1b, p1) twice, k1b, (s1b, k1b, pss) 3 times, (k1, p1) 3 times, k1.

32nd row (P1, k1) 4 times, (p1b, k1) twice, (p1b) twice, (k1, p1b) twice.

33rd row (K1b, p1) twice, (s1b, k1b, pss) 3 times, (k1, p1) 4 times.

34th row (K1, p1) 4 times, (k1, p1b) 5 times.

35th row K1b, p1, k1b, (s1b, k1b, pss) 3 times, (k1, p1) 4 times, k1.

36th row (P1, k1) 5 times, (p1b, k1) twice, (p1b) twice, k1, p1b.

37th row K1b, p1, (s1b, k1b, pss) 3 times, (k1, p1) 5 times.

38th row (K1, p1) 5 times, k1, (p1b, k1) 3 times, p1b.

39th row K1b, (s1b, k1b, pss) 3 times, (k1, p1) 5 times, k1.

40th row (P1, k1) 6 times, (p1b, k1) twice, (p1b) twice.

41st row K1b, (s1f, p1, kssb) 3 times, (p1, k1) 5 times, p1.

42nd row (K1, p1) 5 times, k1, (p1b, k1) 3 times, p1b.

43rd row K1b, p1, s1f, k1b, kssb, (s1f, p1, kssb) twice, (p1, k1) 5 times.

44th row (P1, k1) 5 times, (p1b, k1) twice, (p1b) twice, k1, p1b.

45th row K1b, p1, k1b, (s1f, p1, kssb) 3 times, (p1, k1) 4 times, p1.

46th row (K1, p1) 4 times, k1, (p1b, k1) 4 times, p1b.

47th row (K1b, p1) twice, s1f, k1b, kssb, (s1f, p1, kssb) twice, (p1, k1) 4 times.

48th row (P1, k1) 4 times, (p1b, k1) twice, (p1b) twice, (k1, p1b) twice.

49th row (K1b, p1) twice, k1b, (s1f, p1, kssb) 3 times, (p1, k1) 3 times, p1.

50th row (K1, p1) 3 times, k1, (p1b, k1) 5 times, p1b.

Repeat from row 3*.

Short zigzag

1st row K1b, p5, (k1b, p1) 3 times, p1, (k1b, p1) 3 times.

2nd row *(K1, p1b) 3 times, k2, (p1b, k1) twice, p1b, k5, p1b.

3rd row K1b, p4, (s1b, k1b, pss) 3 times, p1, (s1b, k1b, pss) 3 times, p1.

4th row K2, (p1b, k1) twice, p1b, k2, (p1b, k1) twice, p1b, k4, p1b.

5th row K1b, p3, (s1b, k1b, pss) 3 times, p1, (s1b, k1b, pss) 3 times, p2.

6th row K3, (p1b, k1) twice, p1b, k2, (p1b, k1) twice, p1b, k3, p1b.

7th row K1b, p2, (s1b, k1b, pss) 3 times, p1, (s1b, k1b, pss) 3 times, p3.

8th row K4, (p1b, k1) twice, p1b, k2, (p1b, k1) twice, p1b, k2, p1b.

9th row K1b, p1, (s1b, k1b, pss) 3 times, p1, (s1b, k1b, pss) 3 times, p4.

10th row K5, (p1b, k1) twice, p1b, k2, (p1b, k1) 3 times, p1b.

11th row K1b, (s1b, k1b, pss) 3 times, p1, (s1b, k1b, pss) 3 times, p5.

12th row K6, (p1b, k1) twice, p1b, k2, (p1b, k1) twice, (p1b) twice.

13th row K1b, (s1f, p1, kssb) 3 times, p1, (s1f, p1, kssb) 3 times, p5.

14th row K5, (p1b, k1) twice, p1b, k2, (p1b, k1) 3 times, p1b.

15th row K1b, p1, (s1f, p1, kssb) 3 times, p1, (s1f, p1, kssb) 3 times, p4.

16th row K4, (p1b, k1) twice, p1b, k2, (p1b, k1) twice, p1b, k2, p1b.

17th row K1b, p2, (s1f, p1, kssb) 3 times, p1, (s1f, p1, kssb) 3 times, p3.

18th row K3, (p1b, k1) twice, p1b, k2, (p1b, k1) twice, p1b, k3, p1b.

19th row K1b, p3, (s1f, p1, kssb) 3 times, p1, (s1f, p1, kssb) 3 times, p2.

20th row K2, (p1b, k1) twice, p1b, k2, (p1b, k1) twice, p1b, k4, p1b.

21st row K1b, p4, (s1f, p1, kssb) 3 times, p1, (s1f, p1, kssb) 3 times, p1.

22nd row (K1, p1b) 3 times, k2, (p1b, k1) 3 times, k4, p1b.

23rd row K1b, p5, (s1f, p1, kssb) 3 times, p1, (s1f, p1, kssb) 3 times.

24th row (P1b, k1) twice, p1b, k2, (p1b, k1) twice, p1b, k6, p1b.

25th row K1b, p5, (s1b, k1b, pss) 3 times, p1, (s1b, k1b, pss) 3 times.

Repeat from row 2.*

ARAN PATTERN XIII
Straffen

Figure 158
Multiple of 66

The pattern given below was knitted from a tracing taken from a picture lent by Miss Gahan, and drawn by Miss Rivers. The tracing was done on greaseproof paper whilst I was in Ireland.

Good use has been made of single cross stitch travelling stitches, worked in diamond and zigzag patterns, which are repeated across the guernsey.

Like most of the Aran patterns knitted without written instructions, they do not repeat at the same time, this makes the written instructions more difficult to follow. The two outside panels take 44 rows to complete and are 18 stitches wide. Single stars show the repeat row.

The centre pattern is 30 stitches wide, takes 24 rows to complete. The repeat rows are shown by double stars. It is worked from the 19th stitch across.

Welt pattern can be worked from page 157 Aran XI.

1st row *P1, (k1b, p1) 5 times, k1b, (p1, k1) twice, (p1, k1b) 3 times, p2, k1b, p1, k1b, p12, k1b, p1, k1b, p2, (k1b, p1) twice, k1b, (p1, k1) twice, p1, (k1b, p1) 6 times.

2nd row **K1, (p1b, k1) 6 times, (p1, k1) twice, p1b, (k1, p1b) twice, k2, p1b, k1, p1b, k12, p1b, k1, p1b, k2, (p1b, k1) twice, p1b, (k1, p1) twice, k1, (p1b, k1) 6 times.

3rd row (P1, k1b) 4 times, (s1b, k1b, pss) twice, (k1, p1) twice, k1, k1b, p1, (s1f, p1, kssb) twice, p1, (s1f, p1, kssb) twice, p10, (s1b, k1b, pss) twice, p1, (s1b, k1b, pss) twice, p1, k1b, (k1, p1) twice, k1, (s1f, p1, kssb) twice, (k1b, p1) 4 times.

4th row (K1, p1b) 4 times, (p1b, k1) twice, (p1, k1) twice, p1, (p1b, k2, p1b, k1) twice, k1, (p1b) twice, k10, (p1b, k1, p1b, k2) twice, p1b, (p1, k1) 3 times, p1b, k1, (p1b) twice, (k1, p1b) 3 times, k1.

5th row (P1, k1b) 3 times, p1, (s1b, k1b, pss) twice, (k1, p1) 3 times, k1b, p2, (s1f, p1, kssb) twice, p1, (s1f, p1, kssb) twice, p8, (s1b, k1b, pss) twice, p1, (s1b, k1b, pss) twice, p2, k1b, (p1, k1) 3 times, (s1f, p1, kssb) twice, (p1, k1b) 3 times, p1.

6th row (K1, p1b) 5 times, (k1, p1) 3 times, k1, p1b, k3, p1b, k1, p1b, k2, p1b, k1, p1b, k8, p1b, k1, p1b, k2, p1b, k1, p1b, k3, p1b, (k1, p1) 3 times, k1, (p1b, k1) 5 times.

7th row (P1, k1b) 3 times, (s1b, k1b, pss) twice, (k1, p1) 3 times, k1, k1b, p3, (s1f, p1, kssb) twice, p1, (s1f, p1, kssb) twice, p6, (s1b, k1b, pss) twice, p1, (s1b, k1b, pss) twice, p3, k1b, (k1, p1) 3 times, k1, (s1f, p1, kssb) twice, (k1b, p1) 3 times.

8th row (K1, p1b) 3 times, p1b, k1, p1b, (k1, p1) 4 times, p1b, k4, p1b, k1, p1b, k2, p1b, k1, p1b, k6, p1b, k1, p1b, k2, p1b, k1, p1b, k4, p1b, (p1, k1) 4 times, p1b, k1, (p1b) twice, (k1, p1b) twice, k1.

9th row (P1, k1b) twice, p1, (s1b, k1b, pss) twice, (k1, p1) 4 times, k1b, p4, (s1f, p1, kssb) twice, p1, (s1f, p1, kssb) twice, p4, (s1b, k1b, pss) twice, p1, (s1b, k1b, pss) twice, p4, k1b, (p1, k1) 4 times, (s1f, p1, kssb) twice, (p1, k1b) twice, p1.

10th row (K1, p1b) 4 times, (k1, p1) 4 times, k1, p1b, k5, p1b, k1, p1b, k2, p1b, k1, p1b, k4, p1b, k1, p1b, k2, p1b, k1, p1b, k5, p1b, (k1, p1) 4 times, k1, (p1b, k1) 4 times.

11th row (P1, k1b) twice, (s1b, k1b, pss) twice, (k1, p1) 4 times, k1, k1b, p5, (s1f, p1, kssb) twice, p1, (s1f, p1, kssb) twice, p2, (s1b, k1b, pss) twice, p1, (s1b, k1b, pss) twice, p5, k1b, (k1, p1) 4 times, k1, (s1f, p1, kssb) twice, (k1b, p1) twice.

12th row (K1, p1b) twice, p1b, k1, p1b, (k1, p1) 5 times, p1b, k6, (p1b, k1, p1b, k2) 4 times, k4, p1b, (p1, k1) 5 times, p1b, k1, (p1b) twice, k1, p1b, k1.

13th row P1, k1b, p1, (slb, k1b, pss) twice, (k1, p1) 5 times, k1b, p6, (slf, p1, kssb) twice, p1, (slf, p1, kssb) twice, (slb, k1b, pss) twice, p1, (slb, k1b, pss) twice, p6, k1b, (p1, k1) 5 times, (slf, p1, kssb) twice, p1, k1b, p1.

14th row K1, (p1b, k1) 3 times, (p1, k1) 5 times, p1b, k7, p1b, k1, p1b, k2, p1b, k1, (p1b) twice, k1, p1b, k2, p1b, k1, p1b, k7, p1b, (k1, p1) 5 times, k1, (p1b, k1) 3 times.

15th row P1, k1b, (slb, k1b, pss) twice, (k1, p1) 5 times, k1, k1b, p6, (slb, k1b, pss) twice, p1, (slb, k1b, pss) twice, (slf, p1, kssb) twice, p1, (slf, p1, kssb) twice, p6, k1b, (p1, k1) 5 times, k1, (slf, p1, kssb) twice, k1b, p1.

16th row K1, (p1b) twice, k1, p1b, (k1, p1) 6 times, p1b, k6, (p1b, k1, p1b, k2) 3 times, p1b, k1, p1b, k6, p1b, (p1, k1) 6 times, p1b, k1, (p1b) twice, k1.

17th row P1, k1b, (slf, p1, kssb) twice, (p1, k1) 5 times, p1, k1b, p5, (slb, k1b, pss) twice, p1, (slb, k1b, pss) twice, p2, (slf, p1, kssb) twice, p1, (slf, p1, kssb) twice, p5, k1b, (p1, k1) 5 times, p1, (slb, k1b, pss) twice, k1b, p1.

18th row (K1, p1b) 3 times, (k1, p1) 5 times, k1, p1b, k5, p1b, k1, p1b, k2, p1b, k1, p1b, k4, p1b, k1, p1b, k2, p1b, k1, p1b, k5, p1b, (k1, p1) 5 times, k1, (p1b, k1) 3 times.

19th row P1, k1b, p1, slf, k1b, kssb, slf, p1, kssb, (p1, k1) 5 times, k1b, p4, (slb, k1b, pss) twice, p1, (slb, k1b, pss) twice, p4, (slf, p1, kssb) twice, p1, (slf, p1, kssb) twice, p4, k1b, (k1, p1) 5 times, slb, k1b, pss, slb, k1b, kssb, p1, k1b, p1.

20th row (K1, p1b) twice, p1b, k1, p1b, (k1, p1) 5 times, p1b, k4, p1b, k1, p1b, k2, p1b, k1, p1b, k6, p1b, k1, p1b, k2, p1b, k1, p1b, k4, p1b, (p1, k1) 5 times, p1b, k1, (p1b) twice, k1, p1b, k1.

21st row (P1, k1b) twice, (slf, p1, kssb) twice, (p1, k1) 4 times, p1, k1b, p3, (slb, k1b, pss) twice, p1, (slb, k1b, pss) twice, p6, (slf, p1, kssb) twice, p1, (slf, p1, kssb) twice, p3, k1b, (p1, k1) 4 times, p1, (slb, k1b, pss) twice, (k1b, p1) twice.

22nd row (K1, p1b) 4 times, (k1, p1) 4 times, k1, p1b, k3, p1b, k1, p1b, k2, p1b, k1, p1b, k8, p1b, k1, p1b, k2, p1b, k1, p1b, k3, p1b, (k1, p1) 4 times, p1, (p1b, k1) 4 times.

158   Good use of zigzags forming centre diamond and side panels

23rd row (P1, k1b) twice, p1, s1f, k1b, kssb, s1f, p1, kssb, (p1, k1) 4 times, k1b, p2, (s1b, k1b, pss) twice, p1, (s1b, k1b, pss) twice, p8, (s1f, p1, kssb) twice, p1, (s1f, p1, kssb) twice, p2, k1b, (k1, p1) 4 times, s1b, k1b, pss, s1b, k1b, kssb, (p1, k1b) twice, p1.

24th row (K1, p1b) 3 times, p1b, k1, p1b, (k1, p1) 4 times, (p1b, k2, p1b, k1) twice, p1b, k10, (p1b, k1, p1b, k2) twice, p1b, (p1, k1) 4 times, p1b, k1, (p1b) twice, (k1, p1b) twice, k1.

25th row (P1, k1b) 3 times, (s1f, p1, kssb) twice, (p1, k1) 3 times, p1, k1b, p1, (s1b, k1b, pss) twice, p1, (s1b, k1b, pss) twice, p10, (s1f, p1, kssb) twice, p1, (s1f, p1, kssb) twice, p1, k1b, (p1, k1) 3 times, p1, (s1b, k1b, pss) twice, (k1b, p1) 3 times. ** Repeat centre from row 2.

26th row (K1, p1b) 5 times, (k1, p1) 3 times, (k1, p1b) 3 times, k2, p1b, k1, p1b, k12, p1b, k1, p1b, k2, (p1b, k1) twice, p1b, (k1, p1) 3 times, k1, (p1b, k1) 5 times.

27th row (P1, k1b) 3 times, p1, s1f, k1b, kssb, s1f, p1, kssb, (p1, k1) 3 times, k1b, (s1f, p1, kssb) twice, p1, (s1f, p1, kssb) twice, p10, (s1b, k1b, pss) twice, p1, (s1b, k1b, pss) twice, p1, k1b, k1, p1) 3 times, s1b, k1b, pss, s1b, k1b, kssb, (p1, k1b) 3 times, p1.

28th row (K1, p1b) 4 times, p1b, k1, p1b, (k1, p1) 3 times, (p1b, k2, p1b, k1) twice, p1b, k10, (p1b, k1, p1b, k2) twice, p1b, (p1, k1) 3 times, p1b, k1, (p1b) twice, (k1, p1b) 3 times, k1.

29th row (P1, k1b) 4 times, (s1f, p1, kssb) twice, (p1, k1) twice, p1, k1b, p2, (s1f, p1, ssb) twice, p1, (s1f, p1, kssb) twice, p8, (s1b, k1b, pss) twice, p1, (s1b, k1b, pss) twice, p2, k1b, (p1, k1) twice, p1, (s1b, k1b, p1) twice, (k1b, p1) 4 times.

30th row (K1, p1b) 6 times, (k1, p1) twice, k1, p1b, k3, p1b, k1, p1b, k2, p1b, k1, p1b, k8, p1b, k1, p1b, k2, p1b, k1, p1b, k3, p1b, (k1, p1) twice, k1, (p1b, k1) 6 times.

31st row (P1, k1b) 4 times, p1, s1f, k1b, kssb, s1f, p1, kssb, (p1, k1) twice, k1b, p3, (s1f, p1, kssb) twice, p1, (s1f, p1, kssb) twice, p6, (s1b, k1b, pss) twice, p1, (s1b, k1b, pss) twice, p3, k1b, (k1,

p1) twice, s1b, k1b, pss, s1b, k1b, kssb, (p1, k1b) 4 times, p1.

32nd row (K1, p1b) 5 times, p1b, k1, p1b, (k1, p1) twice, p1b, k4, p1b, k1, p1b, k2, p1b, k1, p1b, k6, p1b, k1, p1b, k2, p1b, k1, p1b, k4, p1b, (p1, k1) twice, p1b, k1, (p1b) twice, (k1, p1b) 4 times, k1.

33rd row (P1, k1b) 5 times, (s1f, p1, kssb) twice, p1, k1, p1, k1b, p4, (s1f, p1, kssb) twice, p1, (s1f, p1, kssb) twice, p4, (s1b, k1b, pss) twice, p1, (s1b, k1b, pss) twice, p4, k1b, p1, k1, p1, (s1b, k1b, pss) twice, (k1b, p1) 5 times.

34th row (K1, p1b) 7 times, k1, p1, k1, p1b, k5, p1b, k1, p1b, k2, p1b, k1, p1b, k4, p1b, k1, p1b, k2, p1b, k1, p1b, k5, p1b, k1, p1, k1, (p1b, k1) 7 times.

35th row (P1, k1b) 5 times, p1, s1f, k1b, kssb, s1f, p1, kssb, p1, k1, k1b, p5, (s1f, p1, kssb) twice, p1, (s1f, p1, kssb) twice, p2, (s1b, k1b, pss) twice, p1, (s1b, k1b, pss) twice, p5, k1b, k1, p1, s1b, k1b, pss, s1b, k1b, kssb, (p1, k1b) 5 times p1.

36th row (K1, p1b) 6 times, p1b, k1, p1b, k1, p1, p1b, k6, (p1b, k1, p1b, k2) 3 times, p1b, k1, p1b, k6, p1b, p1, k1, p1b, k1, (p1b) twice, (k1, p1b) 5 times, k1.

37th row (P1, k1b) 6 times, (s1f, p1, kssb) twice, p1, k1b, p6, (s1f, p1, kssb) twice, p1, (s1f, p1, kssb) twice, (s1b, k1b, pss) twice, p1, (s1b, k1b, pss) twice, p6, k1b, p1, (s1b, k1b, pss) twice, (k1b, p1) 6 times.

38th row (K1, p1b) 9 times, k7, p1b, k1, p1b, k2, p1b, k1, (p1b) twice, k1, p1b, k2, p1b, k1, p1b, k7, (p1b, k1) 9 times.

39th row (P1, k1b) 6 times, (s1b, k1b, pss) twice, k1, k1b, p6, (s1b, k1b, pss) twice, p1, (s1b, k1b, pss) twice, (s1f, p1, kssb) twice, p1, (s1f, p1, kssb) twice, p6, k1b, k1, (s1f, p1, kssb) twice, (k1b, p1) 6 times.

40th row (K1, p1b) 6 times, (p1b, k1) twice, p1, p1b, k6, (p1b, k1, p1b, k2) 3 times, p1b, k1, p1b, k6, p1b, p1, k1, p1b, k1, (p1b) twice, (k1, p1b) 5 times, k1.

41st row (P1, k1b) 5 times, p1, (s1b, k1b, pss) twice, k1, p1, k1b, p5, (s1b, k1b, pss) twice, p1, (s1b, k1b, pss) twice, p2, (s1f, p1, kssb) twice, p1, (s1f, p1, kssb) twice, p5, k1b, p1, k1, (s1f, p1, kssb) twice, (p1, k1b) 5 times, p1.

42nd row (K1, p1b) 7 times, k1, p1, k1, p1b, k5, p1b, k1, p1b, k2, p1b, k1, p1b, k4, p1b, k1, p1b, k2, p1b, k1, p1b, k5, p1b, k1, p1, k1, (p1b, k1) 7 times.

43rd row (P1, k1b) 5 times, (s1b, k1b, pss) twice k1, p1, k1, k1b, p4, (s1b, k1b, pss) twice, p1, (s1b, k1b, pss) twice, p4, (s1f, p1, kssb) twice, p1, (s1f, p1, kssb) twice, p4, k1b, k1, p1, k1, (s1f, p1, kssb) twice, (k1b, p1) 5 times.

44th row (K1, p1b) 5 times, (p1b, k1) twice, p1, k1, p1, p1b, k4, p1b, k1, p1b, k2, p1b, k1, p1b, k6, p1b, k1, p1b, k2, p1b, k1, p1b, k4, p1b, (p1, k1) twice, p1b, k1, (p1b) twice, (k1, p1b) 4 times, k1.

*Repeat two outside patterns from row 1. The centre pattern can be worked up to the 44th row from these directions, and is centre of guernsey front and back.

ARAN PATTERN XIV

Creggiehaven

Figure 159

Multiple of 79

The single cross-over pattern is repeated and crossed every 16th row from the first cross-over.

The double cross-over is repeated and crossed every 18th row from the first cross-over.

The double cross-stitch cable is crossed every 8th row.

The trellis pattern is repeated after row 34—from row 3.

1st row P2, k1b, p7, k1b, p2, (k1b, p1, k1b, p2) twice, k6b, p1, k6b, p6, k4b, p8, k4b, p6, k6b, p1, k6b p2.

2nd row K2, p6b, k1, p6b, k6, p4b, k8, p4b, k6, p6b, k1, p6b, k2, (p1b, k1, p1b, k2) twice, p1b, k7, p1b, k2.

3rd row *P2, s1f, p1, kssb, p5, s1b, k1b, pss, p2, (k1b, p1, k1b, p2) twice, k6b, p1, k6b, p5, s1b, k2b, pss, s2f, p1, k2, ssb, p6, s1b, k2b, pss, s2f, p1, k2, ssb, p5, k6b, p1, k6b, p2.

4th row K2, p6b, k1, p6b, k5, p2b, k2, p2b, k6, p2b, k2, p2b, k5, p6b, k1, p6b, k2, p1b, k1, p1b, k2, p1b, k1, p1b, k3, p1b, k5, p1b, k3.

5th row P3, s1f, p1, kssb, p3, s1b, k1b, pss, p3, (k1b, p1, k1b, p2) twice, k6b, p1, k6b, p4,** s1b, k2b, pss, p2, s2f, p1, k2, ssb, p4,** repeat once between stars, finish k6b, p1, k6b, p2.

6th row K2, p6b, k1, p6b, k4, (p2b, k4) 4 times, p6b, k1, p6b, k2, p1b, k1, p1b, k2, p1b, k1, p1b, k4, p1b, k3, p1b, k4.

7th row P4, s1f, p1, kssb, p1, s1b, k1b, pss, p4, (k1b, p1, k1b, p2) twice, k6b, p1, k6b, p3,** s1b, k2b, pss, p4, s2f, p1, k2, ssb, p2,** repeat once between stars, finish p3, k6b, p1, k6b, p2.

8th row K2, s3b, p3b, p3, ssb, k1, s3f, p3b, p3, ssb, k3, p2b, k6, p2b, k2, p2b, k6, p2b, k3, s3b, p3b, p3, ssb, k1, s3f, p3b, p3, ssb, k2, p1b, k1, p1b, k2, p1b, k1, p1b, k5, p1b, k1, p1b, k5.

9th row P5, s2f, k1b. Purl 2nd stitch on slip needle, and knit into the back of other slip stitch, p5, (k1b, p1, k1b, p2) twice, k6b, p1, k6b, p2, s1b, k2b, pss, p6, s2f, p1, k2, ssb, s1b, k2b, pss, p6, s2f, p1, k2, ssb, p2, k6b, p1, k6b, p2.

10th row K2, p6b, k1, p6b, k2, p2b, k8, s2f, p2b, p2, ssb, k8, p2b, k2, p6b, k1, p6b, k2, p1b, k1, p1b, k2, (p1b, k1, p1b, k5) twice.

11th row P4, s1b, k1b, pss, p1, s1f, p1, kssb, p4, (k1b, p1, k1b, p2) twice, k6b, p1, k6b, p2, s2f, p1, k2, ssb, p6, s1b, k2b, pss, s2f, p1, k2, ssb, p6, s1b, k2b, pss, p2, k6b, p1, k6b, p2.

12th row K2, p6b, k1, p6b, k3, p2b, k6, p2b, k2, p2b, k6, p2b, k3, p6b, k1, p6b, k2, p1b, k1, p1b, k2, p1b, k1, p1b, k4, p1b, k3, p1b, k4.

13th row P3, s1b, k1b, pss, p3, s1f, p1, kssb, p3, (k1b, p1, k1b, p2) twice, k6b, p1, k6b, p3, s2f, p1, k2, ssb, p4, s1b, k2b, pss, p2, s2f, p1, k2, ssb, p4, s1b, k2b, pss, p3, k6b, p1, k6b, p2.

14th row K2, p6b, k1, p6b, k4, (p2b, k4) 4 times, p6b, k1, p6b, k2, p1b, k1, p1b, k2, p1b, k1, p1b, k3, p1b, k5, p1b, k3.

15th row P2, s1b, k1b, pss, p5, s1f, p1, kssb, p2,** slip next 3 stitches on to spare needle and drop to the front, decrease next 2 purl stitches by slipping one stitch over the other, knit into the back of this purl stitch, purl the next knit stitch, knit into the back of next purl stitch, and purl next stitch. Then knit into the back of 1st stitch on spare needle, purl the next, and knit into the back of the 3rd stitch.** This crosses the pattern and is worked every 15th row. P2, k6b, p1, k6b, p4, s2f, p1, k2, ssb, p2, s1b, k2b, pss, p4, s2f, p1, k2, ssb, p2, s1b, k2b, pss, p4, k6b, p1, k6b, p2.

16th row K2, s3b, p3b, p3, ssb, k1, s3f, p3b, p3, ssb, k5, p2b, k2, p2b, k6, p2b, k2, p2b, k5, s3b, p3b, p3, ssb, k1, s3f, p3b, p3, ssb, k2, (p1b, k1) 3 times, p1b, k2, p1b, k7, p1b, k2. The cables cross every 8th row.

17th row P2, k1b, p7, k1b, p2, k1b, p1, k1b. Increase one by lifting, purl this increase and the next stitch. K1b, p1, k1b, p2, k6b, p1, k6b, p5, s2f, p1, k2, ssb, s1b, k2b, pss, p6, s2f, p1, k2, ssb, s1b, k2b, pss, p5, k6b, p1, k6b, p2.

18th row K2, p6b, k1, p6b, k6, s2f, p2b, p2, ssb, k8, s2f, p2b, p2, ssb, k6, p6b, k1, p6b, k2, (p1b, k1, p1b, k2) twice, p1b, k7, p1b, k2.

19th row P2, s1f, p1, kssb, p5, s1b, k1b, pss, p2, (k1b, p1, k1b, p2) twice, k6b, p1, k6b, p5, s1b, k2b, pss, s2f, p1, k2, ssb, p6, s1b, k2b, pss, s2f, p1, k2, ssb, p5, k6b, p1, k6b, p2.

20th row K2, p6b, k1, p6b, k5, p2b, k2, p2b, k6, p2b, k2, p2b, k5, p6b, k1, p6b, k2, p1b, k1, p1b, k2, p1b, k1, p1b, k3, p1b, k5, p1b, k3.

21st row P3, s1f, p1, kssb, p3, s1b, k1b, pss, p3, (k1b, p1, k1b, p2) twice, k6b, p1, k6b, p4,** s1b, k2b, pss, p2, s2f, p1, k2, ssb, p4,** repeat between stars once, k6b, p1, k6b, p2.

22nd row K2, p6b, k1, p6b, (k4, p2b) 4 times, k4, p6b, k1, p6b, k2, p1b, k1, p1b, k2, p1b, k1, p1b, k4, p1b, k3, p1b, k4.

23rd row P4, s1f, p1, kssb, p1, s1b, k1b, pss, p4, (k1b, p1, k1b, p2) twice, k6b, p1, k6b, p3,**s, 1b, k2b, pss, p4, s2f, p1, k2, ssb, p2,** repeat once between stars, ending p3, then k6b, p1, k6b, p2.

24th row K2, s3b, p3b, p3, ssb, k1, s3f, p3b, p3, ssb, k3, p2b, k6, p2b, k2, p2b, k6, p2b, k3, s3b, p3b, p3, ssb, k1, s3f, p3b, p3, ssb, k2, p1b, k1, p1b, k5, p1b, k1, p1b, k5.

25th row P5, s2f, k1b, purl 2nd stitch on slip needle, knit into back of the other slipped stitch, p5, (k1b, p1, k1b, p2) twice, k6b, p1, k6b, p2, s1b, k2b, pss, p6, s2f, p1, k2, ssb, s1b, k2b, pss, p6, s2f, p1, k2, ssb, p2, k6b, p1, k6b, p2.

26th row K2, p6b, k1, p6b, k2, p2b, k8, s2f, p2b, p2, ssb, k8, p2b, k2, p6b, k1, p6b, k2, p1b, k1, p1b, k2, (p1b, k1, p1b, k5) twice.

27th row P4, s1b, k1b, pss, p1, s1f, p1, kssb, p4, (k1b, p1, k1b, p2) twice, k6b, p1, k6b, p2, s2f, p1, k2, ssb, p6, s1b, k2b, pss, s2f, p1, k2, ssb, p6, s1b, k2b, pss, p2, k6b, p1, k6b, p2.

28th row K2, p6b, k1, p6b, k3, p2b, k6, p2b, k2, p2b, k6, p2b, k3, p6b, k1, p6b, k2, p1b, k1, p1b, k2, p1b, k1, p1b, k4, p1b, k3, p1b, k4.

29th row P3, s1b, k1b, pss, p3, s1f, p1, kssb, p3, (k1b, p1, k1b, p2) twice, k6b, p1, k6b, p3, s2f, p1, k2, ssb, p4, s1b, k2b, pss, p2, s2f, p1, k2, ssb, p4, s1b, k2b, pss, p3, k6b, p1, k6b, p2.

30th row K2, p6b, k1, p6b, (k4, p2b) 4 times, k4, p6b, k1, p6b, k2, p1b, k1, p1b, k2, p1b, k1, p1b, k3, p1b, k5, p1b, k3.

31st row P2, s1b, k1b, pss, p5, s1f, p1, kssb, p2, (k1b, p1, k1b, p2) twice, k6b, p1, k6b, p4, s2f, p1, k2, ssb, p2, s1b, k2b, pss, p4, s2f, p1, k2, ssb, p2, s1b, k2b, pss, p4, k6b, p1, k6b, p2.

32nd row K2, s3b, p3b, p3, ssb, k1, s3f, p3b, p3, ssb, k5, p2b, k2, p2b, k6, p2b, k2, p2b, k5, s3b, p3, p3, ssb, k1, s3f, p3b, p3, ssb, k2, (p1b, k1, p1b, k2) twice, p1b, k7, p1b, k2.

33rd row P2, s1f, p1, kssb, p5, s1b, k1b, pss, p2, repeat directions once between stars in row 15,

then continue p2, k6b, p1, k6b, p5, s2f, p1, k2, ssb, s1b, k2b, pss, p6, s2f, p1, k2, ssb, s1b, k2b, pss, p5, k6b, p1, k6b, p2.

34th row K2, p6b, k1, p6b, k6, s2f, p2b, p2, ssb, k8, s2f, p2b, p2, ssb, k6, p6b, k1, p6b, k2, (p1b, k1) 3 times, p1b, k3, p1b, k5, p1b, k3, *trellis pattern repeats from row 3.*

35th row P3, s1f, p1, kssb, p3, s1b, k1b, pss, p3, k1b, p1, k1b. Increase 1 by lifting, purl increase, and purl next stitch, k1b, p1, k1b, p2, k6b, p1, k6b, p5, s1b, k2b, pss, s2f, p1, k2, ssb, p6, s1b, k2b, pss, s2f, p1, k2, ssb, p5, k6b, p1, k6b, p2.

36th row K2, p6b, k1, p6b, k5, p2b, k2, p2b, k6, p2b, k2, p2b, k5, p6b, k1, p6b, k2, p1b, k1, p1b, k2, p1b, k1, p1b, k4, p1b, k3, p1b, k4.

159   Centre trellis patterns with cables and single and double cross-overs

160   Child's cap

ARAN PATTERN XIV

Figure 160

32 stitches

1st row S1, (k1, p1) twice, k1, (k1b, p1) 3 times, k3, k1b, p1, k1b, p4, k3, p1, (k1b, p1) twice, k1, p1.

2nd row K1, p1, (k1, p1b) twice, k1, p3, k4, p1b, k1, p1b, p3, (k1, p1b) 3 times, (p1, k1) twice, p2.

3rd row S1, (p1, k1) twice, (p1, k1b) 3 times, p1, k3, s1f, p1, k1ssb, s1f, p1, kssb, p3, k3, (p1, k1b) twice, p2, k1.

4th row P1, k2, (p1b, k1) twice, p3, k3, (p1b, k1) twice, p3, (k1, p1b) 3 times, (k1, p1) 3 times.

5th row S1, (k1, p1) twice, k1, k1b, p1, slip next 2 stitches onto spare needle, and drop to front, k1b, p1, (the purl stitch on spare needle), k1b, (off spare needle), p1. Make a bobble, by knitting into front, back, front, back and front of the next stitch—thus making 5 stitches out of one. K1, turn and purl 5. Turn and knit 5. Turn and purl 5, then slip 2nd, 3rd, 4th and 5th stitches over 1st stitch, knit into back of bobble stitch. K1, this completes the bobble. P1, ssf, p1, kssb, s1f, p1, kssb, p2. Make another bobble. K1, p1, s2f, k1b, p2nd stitch off spare needle, kssb, k1, p1.

*6th row** K1, p1, (k1, p1b) twice, k1, p3, k2, (p1b, k1) twice, k1, p3, (k1, p1b) 3 times, (p1, k1) twice, p2.

7th row S1, (p1, k1) twice, p1, (k1b, p1) 3 times, k3, p2, (ssf, p1, kssb) twice, p1, k3, (p1, k1b) twice, p2, k1.

8th row P1, k2, (p1b, k1) twice, p3, (k1, p1b) twice, k3, p3, (k1, p1b) 3 times, (k1, p1) 3 times.

9th row S1, (k1, p1) twice, k1, (k1b, p1) 3 times, k3, p3, (s1f, p1, kssb) twice, k3, (p1, k1b) twice, p1, k1, p1.

10th row K1, p1, (k1, p1b) twice, k1, p3, p1b, k1, p1b, k4, p3, (k1, p1b) 3 times, (p1, k1) twice, p2.

11th row S1, (p1, k1) twice, p1, k1b, p1, cross next 3 stitches as in row 5. P1. Make a bobble as in row 5. K1, p3, (s1b, k1b, pss) twice. Make another bobble, k1, p1, cross next 3 stitches, p2, k1.

12th row P1, k1, (k1, p1b) twice, k1, p3, (k1, p1b) twice, k3, p3, (k1, p1b) 3 times, (k1, p1) 3 times.

13th row S1, (k1, p1) twice, k1, (k1b, p1) 3 times, k3, p2, (s1b, k1b, pss) twice, p1, k3, (p1, k1b) twice, p1, k1, p1.

14th row K1, p1, (k1, p1b) twice, k1, p3, k2, p1b, k1, p1b, k2, p3, (k1, p1b) 3 times, (p1, k1) twice, p2.

15th row S1, (p1, k1) twice, p1, (k1b, p1) 3 times, k3, p1, (s1b, k1b, pss) twice, p2, k3, (p1, k1b) twice, p2, k1.

16th row P1, k2, (p1b, k1) twice, p3, k3, (p1b, k1) twice, p3, (k1, p1b) 3 times, (k1, p1) 3 times.

17th row S1, (k1, p1) twice, k1, k1b, p1, s2f, k1b, p 2nd ss, k 1st ssb, p1. Make a bobble. K1, (s1b, k1b, pss) twice, p3. Make another bobble. K1, p1, s2f, k1b, p 2nd ss, k 1st ssb, p1, k1, p1.

Now repeat from row 6**. Work these 11 rows until the cap is big enough to meet round the head. It is joined together, and the stitches for the crown are picked up along the edge of the narrow moss stitch. The crown of the cap is worked in plain knitting. Decreasing to shape all round.

Hebrides

Figure 161 shows a white Barra guernsey knitted on fine needles with a variety of patterns including steps and marriage lines in the lower part and moss stitch diamonds Tree of Life and a diamond shaped pattern showing the window of the house, with cable stitch and horseshoe imprints dividing the yoke patterns. This guernsey is the typical square shape worn by fishermen with a lovely choice of patterns. The direction for knitting the horseshoe imprint follows:

Cast on stitches divisible by 10 and 1 over.

1st row K1, *wo, k3, s1, k2 tog, psso, k3, wo, k1*. Repeat between stars.

2nd row and all even rows purl.

3rd row K1, *k1, wo, k2, s1, k2 tog, psso, k2, wo, k2*. Repeat.

5th row K1, *k2, wo, k1, s1, k2 tog, psso, k1, wo, k1*. Repeat.

7th row K1, *k3, wo, s1, k2 tog, psso, k4*. Repeat.

8th row Purl. Repeat these eight rows as needed.

wo = wool over to make a stitch.

162